ACCESS FOR ALL

SÃO PAULO'S ARCHITECTURAL INFRASTRUCTURES

Edited by Andres Lepik and Daniel Talesnik

With photographs by Ciro Miguel

A.M.

PARK BOOKS

Concept: Andres Lepik and Daniel Talesnik editors, Marcelo Della Giustina assistant editor, João Bittar Fiammenghi reasearcher
Translations: Dr. Billaudele and Partner Translation Services
Copy editing: John Wriedt (English), Carolina Alfaro de Carvalho (Portuguese)
Proofreading: Charlotte Eckler
Design: Kathryn Gillmore
Lithography, printing, and binding: DZA Druckerei zu Altenburg GmbH, Thüringen

Cover image: Terrace, SESC 24 de Maio © Ciro Miguel

Park Books
Niederdorfstrasse 54
8001 Zurich
Switzerland
www.park-books.com

Park Books is being supported by the Federal Office of Culture with a general subsidy for the years 2016–2020.

ISBN 978-3-03860-163-0

INDEX

FOREWORD

ANDRES LEPIK

Every city has its own character—based on historical, geographical, sociological, economic, and other factors. However, a city can never be defined solely by the numbers, facts, plans, and statistics related to these factors. The particular character of each city constitutes itself beyond these factual, objectively measurable conditions from the daily interactions of its citizens and visitors. Urban sociologists call this circumstance the "intrinsic logic" of a city. To perceive, analyze, and understand this logic in its deeper dimensions, one needs specific instruments and observational methods. First, one needs perception in person, the physiological experience of the rhythm of a city's inhabitants and traffic, its hum and smell. The best method, however, is often to search out those places in which the particular profile of a city is condensed in specific spatial configurations.

São Paulo's estimated twelve million inhabitants make it the largest city on the South American continent; it long ago reached dimensions that exceed human imagination. Like other ever-growing megacities of the twenty-first century, São Paulo has a specific character recognizable within its highly complex spatial and social conditions. But this character is not encountered in the shopping malls, the repetitive high-rises of mass housing, nor in the elitist gated communities—building types which resemble each other across the globe. Those who want to find and understand São Paulo's particular character should venture to one of the built projects we present in this exhibition, "Access for All," and the accompanying catalogue. Once one has experienced on a regular weekday how "Paulistas" of different ages and social backgrounds at SESC Pompéia lie on a chair on the sun deck, while others read books next door in the library or take part in craft courses, one will quickly realize that this compound is unique in its mixture of leisure, education, sports, culture, and diverse encounters. There, one can experience a dense coexistence of offerings for an urban population which gladly takes advantage of them. Beyond the city's structures for working and living, these spaces assert the identity of their users as an urban society.

There are several such places in the city, which take on similarly complex tasks. They are "social condensers" (to use a central term from Russian Constructivist architecture) in a current, expanded sense. Hence, the first thesis of our exhibition: the megacity of São Paulo creates a surplus value for its inhabitants with these projects, which offer a necessary compensation for the extreme urban conditions of spatial and social density. At the same time, these projects are representative of the character of the city at large. They are spaces of inclusion, which foster encounters between inhabitants of diverse economic and social backgrounds, and they create added societal value that exceeds their individual programmatic offerings. From this conclusion derives our second thesis: these projects render São Paulo as exemplary, since they contain a message that is essential for the future of other large cities. In times of growing social inequality, we need many more such spaces where diverse local communities meet.

With the exhibition "Access for All," the Architecture Museum of the TUM takes up once more the question of architecture's potential to positively influence societal conditions through concrete, built structures. This spectrum ranges from Oscar Niemeyer's canopy covering the Ibirapuera Park (1954) and the SESC Pompeia by Lina Bo Bardi (1977-1986) to the Centro Cultural São Paulo (1972-1982) and the recently opened Instituto Moreira Salles on the Avenida Paulista. These buildings are also architecturally formed spaces where the architects' aim was not focused on iconic façades, but on the needs of urban users. We propose to read all these projects as a network of social infrastructures.

The exhibition and accompanying catalogue emerged from a seminar led by the curator, Daniel Talesnik, at the TU Munich during the fall semester 2018/19. He further sharpened and expanded the concept with support and suggestions from colleagues in São Paulo and during a workshop at the Goethe Institute São Paulo. We thank him for his intense engagement and hope that this exhibition and catalogue can spark a discussion about these projects and ideas well beyond São Paulo.

INTRODUCTION

Just what is it that makes today's São Paulo so different, so appealing?

DANIEL TALESNIK, CURATOR

"São Paulo é um país inteiro." ("Sao Paulo is a whole country.")

- Taxi driver in São Paulo, March 2019

The epigraph that opens this Introduction can be understood in at least two ways. The first is that São Paulo has grown so big that it could be a country.[1] The other reading has to do with the diversity of its inhabitants, mainly since São Paulo is a destination for domestic migration in Brazil, where "all" the country is represented in its population—a diversity that can be extended to include the richness of different nationalities among the inhabitants, including the largest Japanese immigrant population in a city in the world.

As one of the worlds megacities, São Paulo has for decades seen an investment in architectural infrastructures that attempt to mitigate its open space shortages as well as fulfill the constant need for recreational, cultural, and sports programs. This exhibition catalogue presents buildings and infrastructural projects at different scales, focusing on their programmatic characteristics rather than the formal qualities usually emphasized in scholarship on Brazilian architecture. These buildings and open spaces—which can be public, semi-public, or privately owned—arguably attempt to create inclusive places for urban society. While many cities around the world are still chasing the so-called "Bilbao Effect"—the creation of a monofunctional "signature" architectural work by a famous architect that can attract tourism—this exhibition advocates for architectural infrastructure that adds programs of different natures, and that are aimed at social sustainability for local citizens. This aspect of urban growth in São Paulo —quite a vertical and densely-populated city; a city of great resources and also tremendous poverty; a city with high crime rates; a city with severe traffic issues; a city with public-health problems—illustrates how architecture and infrastructure can contribute to a city's urban development in multiple ways.

This exhibition occurs at the crossroads of the Architecture Museum of the Technical University of Munich's longstanding interest in the social impact of architecture and my personal interest in "big buildings" that are heavily programmed, often creating encounters and frictions between program elements that do not usually meet in run-of-the-mill architecture, in dialogue with their immediate surroundings and the city at large. This interest was expanded to the "open spaces" that are found within some buildings in São Paulo, and that provide much needed areas of encounter and leisure for citizens. By the same token, the concept was expanded to include the Minhocão expressway in its Sunday and evening incarnations, when it is closed to vehicular traffic and offered as mitigating open space that enables a vibrant urban scene.

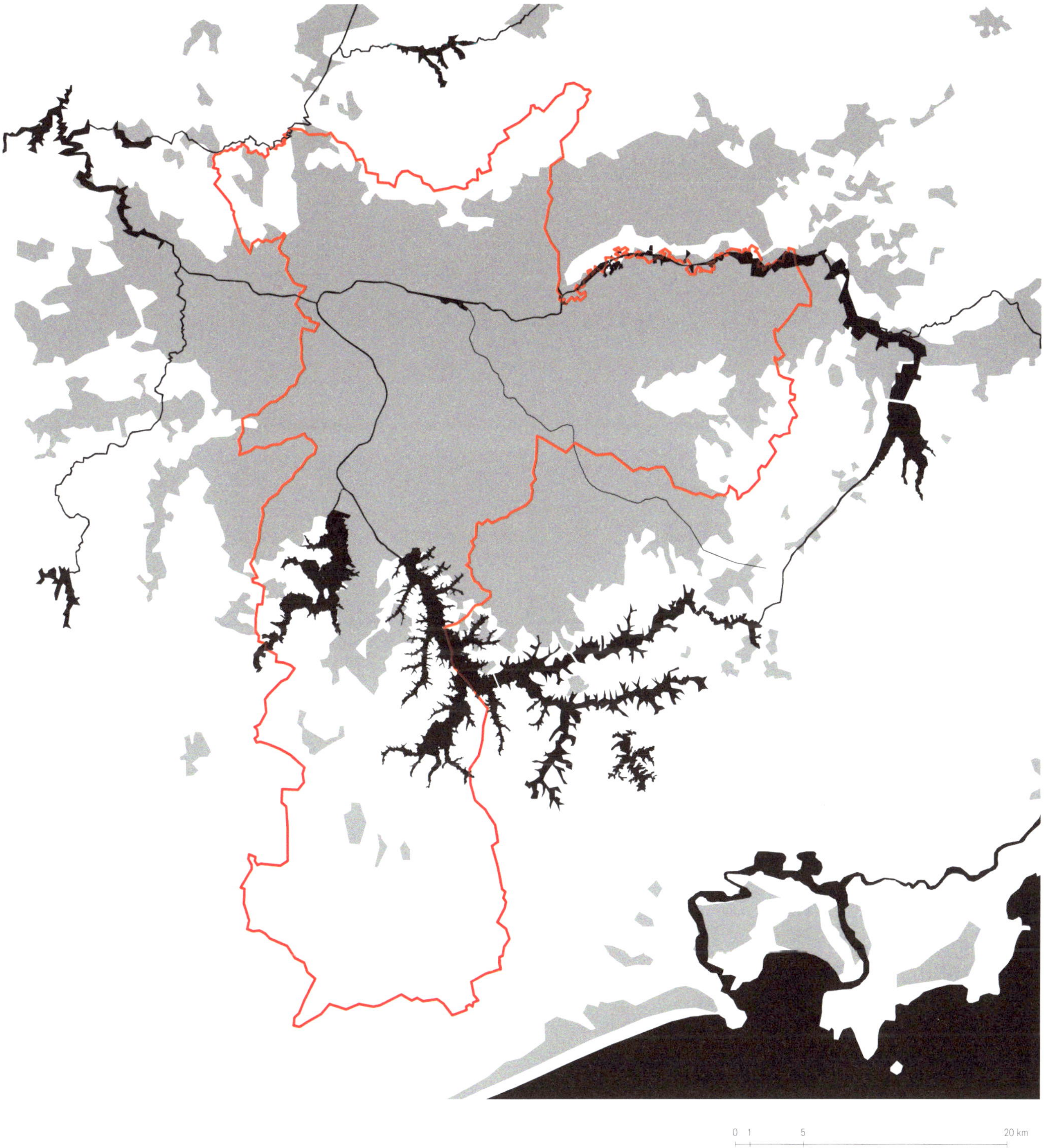

Map of São Paulo inside the metropolitan area
© Guilherme Pianca, Gabriel Sepe and team

Alexander Deyneka, V rayonnom klube (At the local club), illustration for *Bezbozhnik u stanka* (Atheist and the Machine), No. 3 (Moscow, 1927).

The Sunday Minhocão leads us directly to Avenida Paulista, which has also been closed to vehicular traffic on Sundays and that provides an example for coordinated strategies between open spaces provided by buildings and the sidewalk and street space at multiple levels (some physical and some visual). The examples selected were built from the 1950s to the present, meaning that the exhibition is both a historical survey and an analysis of current architectural production. All of the projects, regardless of the period of their origin, have been analyzed in their current state. The exhibition has left out mono-programmatic buildings, with the exception of MASP and the "Free Market Pavilion" at CEAGESP, which are included because their open spaces serve as much more than a museum or a market respectively. Also, housing, transportation, and work-oriented projects have not been our focus, although there are projects like the Conjunto Nacional which incorporates an office tower.

The exhibition and catalogue are structured around three categories:

Big Multi-Programmatic Buildings:
This category is directly inspired by the "social condenser" idea of the Russian Constructivists in the Soviet Union in the 1920s: buildings such as workers' clubs that had the aim of dynamizing society through sports, culture, and education.[2] If one removes (or tones down) the ideological component of these Soviet examples, it is possible to see the kernel for the Serviço Social do Comércio (SESC) buildings, which deliver cultural and recreational services to "workers of commerce" in Brazil. These buildings have proliferated in São Paulo, particularly since the 1960s when the SESC Consolação set the model for the Downtown-

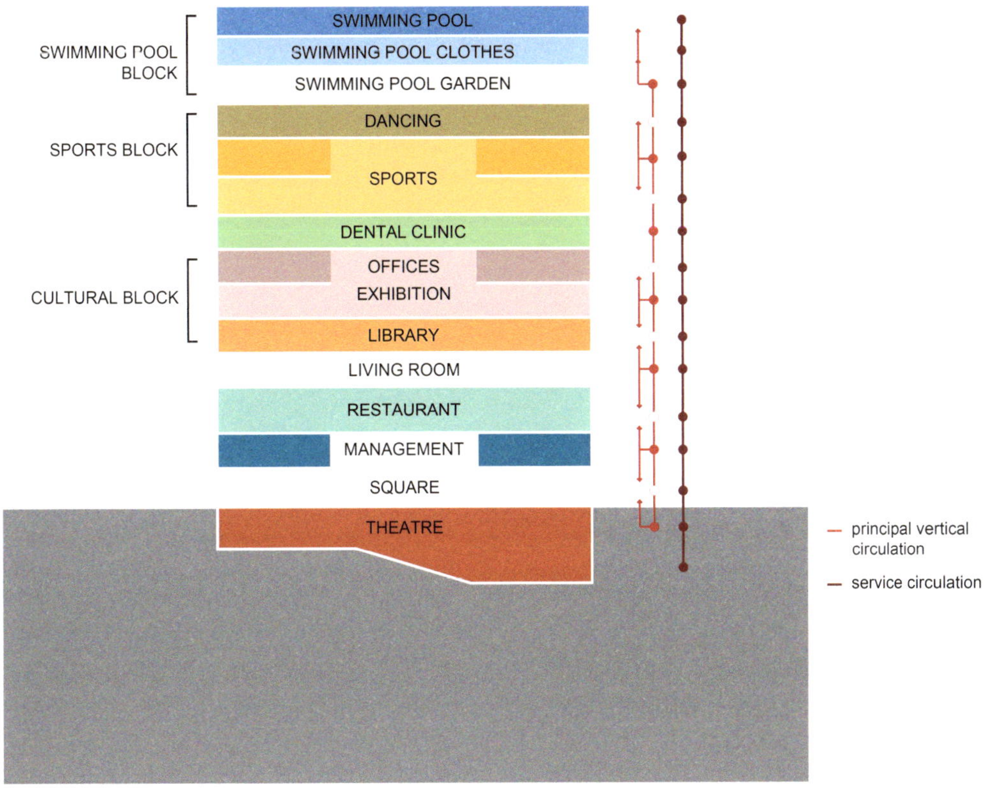

Longitudinal Section with diagram of uses of SESC 24 de Maio © MMBB Arquitetos

Athletic-Club-like approach of these projects.[3] This agglomeration of programs of different natures has seen many variations, including two of the buildings in this section of the exhibition: Lina Bo Bardi and team's SESC Pompéia, finished in 1986, which matched the refurbishment of an existing factory with a new sports tower, and Paulo Mendes da Rocha and MMBB's SESC 24 de Maio. This last project is the outcome of a complex intervention in a preexisting building that, together with the addition of a service tower, results in moments like the double-height gymnasium on top of a single-height dentistry service woven together by a side ramp. Talking to a colleague in São Paulo, I was told that the SESCs were buildings for all ages, and I thought he meant that they cater to all age groups, but he then explained that the real meaning was that one person can go to the same building throughout his entire life and will find suitable activities. In this category, we have also included Eurico Prado Lopes and Luiz Telles's Centro Cultural São Paulo, finished in 1982: a city-commissioned project and a variation on the theme, where the architects distributed an array of cultural, educational, and leisure programs in a whale-like sunken building that is complimented by outdoor plazas and rooftop green areas and a direct connection to the subway. Alexandre Delijaicov and team's Centro Educacional Unificado (CEU) Inácio Monteiro was chosen to represent the network of these facilities distributed on the periphery of the city: school facilities by day which also serve as community centers, universities, and a series of other infrastructures. Finally, Lina Bo Bardi's Museu de Arte de São Paulo (MASP), finished in 1968, is at the juncture of all the categories of this exhibition, but is included in this section due to its almost prototypical aspect. Although a museum, it represents the big multi-programmatic dimension with galleries stacked over an open space which constantly switches uses, above a sunken auditorium, restaurant, and another exhibition area, among other programs. The open space is created by the void between the above and below ground elements and connects to Avenida Paulista, putting an open-space/street strategy at play.

If one looks at the dates of the buildings in the "big multi-programmatic" category, many were designed or completed during the years of dictatorship in Brazil, particularly the SESC Pompeia and the CCSP which were both commissioned during this period. An idea hovering over the exhibition is that buildings can last longer than political systems. Although these buildings do not represent the political system under which they were built via their architecture, it is interesting to see that in these cases the architecture is more stable than the system that built them. Even in times of repression in São Paulo, there was a preoccupation with collective infrastructure, something that is addressed in some of the essays in this catalogue, particularly in Guilherme Wisnik's "Architecture as Infrastructure: The Political Design" and Renato Anelli's "Architecture and Metropolitan Culture: CCSP and SESC Pompéia," essays that analyze a historical dimension of these São Paulo architectures that can give perspective and ideas to critically reflect on architecture and the current political moment in Brazil.

Open Spaces

This category deals with open spaces that are part of the design of buildings and in service of the city. The first example, Oscar Niemeyer's Marquise at the Ibirapuera Park, finished in 1954, has served as a blueprint for open space in São Paulo. Using the simple idea of roofing a sidewalk that varies in width, this space hosts varied sports and leisure activities, while also connecting a series of buildings. The Companhia de Entrepostos e Armazéns Gerais de São Paulo's (CEAGESP) main market, finished in 1964, illustrates how a space for a market can alternate uses and activate its surroundings through the sheer fact of being a completely open building that acts as linear covered plaza. Brasil Arquitectura's open spaces at the Praça das Artes Building, which act as a passage between three streets, offer a much-needed, safe open space for activities and repose in an otherwise rundown area of the city center. Finally, the Minhocão, from 1969-70, is the odd example in the exhibition: this 3.5 kilometer expressway transforms on Sundays when it is closed to cars, making it useful in understanding the range of open space in this city.

Despite great need, not all of the open spaces in São Paulo are successful, as Vanessa Grossman argues in the essay "The Park and the Slab: The Marquise at Ibirapuera by Oscar Niemeyer" in her description of the emblematic failure of open space at the Memorial da América Latina (Latin America Memorial), also designed by Oscar Niemeyer and inaugurated in 1989. The failure of this social, political, and cultural center with vast open spaces between the buildings stands in direct contrast to the success of the Ibirapueira Park's Marquise by the same architect. Ana Luiza Nobre, in her "The Ground as a Project" essay also analyzes the nature of open space in Brazilian architecture, illustrating via a historical analysis the idea of architecture detaching itself from the ground in São Paulo and the type of spaces that can thereby be created.

Avenida Paulista

Inaugurated in 1891, the Avenida Paulista today has only the Casa das Rosas at number 37 as proof of the elitist past when it was lined with mansions. During the 1950s, the plots of land along the avenue started to be developed as high rises. With the addition of the subway, it undoubtedly became the main thoroughfare of the city. Apart from an analysis of the avenue and its multiple dimensions (through hosting the biggest LGBT Pride parade, a yearly run, protests, Carnaval, New Year's Eve festivities, et al.) and the fact that it has a dimension as an open park when it closes to vehicular traffic on Sunday, we have chosen four buildings besides the MASP along the avenue, each representing a different strategy of open space coordinated with the street from within the building. The Instituto Moreira Salles by Andrade Morettin

Big multi-programmatic buildings: Library at the SESC Pompeia

Open Spaces: View of Marquise Ibirapuera with the Museum of Moder Art in the back

Avenida Paulista: View of the stairs of Gazeta building

Arquitetos, inaugurated in 2017, provides an example that accumulates all the strategies developed along the avenue, lifting the first floor to create a plaza and higher-level terraces with visual connections to the street. In other words, it both amplifies horizontally and multiplies vertically the open space of the street inside the building. The 1956 Conjunto Nacional by David Libeskind has a gallery on its first floor that is a literal continuation of the sidewalk into the building and also connects different streets, thus creating an augmentation of public space into the building. The 1966 Gazeta building provides a rare example of theatre-like monumental stairs where people lounge on Sundays, capped by a deep lobby that offers public tables. Meanwhile, at the Federação das Indústrias do Estado de São Paulo (FIESP), (Rino Levi, 1979; partial refurbishment, Paulo Mendes da Rocha and MMBB Arquitetos, 1998), the street level splits when entering the building, creating a variation of the expansion of the street by distributing programs and plazas on two levels.

José Tavares Correia de Lira's "Architecture, Public Space, and Exception" addresses the evolution of Avenida Paulista and other case studies in the exhibition, providing a politically charged and nuanced understanding of the topic. Finally, Fraya Frehse's "In Favor of a (Rare) Aesthetic Contact with the Street in São Paulo" is both a comment on the exhibition's argument and a critique specific to São Paulo.

Despite the fact that the exhibition shows a critical number of projects that represent São Paulo's architectural infrastructures and how it is possible to construct the city from within buildings—and also in the case of the projects in Avenida Paulista to create myriads of interactions between the street and the buildings—we are aware that there is a need for more of these types of infrastructure in such a heavily-populated city. Also, with the exception of the CEU network, the examples presented are all in the central area of São Paulo. The periphery is different. Different sources provide different data, hundreds of thousands of São Paulo's citizens live in slum-like conditions and a critical number of existing housing faces the reality of landslides and flooding. (Although São Paulo generates over 10 percent of Brazil's GDP, conservative estimates establish that a fifth of its population lives in poverty). We started by focusing on the existing knowledge about these buildings in São Paulo and then excavated new evidence to support and illustrate our arguments. We suggest a conception of architecture/architectures that is not only essential to urban processes but one that can, at its best, generate new urban and urbanization processes. This is a reading of architecture that has political undertones and that reaffirms the possible agencies that complexly-programmed buildings have in supporting life in cities, and it is our ambition that our analyses are useful for cities around the world. Although not strictly speaking a "Learning from São Paulo" exhibition, it does have a pedagogical ambition that will become available for future use.

The accessibility of the buildings considered in the exhibition has been a key preoccupation for us. Not all of them have free admission or are completely open, but parts of them usually are. This focus on accessibility was accompanied by surveys conducted by Mariana Lourenço with the management of the buildings in order to understand their biggest challenges, expenditures, the profile of users, etc. Part of the success of these buildings has to do with the way they are administered, the specialized staff, and the fact that through a symbiosis between the architecture and the maintenance/security, they are safe places. We have also commissioned an interview from Enrique Walker with Paulo Mendes da Rocha and Marta Moreira about their SESC 24 de Maio Building.[4] This building was one of the last of the case studies to be opened to the public. On the one hand, it represents the accumulated intelligence of many of the buildings and open spaces in this exhibition and, on the other, the long gestation of the design process produced enough friction between the original building, the project, and the problems that arose along the way to result in some of the best moments of the building. The arguments of the exhibition and the catalogue are supported with archival evidence and new architectural drawings by Guilherme Pianca and Gabriel Sepe, illustrations by Danilo Zamboni, and photographs by Ciro Miguel. The exhibition also includes a series of six on-site interviews by Pedro Kok that weave together critical analyses of the case studies by local experts and some of the designers of the buildings with a sense of place.

Just what is it that makes today's São Paulo so different, so appealing? Beyond a more complete subway system, better control of security, and other such details, what makes the city exciting today, at least in part, can be explained by the analyses of the case studies selected for this exhibition, and a series of other buildings of a similar nature—especially when they are understood as a network that supports life in the city, havens that make the urban intensity more bearable, that favor encounters between people, and that in the most interesting cases empower them via sports, cultural, and educational activities.

1 São Paulo has an area of 1,521 km^2 with circa 12,176,000 inhabitants, and Greater São Paulo has an area of 7,946.96 km^2 with circa 21,571,000 inhabitants. The city of São Paulo consists of 9 administrative zones divided in 32 regional prefectures that are subdivided in 96 districts. Each of the districts with circa 120,000 inhabitants, and some reaching up to 320,000. (The municipality of Guarulhos alone has an area of 318.68 km^2 with circa 1,324,000 inhabitants, which is a good comparison with Munich's 310.43 km^2 and circa 1,464,301 inhabitants).

2 For more on the Constructivist social condensers see the special issue on the topic of *The Journal of Architecture*, 22:3, (2017).

3 For more about the Downtown Athletic Club see Rem Koolhaas, *Delirious New York: A Retroactive Manifesto for Manhattan* (New York: Oxford University Press, 1978).

4 The other architects are Milton Braga and Fernando Mello Franco, partners of Marta Moreira in MMBB Arquitetos.

ARCHITECTURE AS INFRASTRUCTURE – POLITICAL DESIGN

GUILHERME WISNIK

The architecture of the aptly named "Escola Paulista" (or "São Paulo School") includes an exemplary, broadly formulated infrastructural approach in each of its projects. Infrastructure is understood here as the entirety of all large public facilities, which systematically organize the essential comings and goings and services of the city. Educational, leisure, and even residential buildings, for example, are therefore generally designed as if they were components of the urban-development infrastructure: terminals for mass transportation, equipped with large-scale structural elements, such as bridges and viaducts. Hence, the programmatic replacement of stairs with ramps and of windows with skylights in numerous buildings designed by Paulista Architects in the city. A remarkable example is the *Mendes André House* (1966) by João Vilanova Artigas, in which two large hanging-framework units with large open spaces and horizontal and vertical lines, supported on just four pilars, together produced what the architect christened with the epithet, "a beam you can live on."[1]

Since architecture in São Paulo applies itself as a branch of engineering, technology is considered here as a basic requirement for imagination. "Formal changes are impossible to implement if you don't know how," says Paulo Mendes da Rocha. "So, one thinks with the inventiveness of the 'doable', instead of thinking in the autonomous or independent terms of a factory version of these forms,"[2] he adds. In this context, the University of São Paulo's Faculty of Architecture and Urbanism (FAUUSP), with its space designed by Vilanova Artigas, must be seen not only as the point of convergence of a superb understanding of technology (a legacy of the University's Engineering Faculty), but also as an expression of the pronounced humanistic tradition of the Philosophy, Natural Sciences, and Humanities Faculty. This underlying legacy is the contribution of a group of outstanding architects and thinkers, represented at an exceptional level by Artigas, Paulo Mendes da Rocha and Flávio Motta. Designed in 1961, the FAUUSP building was conceived as a reinforced concrete box, which clearly has no doors, within which, however, rooms flow into one another, connected by slightly offset mezzanines and by long ramps that are never perceived as corridors, but rather as rooms of movement, as public spaces in the best possible sense.

São Paulo was never Brazil's capital city—neither in the colonial period nor in the days of empire (1822-1889). The city, therefore, developed independently of the most important political and cultural influences from Europe—the Portuguese Royal Court and the French *Académie des Beaux-Arts*—which influenced other Brazilian institutions. However, due to São Paulo's location, the city became the starting point for exploring and conquering the country's interior. The city sits on a plateau that stretches out from the Serra do Mar

Mendes André house (1966), Architect João Vilanova Artigas
© Nelson Kon

Exterior view of FAUUSP building (1961), Architect Vilanova Artigas
© Nelson Kon

CEU Inácio Monteiro

Interior view of FAUUSP building
© FAUUSP Library

mountain range. The Tietê River runs through São Paulo, but, unlike most other rivers, flows into the interior, where it ultimately merges with the Paraná River. Following rapid growth at the beginning of the twentieth century due to coffee cultivation and industrial development, the city built the country's biggest rail network into the "hinterlândia," which brought a particularly pronounced awareness of the colossal distances on the continent. Architecture was applied as the means of developing this territory, which also entailed a technical conversion of local nature.

When asked to compare the FAUUSP building project with the University of Porto's Architecture Faculty (FAUP, 1987) in Portugal, Álvaro Siza himself pointed out that the two were entirely different projects. In his view, the generous spaces of Vilanova Artigas's project were in line with the "territorial scale of Brazil." In Europe on the other hand, according to Siza, architects work with significantly smaller spaces.[3] However, what also enables one to identify the FAUUSP building with Brazil as a country or São Paulo as a city, in line with Siza's view, is not necessarily the size, but rather the resulting spatial quality—the "character" that a building can attain when the program is interpreted appropriately and is configured as a continuous sequence of spaces around a common "square," which is understood as a place of exchange and cohabitation. Indeed, even the university building erected in Portugal had to be divided into several individual buildings.

These characteristics typical of the heroic generation of architects in Brazil, who erected their buildings during the military dictatorship's years of harsh repression, are also continued in the buildings of more recent generations in São Paulo. Characteristics such as a refusal to rely on exaggerated subdivisions and the ganging together of enclosed rooms (wet rooms, bedrooms) enables the spatial continuity of the building to be maintained and counteracts the excessive restriction of spaces. Plus, not only should the structural elements (the materials used and their installation) be highlighted, but the indivisible surveying of the space (e.g. its continuous material extension from one façade to the next) should not, in particular, stand in the way of any structural removal processes, either. Which, of course, then turns buildings into instruments of measurement, of the perceptive reading of space, and, on a larger scale, of the landscape—which, consequently, explains the frequent occurrence of terms such as "straightening" or "urban development delimitation" in project descriptions by São Paulo's new generation of architects.

Since São Paulo's large-scale new building or urban projects are now postulated as "programmatic arrangements" or simply "spatial arrangements," instead of making the attempt to create an "urban development form," these projects exhibit the systematic vision of an urban development that is determined to protect the irresolution of the term with strategic measures. Which takes us back to Paulo Mendes da Rocha, who describes the "unpredictability of life."[4] A whole range of articles on this new generation are available, arguing for a logic that is rather more "operative" than "linguistic."[5] An eloquent example of this approach is provided by the MMBB and Metro architectural office's project for the "Bairro Novo" ("New Neighborhood," 2004) in São Paulo. The project by this group of architects focused on the "readable" design of the public infrastructure (streets, utility areas, canals, bridges, flyovers, treatment plants) and refused to feign compliance with the practically unyielding models for the part of the city that is reserved for private "occupation," i.e., the real-estate market. This position, characterized by a certain strategic realism, very consciously distances itself from both the nostalgic revival pose of historicist role models and the universal, abstract orderliness of modern urban development.

A further remarkable example: The Centros Educacionais Unificados (CEUs), a complex of public schools, designed in 2001 by the team of architects of the São Paulo Prefecture (EDIF) under the coordinated collaboration of Alexandre Delijaicov, André Takiya, and Wanderley Ariza. A rational approach to the construction and speed of completion of a significant number of units (forty-five in just two years) took priority here. The project therefore had a clear preference for turnkey construction, where precast concrete parts and metal stairs were used. The CEUs situated in São Paulo's poorer periphery characterized by low height and irregular building development are points of attraction for people from the respective neighborhoods. During the week, there are school lessons here, but, at the weekend, leisure activities and cultural events are held, attracting droves of people from the immediate surroundings. The CEUs have therefore become a form of community center. The ethical legacy of the Escola Paulista here enabled the erection of a "real" system of urban development facilities, which function extremely effectively as building blocks of a more spacious, more collective urban cohabitation.

The FAUUSP building, which connects the argument of this text again with the original role model of the Escola Paulista, is instilled with a civilizing ideal which relates to the importance and responsibility of a form of cohabitation in which freedom is neither an easy-to-achieve nor an immediately-available attribute, but rather—and far more to the point—something that must be taken piece by piece. "Shout in the building's interiors and you destroy its wholeness and feel responsible for [your own actions]," remarks Artigas in a memorandum on the project. "The individual learns here, acquires good manners and team spirit,"[6] he adds. The notion of good manners must be emphasized here, as the enormous feeling of freedom that the building imparts, also demands respect for the space of the other in the joint sharing of freedom. One of the principal characteristics of the Escola Paulista is exhibited here—the struggle against the supremacy that the private domain exercises over the public domain in Brazil. In social theory, we call this patrimonialism: the tendency, so typical of countries molded by colonialism and traditional forms of slavery, to handle public affairs on the basis of personal relationships, founded on favor. It is not by chance that Artigas has designed so many buildings that contrast head-on with the domestic idyll, the fetish of the private sphere, as well as the concepts of private isolation, separation, and subdivision into small units, and the comfort of the bourgeoisie. These goals were best achieved with an architecture designed as infrastructure. And he created an architecture "school" that is the most long-lived and active in today's Brazil. A "school" whose adherents consider that designing a building is not just a formal and volumetric exercise, but indeed—and above all—a political activity.

1 See Álvaro Puntoni, Ciro Pirondi, Giancarlo Latorraca, Rosa Artigas, eds, *Vilanova Artigas*. (São Paulo: Instituto Lina Bo e P. M. Bardi e Fundação Vilanova Artigas, 1997), 125

2 Paulo Mendes da Rocha, "Genealogia da imaginação," in *Paulo Mendes da Rocha: projetos 1957-1999*, ed. Rosa Artigas (São Paulo: Cosac Naify, 2000), 71-72.

3 Álvaro Siza, "Entrevista com Álvaro Siza," in *Caramelo*. 9 (São Paulo: GFAU, 1997).

4 "The unpredictability of life is expressed by a neat and strictly technical building, with which, however, nothing can be said about the why, from where, how or the program itself. This protects the irresolution, the unpredictability of the freedom of the individual." Paulo Mendes da Rocha, "A cidade para todos," in *Paulo Mendes da Rocha: projetos 1957-1999*, ed. Rosa Artigas (S.o Paulo: Cosac Naify, 2000) 171-172.

5 See, e.g., Ana Vaz Milheiro, Ana Luiza Nobre, and Guilherme Wisnik, eds . *Coletivo: arquitetura paulista contemporânea*, (São Paulo: Cosac Naify, 2006).

6 Álvaro Puntoni, Ciro Pirondi, Giancarlo Latorraca, and Rosa Artigas eds., *Vilanova Artigas*, (São Paulo: Instituto Lina Bo e P. M. Bardi e Fundação Vilanova Artigas, 1997), 101.

ARCHITECTURE AND METROPOLITAN CULTURE: CCSP AND SESC POMPÉIA

RENATO ANELLI

The Centro Cultural de São Paulo (CCSP) and the Serviço Social do Comércio Pompéia (SESC Pompéia) were designed and constructed almost in parallel. Both cultural centers are perfect examples of an architecture that is used and admired by the general public, and which is compatible with the metropolitan dimension that São Paulo had only just attained at the time of their conception. The CCSP was designed and built by Eurico Prado Lopes and Luiz Telles between 1977 and 1982.[1] The project by Lina Bo Bardi and her team for the SESC Pompéia, was completed in two phases: from 1977 to 1982 and from 1982 to 1986.[2]

It may sound surprising that these two projects with their freely accessible open spaces were erected during a military dictatorship. But it is essential to consider these structures with regard to the very special characteristics of their historical context, so that we are not tempted to conflate architecture with politics. The economic growth that had characterized the first half of the 1970s stagnated during the second half. In response, the state reacted to the increase in social and trade union movements with new strategies, but also endeavored to nip radical attempts at regime change in the bud. Against this background, both the São Paulo city government, appointed without elections, and the SESC, a non-profit private institution, introduced new social policies.

São Paulo's rapid growth in population—from 1.3 million in 1940 to 8.5 million in 1980—was the result of a national resettlement program from the countryside into the increasingly industrialized city and its peripheral areas, where poverty and hardship were the order of the day. Here, once again, we can see the intimate connection between growth and poverty.[3] The settlement of outlying areas of the city required a decentralization of public facilities for essentials such as health, education, sports, and culture. Locations for these functions were chosen that acted as interfaces between the center and the periphery and which further facilitated decentralization. With this intention, the CCSP was built on the city's southern axis on an old street running towards the coast; and for the construction of its second location in São Paulo, the SESC chose the Pompéia working-class quarter, placed further inland on the city's western axis, where there were plenty of factories lying idle.[4]

Uses

The CCSP was initially intended as an extension of the Mário de Andrade municipal library in the center of the city, but the program was expanded and reoriented in 1979. Four theaters, two concert halls, an amphitheater, exhibition spaces and storage space for cultural assets, as well as wide, freely accessible areas were added to the library. This programmatic reorientation resulted from the "Projeto Periferia" program, in which cultural

Rooftop garden at Centro Cultural de São Paulo (CCSP)

Interior view of the main space at CCSP

View of the entrance of Serviço Social do Comércio (SESC Pompéia)

View of the library of SESC Pompéia

Original layout of the logo for SESC Pompéia Factory

centers located in the individual districts of the city were connected with central institutions.[5]

The SESC in the Pompéia quarter extended the traditional social-services program of that institution which had been established in 1945. Sport, relaxation, and culture were merged under the "leisure" social concept. The idea of offering spaces for workers to relax outside their homes and workplaces can be traced to the French Catholic intellectual, Joffre Dumazedier.[6] This intention solidified with a series of seminars organized at the SESC.[7] The new concept could also be read in the name, which changed from "Centro Cultural e Desportivo Pompéia" (Pompéia Cultural and Sports Center) to "Centro de Lazer – Fábrica da Pompéia" (Pompéia Leisure Center Factory). The center's first logo was a factory chimney sprouting flowers.

Architecture

The architects of both projects, with their opportunities to interpret new architectural programs, followed completely different strategic tacks. Based on a modern-abstract concept, the CCSP is protected from the surrounding urban environment by man-made embankments. A "street" running through the interior—a continuous, straight space—connects the activities occurring on different levels. At SESC Pompéia, a street also runs through the former factory building, but this street was preexisting. Left in its original configuration, it connects various factory sheds, which were converted into a roofed square, a restaurant, a theater, an arts-and-crafts workshop, exhibition spaces, and leads further on to the towers of the facility's sports complex. The architect's strategy was to transform the building's meaning from its original function as an industrial disciplinary working space into a leisure center by introducing new symbolic elements. Here, Lina Bo Bardi drew on her experiences as a stage designer and created figures that could synthesize empathy with visitors. The promenade architecturale was transformed into a symbolic narrative to be filled with life.

The CCSP acts like an urban utility building—a straight "trench," which adjusts to the resulting space, produced from the excavations necessary to build the Vergueiro subway station at the top of the hill and the highway in the valley at the bottom. The space that unfurls between the two parallel embankments is protected by the gardens laid out on the hills adjacent to the two roads, the highway at the bottom, and the avenue at the top. This is the first act of the project. The program is distributed vertically, but also on horizontal levels, the most accessible elements on the upper levels facing the street and those requiring more protection on the lower levels. The public access garden terrace leads the visitor out from the protected area and offers a unique, broad view across the city.

The promenade architecturale along the inner street gives perspectives of the spaces and activities on the upper and lower levels. The amphitheater is quite revolutionary in its arrangement — events are held behind transparent barriers and can be seen but not heard by all visitors to the complex.

Structure

Despite the generously dimensioned spatial arrangement, which opens up the free spaces and transparent barriers, the CCSP's structure also has its deficiencies. Early schemes used reinforced concrete exclusively, but, as the design developed, rolled steel sections were incorporated. The structure's complex geometry surpassed the ability of the planners to work out all the details, especially given the rush with which the project was completed to curry favor in 1982, an election year. The end result is nevertheless inspiring with its experimental orientation.

The SESC Pompéia construction was conducted using a contrasting approach. The architect and her team were constantly at the construction site, making specifications and explaining the details of the project's processes. Since the building was not listed, they could transform the factory almost entirely as they wished, removing plaster from the walls and demolishing and rebuilding parts of the structure. The factory's biggest hall was converted into a roofed square, with the original ceramic tiles partially replaced with glass tiles. Laminated timber furniture such as tables, chairs and benches were conceived as part of the architecture, creating large recreation spaces. Some of the forms were given names like elements in a narrative.[8] The water pond, for example, was named for the Brazilian river, the "Rio São Francisco." The water tower became the "Chaminé" ("Chimney"), and a railing became the "Flor de Mandacaru" ("Mandacaru Flower"). Not only do visitors feel welcome here, but a symbolic dialog with the cultural repertoire is also possible.

Cultural Programs

The CCSP combines a cultural program with an archive of documents that Mário de Andrade had assembled when he was head of the culture department of the São Paulo city government (1935-1938).[9] His ethnographic research on popular and folk culture, which he carried out in the 1930s on trips throughout Brazil, is a superb cultural testament, previously almost unknown as the music, dance, objects that were surveyed had been spread across the entire country. Indeed, the collection of cultural assets that were originally part of the "Biblioteca Mário de Andrade," served husband and wife Pietro and Lina Bardi, as early as the 1940s, as an introduction to the culture of their adopted home.[10] After the CCSP was completed these cultural assets were brought there and have provided a resource for exhibitions, publications, and research.

The exhibitions organized by Lina Bo Bardi after the inauguration of the SESC Pompéia brought the understanding of Brazil's popular culture right up to date. The first of these was the *Design no Brasil: história e realidade* (*Design in Brazil: History and Reality*) exhibition. It went back to her older ideas of a renovation of modern design based on the folk experience of handcrafted utensils, but also integrated more-contemporary design products, such as computers, cars, and airplanes.[11] Subsequent exhibitions intensified the SESC Pompéia's interactions with the rural origins of the city's newly arrived citizens. To address younger populations, other strategies were utilized and festivals were organized, such as "O Começo do Fim do Mundo" ("Beginning of the End of the World"), which documented the power of punk rock in the city's outskirts. In the two years that followed, the theater provided the setting for the "Fábrica do Som" ("Sound Factory") TV program, which allowed young rock bands from São Paulo to develop fame across the country via TV Cultura. The SESC Pompéia therefore developed into a "dream factory,"[12] a dynamic center that attracted the production and dissemination of popular culture in the broadest possible sense, and overcame the restrictions of the colonial roots of Brazilian culture.

Center and Periphery

The CCSP was founded with the idea of allowing culture to emanate from the center out to the periphery. The SESC Pompéia, by contrast, was designed as a center for the interaction and renewal of popular urban culture. In the decades since their inaugurations (the longest democratic period in Brazilian history), these two institutions have served time and again as both references for Brazilian politics and for the architecture that has aimed to reshape São Paulo with culture.

The reasons both attract and accommodate visitors with such great success are not simply due to easy access and the characteristics of their programs. Even if the two buildings employ completely different strategies, it is nevertheless clear that their architectures are largely responsible for the uninterrupted popularity of both cultural centers.

1 Eurico Prado Lopes and Luiz Telles, with the cooperation of: Armando Alberto Prado, Christina de Castro Mello, Ernesto Theodor Walter, José Mario Nogueira de Carvalho, Raul Masatoshi Kan, and Rita de Cássia Vaz Artigas.

2 Lina Bo Bardi, with the cooperation of: Marcelo Ferraz, André Vainer, and Marcelo Suzuki.

3 Luxion Kowarick and Vincius Caldeira Brant, *São Paulo, 1975: Crescimento e pobreza*, (São Paulo: Edições Loyola, 1976).

4 The SESC Consolação was the very first center of its kind in São Paulo. Its first unit was inaugurated in 1967.

5 Cristina Rodrigues Pereira, *Tres obras arquitectónicas y una ciudad en transformación: Estación de Subte São Bento, Centro Cultural São Paulo y SESC Fábrica Pompéia en la ciudad de San Pablo*, Master thesis, Buenos Aires: Universidad Torquato di Tella, 2015; Fernando Serapião, *Centro Cultural São Paulo: espaço e vida*, (São Paulo: Editora Monolito, 2012); Carol Anseloni, "Centro Cultural São Paulo: En tiempos de represión y desarrollo urbano," in *Registros* (Mar del Plata), v. 14, 2018: 48-60.

6 Dumazedier arrived in Brazil at the beginning of the 1960s at the invitation of the "Movimento de Cultura Popular de Pernambuco," with which Lina Bo Bardi prepared the *Exposição Nordeste* in Salvador da Bahia.

7 Renata Carneiro Bechara, *A atuação de Lina Bo Bardi na criação do SESC Pompeia* (1977-1986), Master thesis, São Carlos: Instituto de Arquitetura e Urbanismo USP, 2016; Joffre Dumazeidier, *Vers une civilization du Loisir*, (Paris: Ed. du Seuil, 1962).

8 Brazilian woods from reforestation projects were used here—the system was developed by Vinício Walter Callia in his company, Laminarco.

9 Mário de Andrade (1893-1945), was a Paulistano writer, art critic, and photographer, and a key figure in the Brazilian modernist avant-garde.

10 The husband and wife's publications include numerous references to Mário de Andrade's research work. A first example was the "Ex-votos do Nordeste" article (*Habitat 1*, 1950 colon: 72), which referred to Luis Saia's book *Escultura Popular Brasileira* (São Paulo: Editora Gazeta, 1944).

11 Exhibitions *Nordeste* (1963) and *A Mão do Povo Brasileiro* (1969).

12 The name "fábrica de sonhos" (dream factory) is attributed to Dumazedier by Erivelto Busto Garcia in his text, "Fábrica de Sonhos e o Começo do Fim do Mundo," in *Cidade da Liberdade: Lina Bo Bardi e o SESC Pompéia*, eds. Marcelo Ferraz and André Vainer, (São Paulo, Edições SESC, 2013), 11.

BIG MULTI-PROGRAMMATIC BUILDINGS

CCSP (São Paulo Cultural Center)

SESC Pompéia

CEUs (Structuring Urban Centers)

SESC 24 de Maio

MASP (Museum of Art of São Paulo)

Viewed through the lens of the Constructivist social condensers of the 1920s, which were buildings that had the ambition of supporting and accelerating the life of people through sports, culture, and education (and political indoctrination in the Soviet system), São Paulo's own variety of big multi-programmatic buildings finds its epitome in the Serviço Social do Comércio (SESC) buildings. The SESC buildings, 23 in total in the city of São Paulo and 43 altogether in the State of São Paulo, offer an array of recreational, educational, and cultural programs to SESC members, and at the same time also offer some of the facilities free of charge to everyone. From the blueprint of the SESC Consolação in the 1960s, to Lina Bo Bardi and team's SESC Pompéia in the 1980s, to Paulo Mendes da Rocha and MMBB's SESC 24 de Maio inaugurated in 2017 (the last two included in this catalogue), we can understand how a private-public initiative set the tone for city (public) projects; for example Eurico Prado Lopes and Luiz Telles's Centro Cultural São Paulo from the early 1980s, is truly accessible to all in every one of its dimensions. Alexandre Delijaicov and team's Centro Educacional Unificado (CEU) Inácio Monteiro is one of 45 such buildings in the city's periphery (from the first stages of this initiative in 2003-04), weaving together fragile neighborhoods through education, culture, recreation, and social assistance. Lina Bo Bardi's Museu de Arte de São Paulo (MASP), finished in 1968, is at the juncture of all the categories of this exhibition, but will only be presented in this section. What allows us to call this building multi-programmatic is the open space underneath, which is accessible every day at any time, and has the capacity to host varied programs, usually one at a time—from protests to artistic performances, from markets to a big roof for the tents of the homeless on cold nights.

CCSP (São Paulo Cultural Center)

Name: CCSP (São Paulo Cultural Center)

Address: Rua Vergueiro, 1000

Year of project: 1976-1982

Architects: Eurico Prado Lopes and Luiz Telles

Strucrtural engineers: Maubertec Engenharia e Projetos

Client/who commissioned: city administration

Type of institution: public cultural center owned by the city culture authority

Hours: open spaces (including the "dance corridor"): every day from 9 am to 10 pm; libraries: Tue. - Fri., 10 am - 8 pm / Sat. - Sun. 10 am - 6 pm / closed on holidays; exhibition spaces: Tue. - Fri., 10 am - 8 pm / Sat.- Sun. and holidays, 10 am - 6 pm; rooftop garden: Tue. - Sun., 10 am - 6 pm; restaurant/café: Mon., 9 am - 4 pm / Tue. - Sat., 9 am - 9 pm / Su. and holidays, 9 am - 8 pm.

Number of daily visitors: about 2,500 people (about 70,000 per month)

Project: Eurico Prado Lopes and Luiz Telles won an open competition in 1976, and works began in 1978, ending in 1982. Still under military dictatorship. The mayor was Reynaldo de Barros (not democratically elected) and the culture secretary was Mário Chamie. The project is integrated to the public transportation system (with direct connection to the subway), through the Vergueiro Station, opened in 1975.

Program: three exhibition galleries; five libraries (including second largest one in São Paulo); city collections, such as the City Art Collection, the Oneyda Alvarenga Music Archive, the Multimedia Archive, the CCSP Memory Center and Mário de Andrade Folkloric Research Mission Archive; Sala Adoniran Barbosa with 622 seats (theater), Sala Jardel Filho with 321 seats (theater), Sala Paulo Emilio Salles Gomes with 99 seats (cinema), Sala Lima Barreto with 99 seats (cinema), Espaço Cênico Ademar Guerra up to 200 people (theater); administration, workshop spaces, restaurant/café, garden, rooftop garden.

Area: 46,500 m^2

Interior view of the main space at CCSP

Dedicated in 1982, the Centro Cultural São Paulo was planned on expropriated land resulting from the construction of the subway, using the same trench-in-the-ground approach as the subway. Popular with São Paulo's citizens from the start, it has seen periods of decline, but as of late it has become once again a destination in the city, both for immediate neighbors as well as for people from all over the city due to its accessibility via the subway. Particularly popular as a library, exhibition space, and lunch spot, it has become an epicenter of alternative youth cultures that practice dance routines in small groups, distributing themselves throughout the building's open spaces. As happens with heavily-used public facilities today, free wifi is as important as some of the physical qualities of the building. The maintenance of the building is a critical issue, both in terms of ensuring the security of the users with specialized personnel as well as the upkeep of the heavily used facilities (namely the restrooms are a critical issue), resulting in maintenance being a top priority of the administration. The CCSP is a paradigmatic example of public architecture—at the limits of civic urbanism and civic architecture—at the scale of the city.

Interior view of the main space at CCSP looking at library tables on the inside and cafeteria tables and sunken terrace on the outside

Karate practice at the rooftop garden

Interior view of the library tables, exterior view of cafeteria tables

View of the cafeteria terrace

View of one of the sunken terraces

View of the rooftop terrace garden

Elevations CCSP
© FAUUSP Library

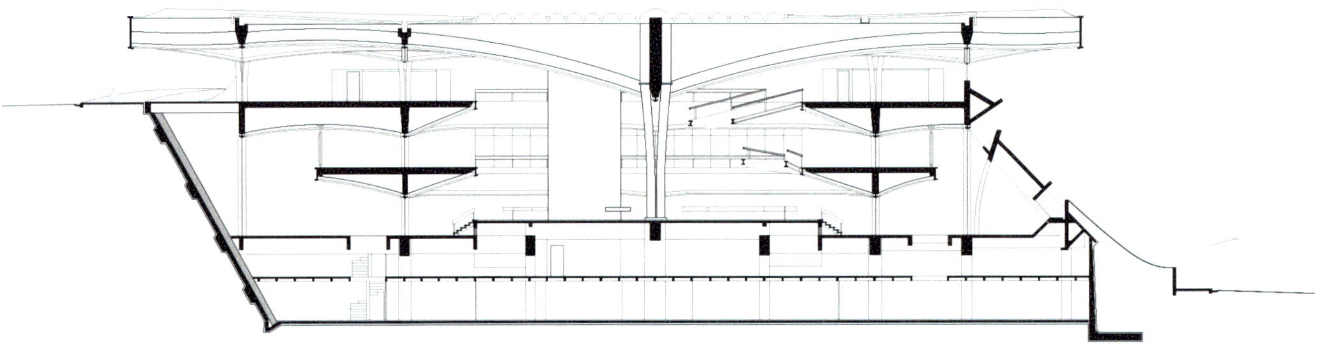

Transverse sections 1:500
© Guilherme Pianca, Gabriel Sepe and team

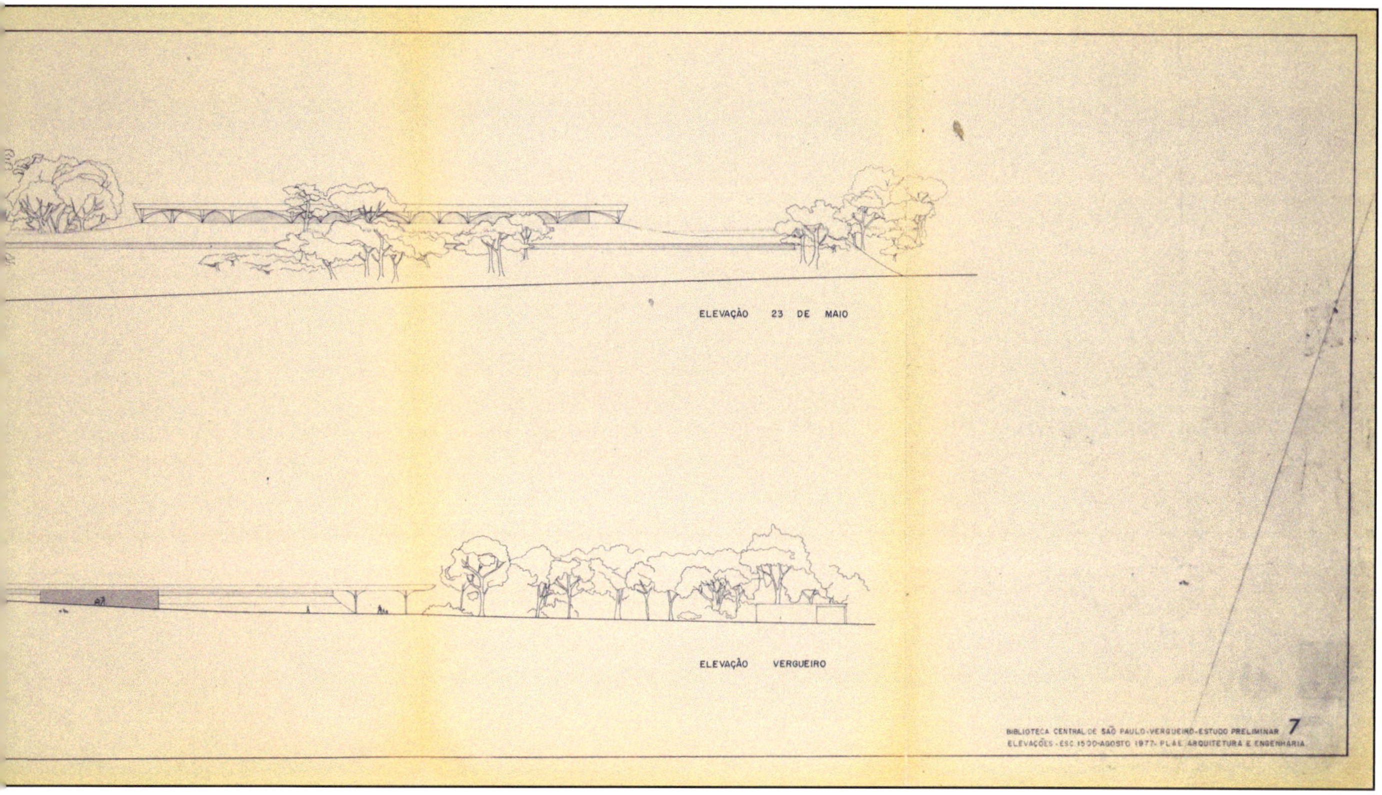
ELEVAÇÃO 23 DE MAIO
ELEVAÇÃO VERGUEIRO
BIBLIOTECA CENTRAL DE SÃO PAULO-VERGUEIRO-ESTUDO PRELIMINAR 7
ELEVAÇÕES - ESC 1:500-AGOSTO 1977- PL.AE. ARQUITETURA E ENGENHARIA

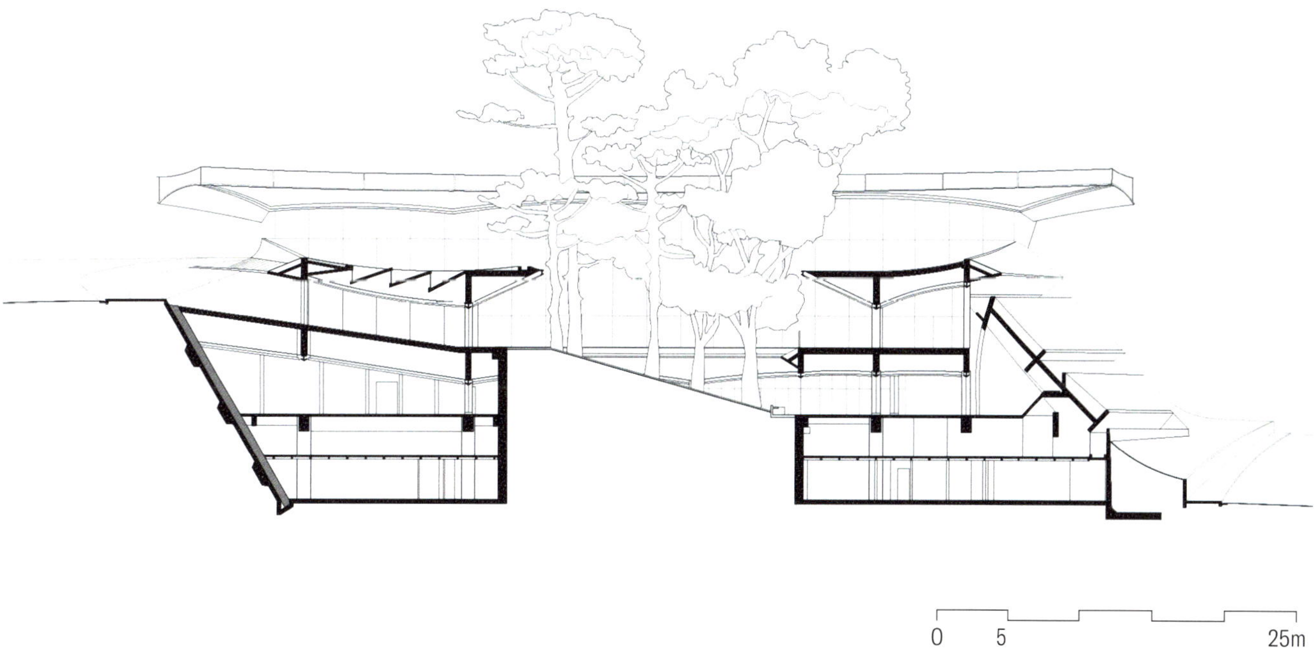
0
5
25m

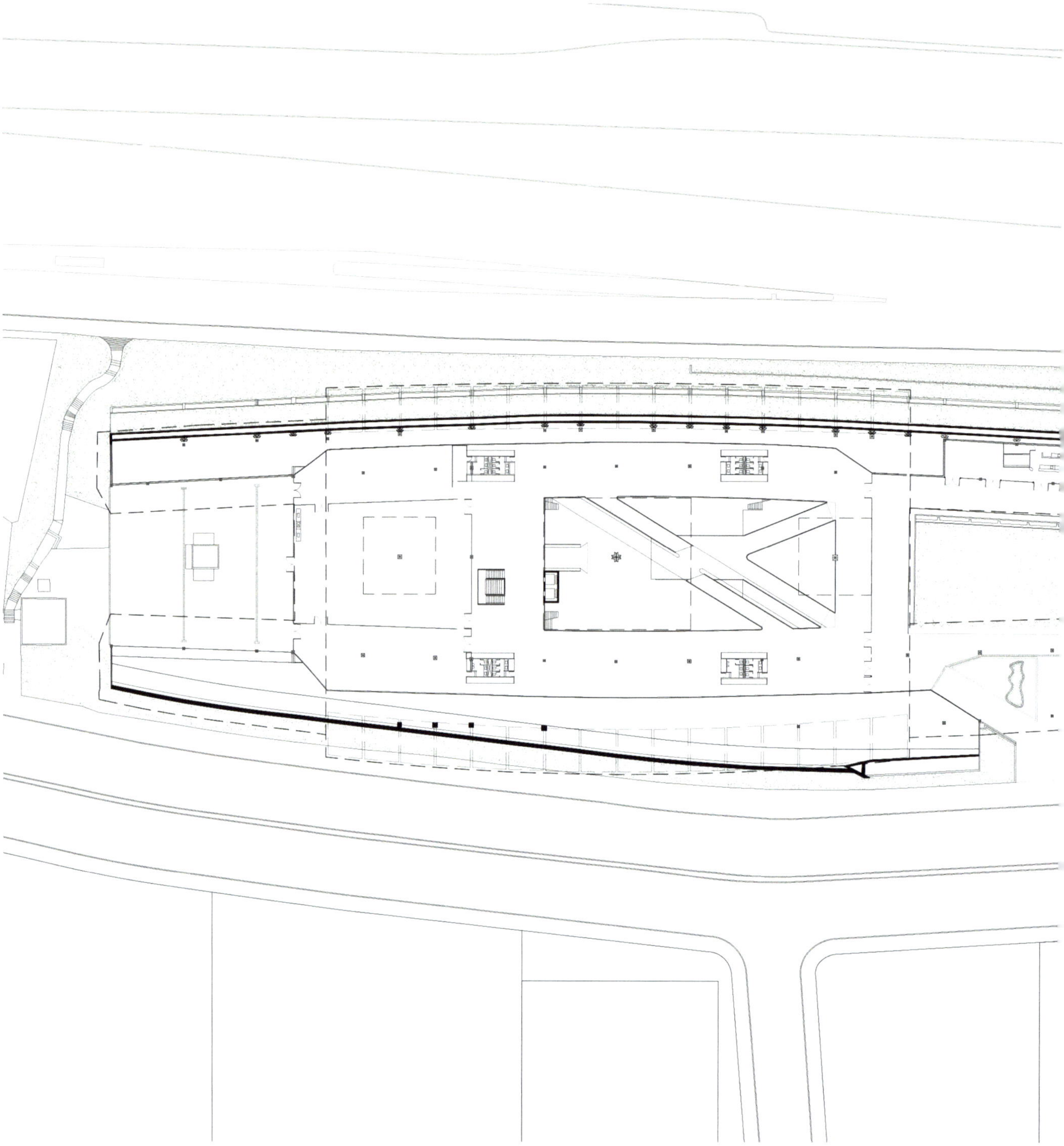

Ground floor plan 1:1,000
© Guilherme Pianca, Gabriel Sepe and team

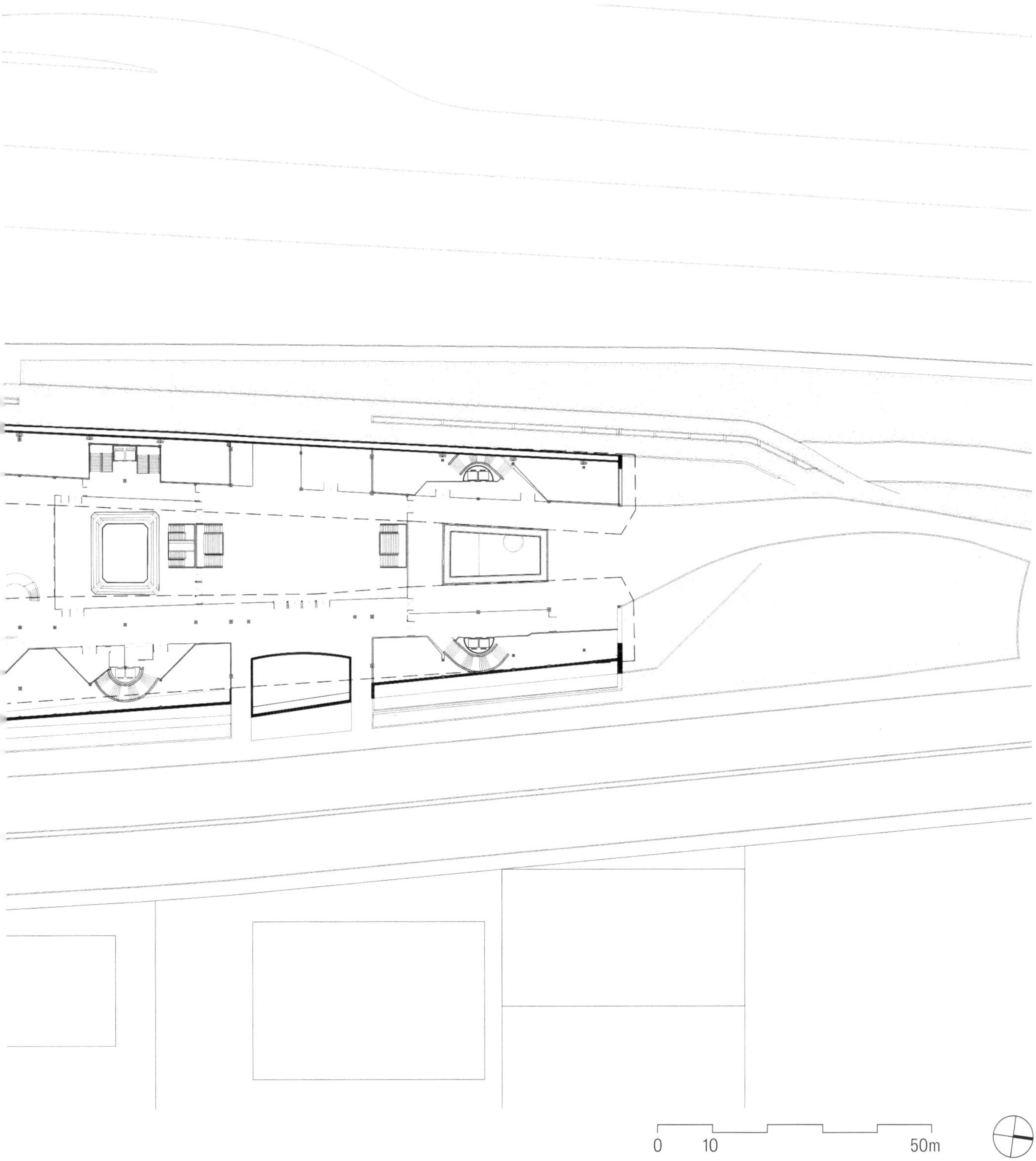
0
10
50m

Exploded perspective drawing
© Danilo Zamboni

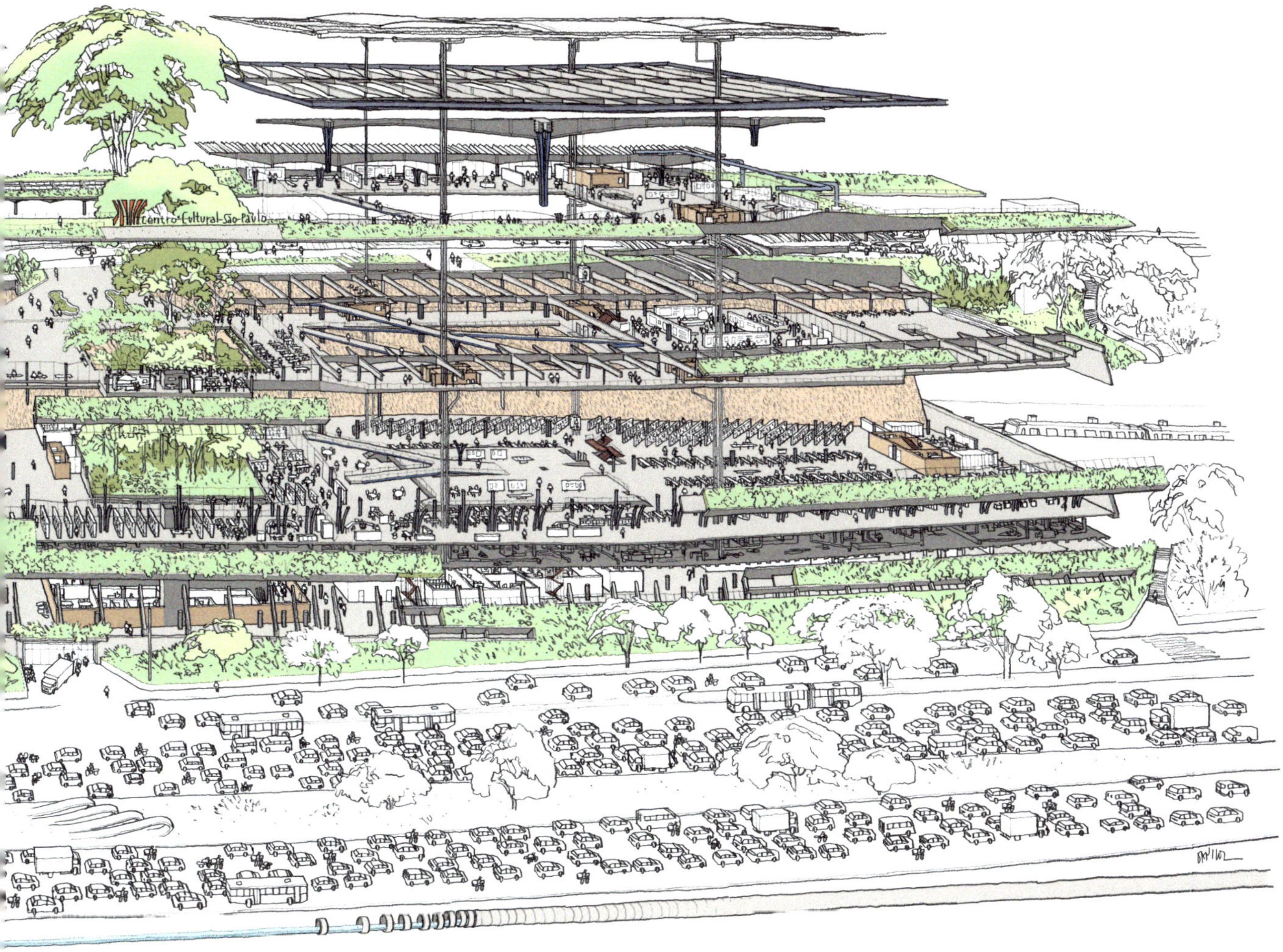
Centro Cultural São Paulo

SESC Pompéia

Name: Serviço Social do Comércio (SESC) Pompéia

Address: Rua Clélia 93

Year of project: 1977-1986

Architect: Lina Bo Bardi, with Marcelo Ferraz, André Vainer and Marcelo Suzuki.

Engineer: José Carlos de Figueiredo Ferraz

Client/who commissioned: Serviço Social do Comércio - SESC (Social Service of Commerce)

Type of institution: private non-profit company financed with public federal or state founds

Hours: Tue. - Sat., 9 am - 10 pm; Sun. and holidays, 9 am - 8 pm; Mon., closed.

Number of daily visitors: Between 1,000-5,000 depending on the day.

Project: Lina Bo Bardi, 1977-1982 (restoration and intervention in the old barrels and refrigerators factory from early twentieth century with a François Hennebique reinforced concrete system), 1982-1986 (sport facilities, engineer: José Carlos de Figueiredo Ferraz)

Program: in the restored old factory: restaurant, bar and café for 800 people, souvenir and book store, ticket shop, foyer, theater with 746 seats, exhibition room, arts and crafts workshop (to attend workshops it's necessary to register and pay, but the room is open for all, with temporary exhibitions too), indoor playground, reading and studying space, library, administration, five dental care clinics (just for trade and services workers with credential). In the sports facilities blocks (access just for trade and services workers with credential): swimming pool for 600 people, three multi-sport courts, gym and yoga rooms. Open space (access for all): inner street and deck-solarium.

Area: building land 16,573 m^2, old factory 12,211 m^2, new constructions 23,571 m^2.

View of the urban beach with the refurbished old factory buildings to the left and sports towers at the backcround at Sesc Pompéia.

With the first phase dedicated in 1982 and the second phase dedicated in 1986, the compound is located in the western part of the city in what used to be the traditional working-class neighborhood of Vila Pompéia. The site was originally used by a German company that originally produced cottonseed oil drums, later evolving to the production of consumer goods. SESC bought the plot with the factory in the 1960s. Later, when Lina Bo Bardi was engaged to do the design, an early decision was made to keep the factory facilities and intervene within them, although a sports tower was eventually added. Like all the SESC's buildings in São Paulo, it caters to people of all ages, offering the members workshops, sports facilities, subsidized food, and reduced-priced cultural spectacles. At the same time, the building is popular with the general public, which produces a vibrant scene on weekends, particularly in summer, when the "urban beach" at the end of the plot comes alive.

The programmatic success is combined in this case with an architecture of particular quality, with a bold use of reinforced concrete in a brutalist tradition, and the customized design of everything from the railings to the furniture. Unlike the prototype-like edge of Lina Bo Bardi's MASP, where the power of the idea is greater than the architectural execution of it, the SESC Pompeia is an example of design mastery, both in the sensibility of the intervention in the old factory as well as in the design and execution of the sports tower and the circulation and office volume that accompanies it and the bridges that connect both.

View looking towards the main entrance of the internal pedestrian street flanked by the old factory buildings

Interior view of the main entrance building with the library at the background

Interior view of the reading space at the library

Interior view of the workshop space

Sunbathers at the urban beach

View of the pedestrian street

Interior view of sports facilities at the sports tower

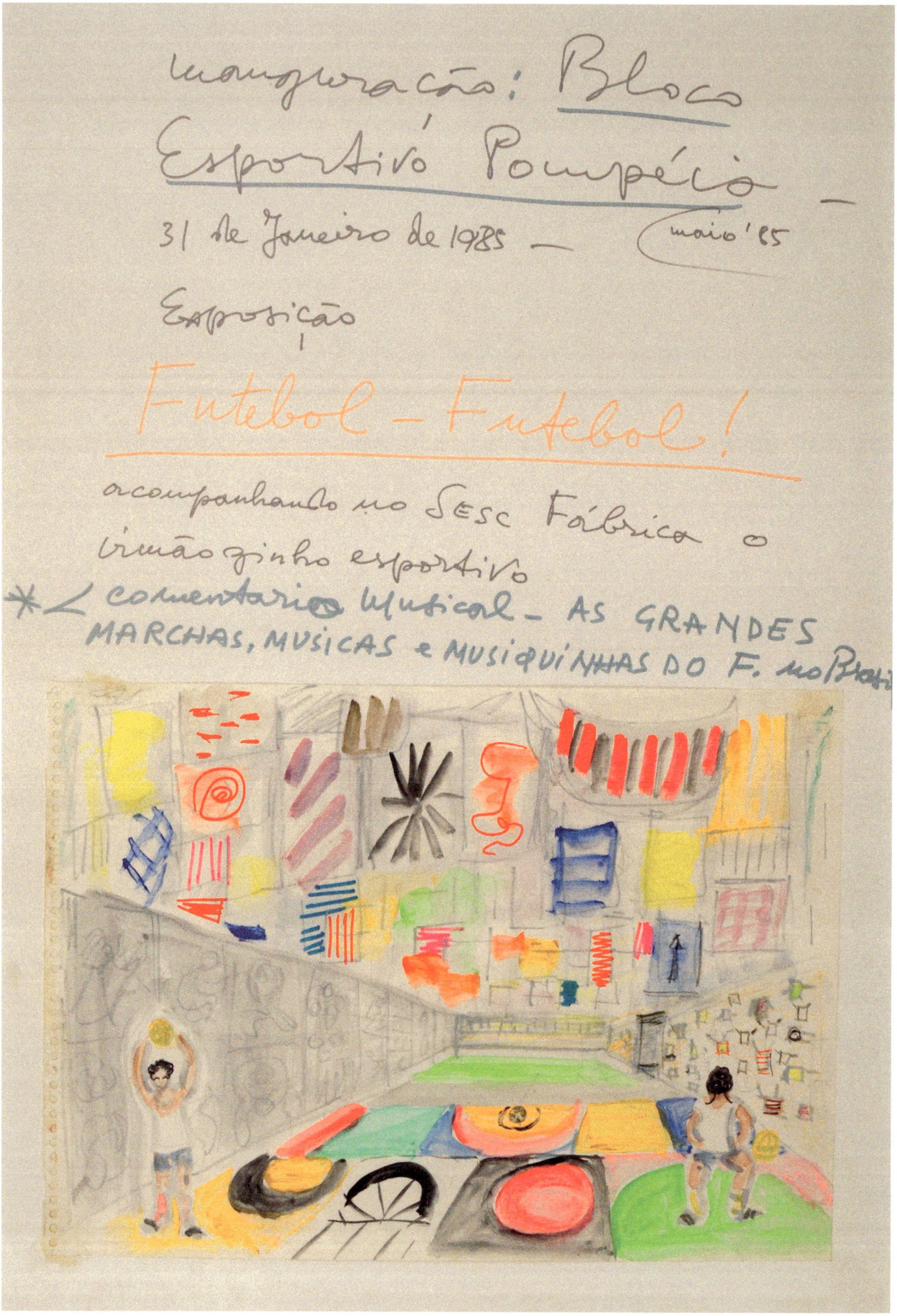

Lina Bo Bardi, Study for the inauguration of the sports center of SESC – Pompeia Factory, 1985
Watercolor, felt tip, graphite and colored pencil on cardboard, parchment, and offset paper 69.5 x 49.7 cm

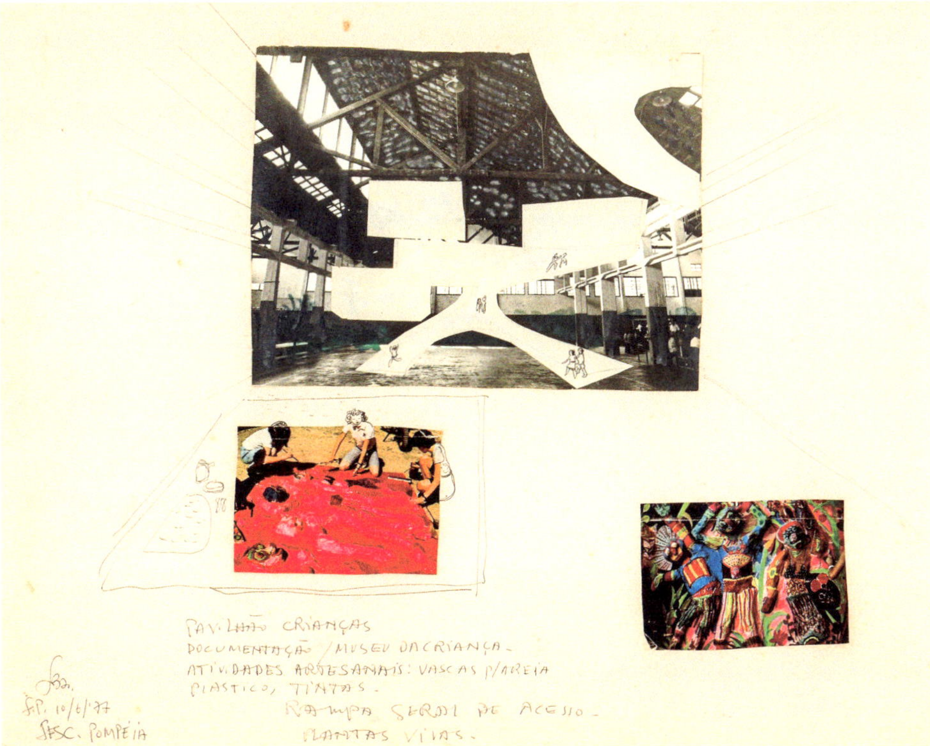

Photomontage of the warehouse of SESC – Pompeia Factory, 1977
Felt tip pen and graphite on cardboard 39 x 56.6 cm. © Instituto Bardi / Photo: Henrique Luz

Internal street of SESC – Pompeia Factory, 1977
Watercolor, ballpoint, and graphite on cardboard 28.5 x 38.5 cm. © Instituto Bardi / Photo: Henrique Luz

Ground floor plan 1:1,000
© Guilherme Pianca, Gabriel Sepe and team

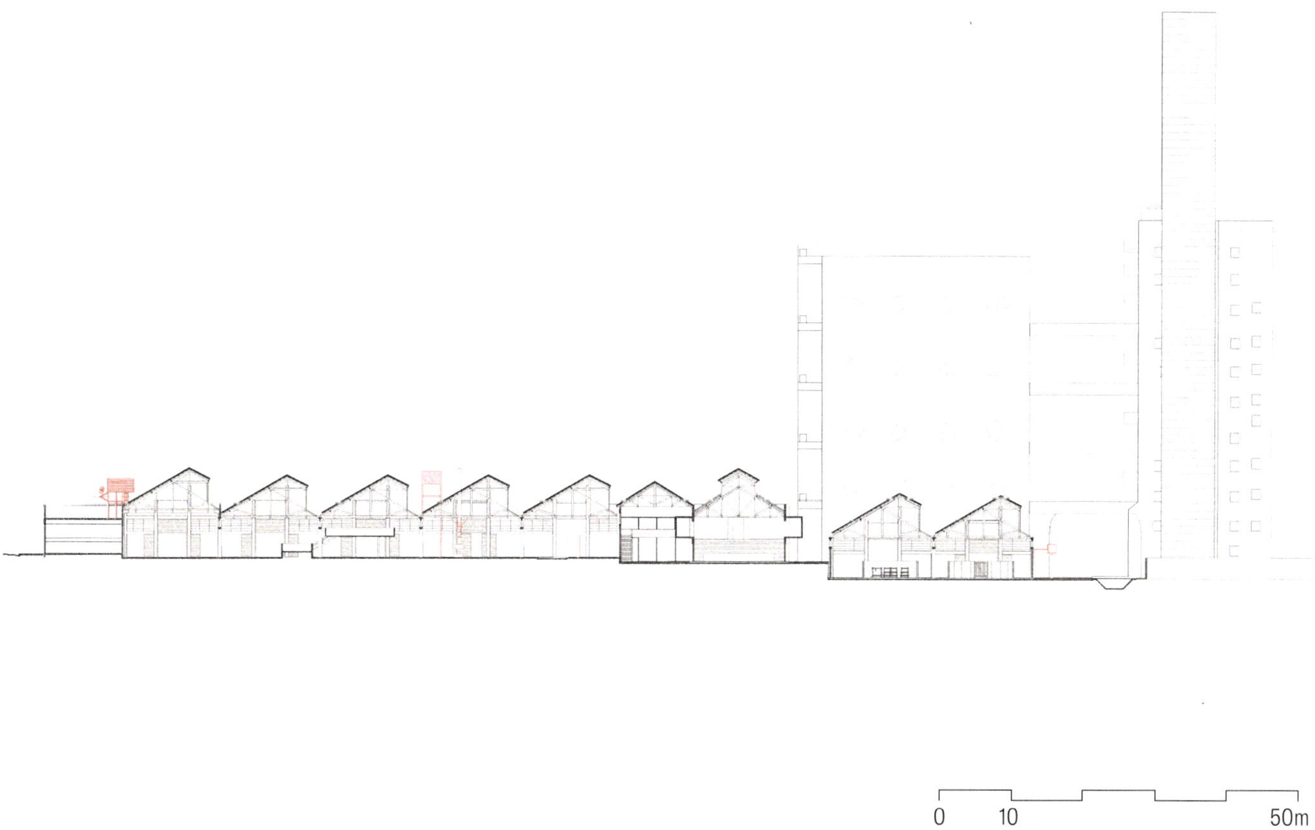

Longitudinal section 1:1,000
© Guilherme Pianca, Gabriel Sepe and team

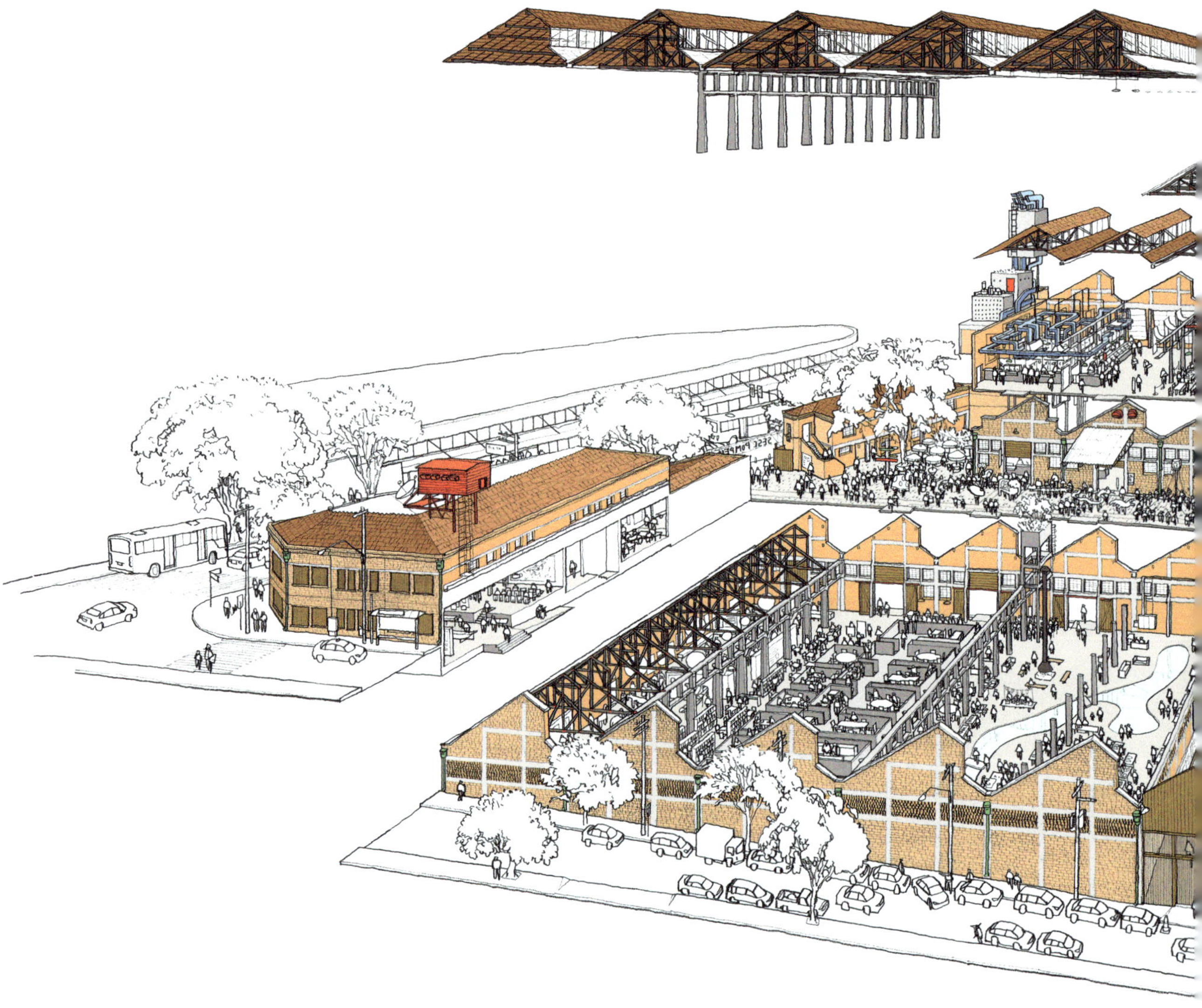

Exploded perspective drawing
© Danilo Zamboni

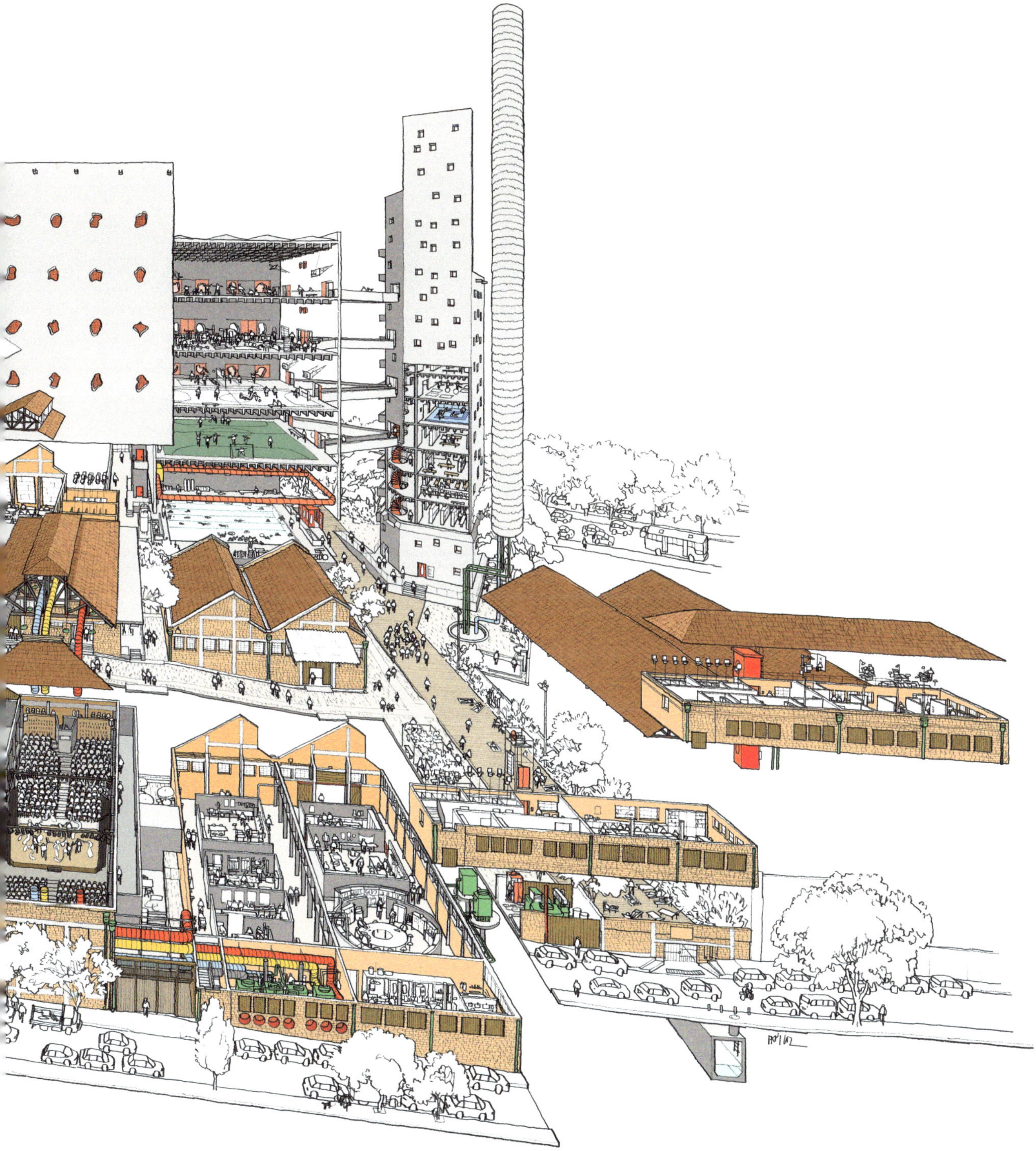

CEUs (Structuring Urban Centers)

Name: Centro Educacional Unificado (CEU) Inácio Monteiro

Address: R. Barão Barroso do Amazonas, s / n – Guaianases

Year of project: 2001-2003

Architect: Alexandre Delijaicov, André Takyia and Wanderley Ariza (team coordination)

Engineer: Péricles Salvatore Palazzi and José Zamarion Diniz (EDIF-SSO-PMSP)

Client/who commissioned: city administration

Type of institution: public educational center owned by the city education authority (the city culture authority also develops activities on CEU units)

Hours: Mon. - Sun., 7 am - 11 pm

Project: Departamento de Edificações - EDIF (building department) from Secretaria Municipal de Infraestrutura Urbana e Obras (Municipal Authority of Urban Infrastructure and Public Works), Alexandre Delijaicov, André Takyia and Wanderley Ariza (team coordination), 2001-2002 (conception and project), november 2003 (works finished). Between 2001 and 2004 when Marta Suplicy was the mayor (Workers Party) the first 21 CEUs were built. Nowadays 46 CEUs units are built in São Paulo periphery (all units now are also used as UniCEU - universidade nos CEUs, a university "campus" in the CEU units, coordinated by the Federal Government. 15 CEUs house the public system of cinemas, Spcine). The project conceived by the team of architects from the Department of Buildings of the City of São Paulo (EDIF)—who could be considered as heirs of Anísio Teixeira (educator), Hélio Duarte and Diógenes Rebouças (architects) ideals—groups the program into three simple volumetric sets. The largest, in the form of an orthogonal grid, includes classrooms, dining rooms, library, digital inclusion program, bakery school, exhibition areas and living spaces. The smaller, high disk-shaped volume houses the nursery. The third gathers in a five-story compact volume, theater, sports gymnasium and music rehearsal room.

Program: educational center with sports facilities, theater, library, restaurant, nursery, kindergarten, elementary school, technical and vocational high school, university. CEU CEI Josely Maria Cardoso Bento (nursery), CEU EMEI Inácio Monteiro (kindergarten), CEU EMEF Inácio Monteiro (elementary school), ETEC de Itaquera technical and vocational high school), UniCEU (university), theater "Cassia Eller" with 450 seats, library "Adelaide de Castro Alves Guimarães, internet and computer room (digital inclusion program), three swimming pools, closed sport court, open sport court, skate track, gym room, gymnastics hall, dance room.

Area: around 14,000 m^2

Exterior View, CEU Inácio Monteiro

CEU INACIO MONTEIRO

With the first buildings done in 2003-04, the official title of this initiative is Centro Educacional Unificado, literally "Unified Educational Center," but the architect Alexandre Delijaicov prefers to call these buildings Praças de Equipamentos Sociais, literally "Social Equipment Squares." There were 45 units in total built under a single construction bid in 2003-04, with the aim of optimization of the construction sites, machinery, and equipment. Inácio Monteiro (CEU) is one of the buildings from the first stage, and like all of its building-siblings, the aim is to organize the territory around the structure. The idea comes from the 1989-1992 period, originated by Secretary of Education Paulo Freire during the first PT (Workers' Party) administration, and then taken over by the architects Delijaicov, André Takyia, and Wanderley Ariza who gave architectural form to the conception in the program and made the analyses of where to locate them. The first 45 CEUs were located in the neediest and most vulnerable districts of São Paulo, mostly on the periphery of the city. The CEUs, including CEU Inacio Monteiro, are urban centers that structure the neighborhoods around them through school facilities that also serve as community centers, universities, and a series of other infrastructures. They all include a nursery, kindergarten, school, adult education, sports facilities, a theatre, and rehearsal spaces. These compounds not only organize networks of municipal public education, culture, sports, and leisure, but also social welfare and health facilities.

Interior view

View of the sports courtyard

Skatepark with CEU buildings in the back

Exterior view of the swimming pool

View of the sports courtyard

View of the sports courtyard

CEUs 1st phase 2003

1	Jaraguá
2	Perus
3	Paz
4	Pera Marmelo
5	Vila Curuçá
6	Jambeiro
7	Parque Veredas
8	Parque São Carlos
9	Cidade Dutra
10	Três Lagos
11	Pedreira-Alvarenga
12	Grajaú-Navegantes
13	Aricanduva
14	Meninos
15	Rosa da China
16	São Mateus
17	São Rafael
18	Inácio Monteiro
19	Butantã
20	Monte Azul
21	Capão Redondo

CEUs 2nd phase 2004

22	Tremembé
23	Tiquatira
24	Quinta do Sol
25	Três Pontes
26	Lajeado
27	Azul da Cor do Mar
28	Água azul
29	Limoeiro
30	Sapopemba
31	Formosa
32	Caminho do Mar
33	Cidade do Sol
34	Vila Rubi
35	Parelheiros
36	Vila do Sol
37	Guarapiranga
38	Feitiço da Vila
39	Três Marias
40	Paraisópolis
41	Cantos do Amanhecer
42	Estrelão
43	Jaguaré
44	Jardim Britânia
45	Jardim Paulistano

0 1 5 20 km

Location of CEUs in the map of the city of São Paulo inside the metropolitan area.

Aerial views of the first 21 CEUs © David Rego Jr.

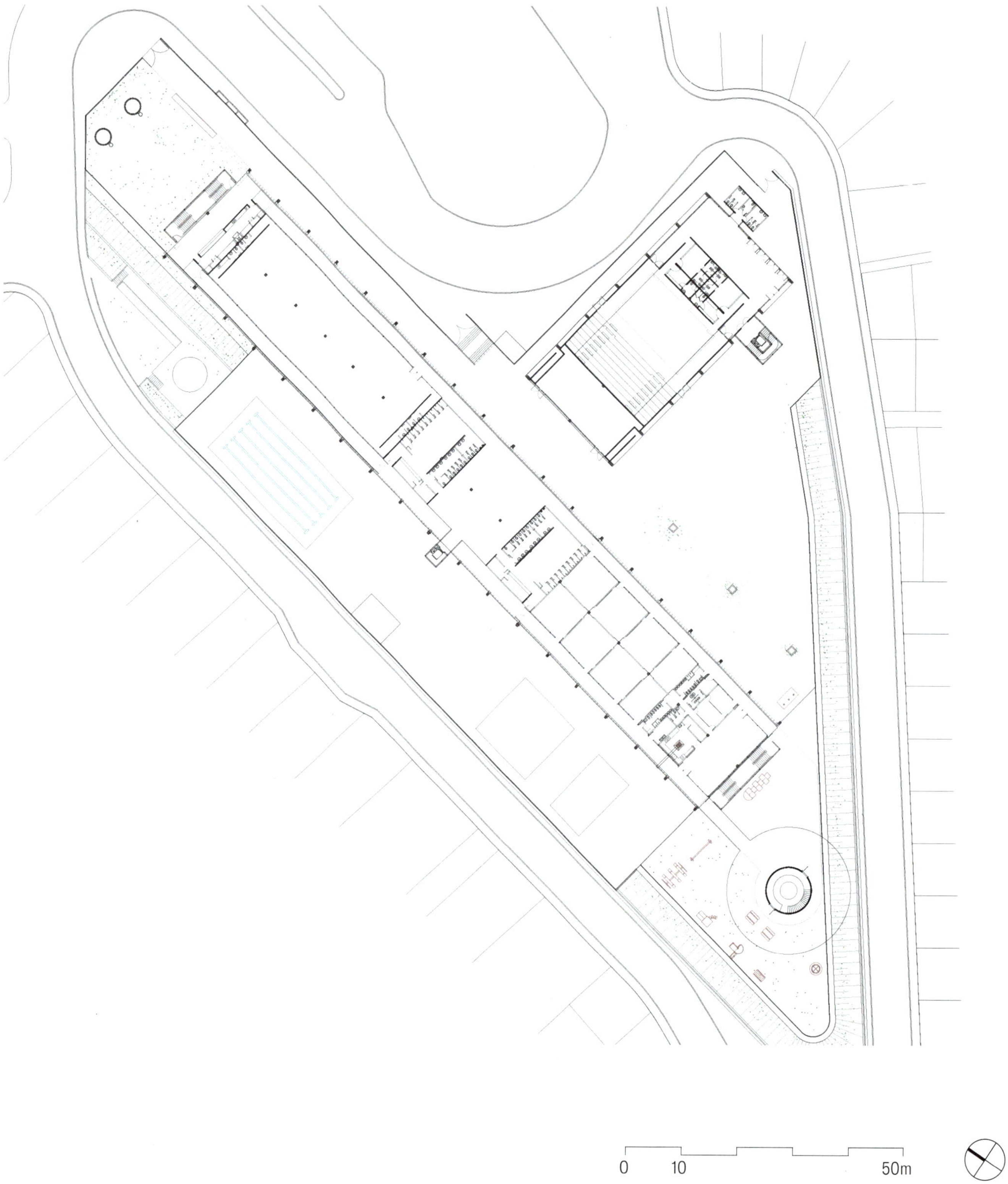

Ground floor plan, CEU Inácio Monteiro 1:1,000
© Guilherme Pianca, Gabriel Sepe and team

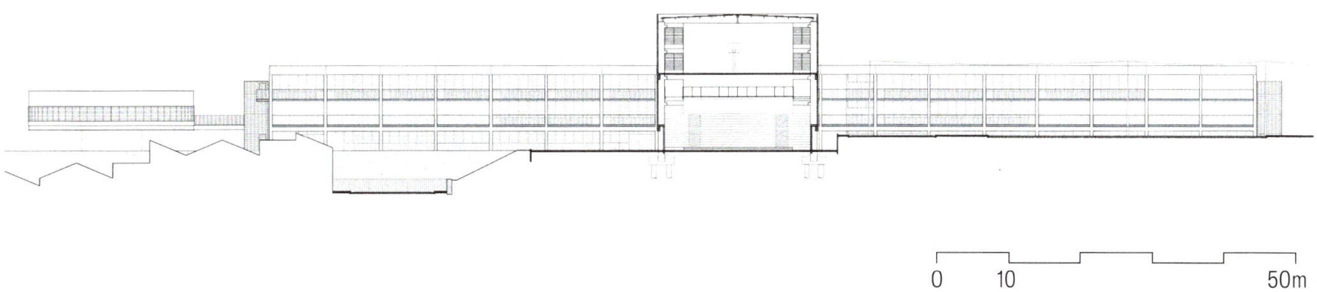

Section and elevation, CEU Inácio Monteiro 1:1,000

Exploded perspective drawing
© Danilo Zamboni

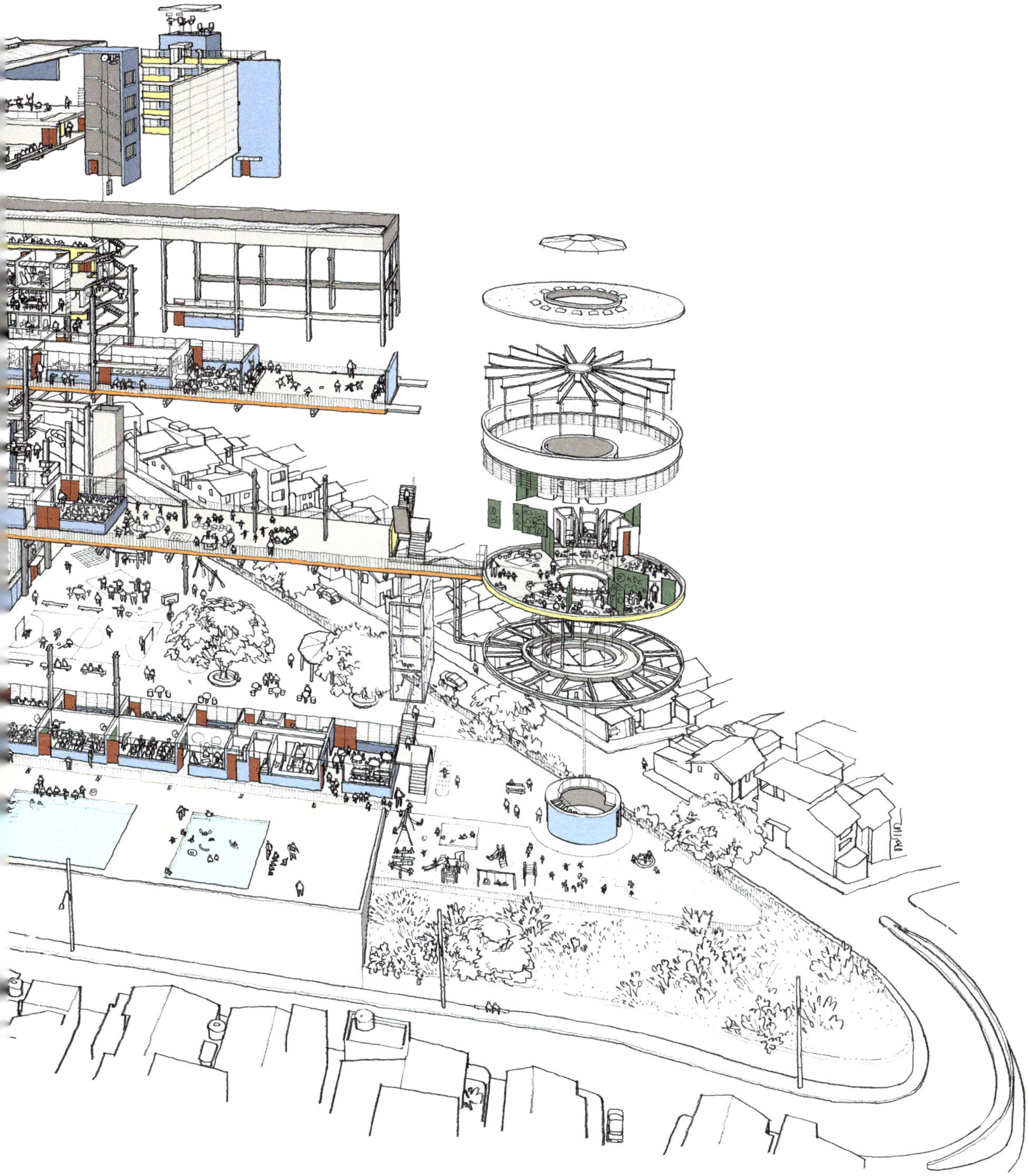

SESC 24 de Maio

Name: Serviço Social do Comércio (SESC) 24 de Maio

Address: Rua 24 de Maio, 109

Year of project: 2001-2017

Architects: Paulo Mendes da Rocha and MMBB Arquitetos (Fernando Mello Franco, Marta Moreira, Milton Braga)

Structural engineers: Kurkdjian e Fruchtengarten Engenheiros Associados

Client/who commissioned: Serviço Social do Comércio - SESC (Social Service of Commerce)

Type of institution: private non-profit company financed with public federal or state funds

Hours: Tue. - Sat., 9 am - 9 pm; Sun. and Holidays, 9 am - 6 pm; Mon. closed.

Number of daily visitors: 10,000

Project: Underground Café, foyer, theater with 216 seats. Entrance square with administrative user services (ground floor); administration offices; restaurant; open third floor square "living area"; library; exhibitions; workshops; dental care clinics (just for trade and services workers with credentials); sport courts (open, but the use is just for trade and services workers with credential); gym and dance room (open, but the use is just for trade and services workers with credential); open eleventh floor swimming pool garden with café, changing rooms (just for trade and services workers with credential); open air rooftop swimming pool for 400 people (just for trade and services workers with credential).

Program: sports facilities, exhibition space, theater, workshop space, dental clinics, library, and restaurant.

Area: building land 2,203 m^2, total built area 29,516 m^2

Third floor and ramp, SESC 24 de Maio

5
Exposições
3
Convivência
Elevador Se

Dedicated in 2017, the SESC 24 de Maio was designed as an intervention in an existing department store building to which an additional service tower was added. The building is in the center of São Paulo close to Praça da República, the Mario de Andrade Public Library, Praça do Patriarca, the Municipal Theatre (and the Praça das Artes), and connected to the Viaduto do Chá.

This building stacks up from the basement with the following elements: a theatre, store, and café independently accessible by stairs and elevators; an entrance plaza at street level (and from this floor up, all program elements on the remaining 11 floors are connected by a side ramp); management offices; cafeteria; open lounge floor; library; exhibition space; offices; dental clinic; sport facilities; dance studio; swimming pool plaza with cafeteria; changing rooms (twelfth floor); and a rooftop swimming pool (thirteenth and last floor).

The existing Mesbla department store was a forty-by-forty-meter square building with a central void measuring fourteen by fourteen meters, in the corners of which the architects located four new columns extending below street level to open up a space for a theater and extending all the way to the roof to support the weight of a swimming pool, with the rest of the program stacked between the two. Parallel to the intervention in the old building, a plot of land was cleared on the side to make way for a service tower with bathrooms and other such program elements. The circulation ramp between the old and the new building is one of the innovations of this project, allowing a "street life" type of atmosphere to mount through the building and invigorating the programs it connects, including some intermediate spaces like that of the ground floor, third floor, and eleventh floor lounges where people can take breaks or engage in more informal activities.

The centrality in the city, the quality of the facilities including the beach-like rooftop swimming pool in the middle of an office-and-retail area of the city, and the intense use of all of the remaining program elements (including the cafeteria which offers reduced price meals to the members), turn this building into a pole of attraction in São Paulo. It is an everyday or weekly place of pilgrimage for many, as well as an occasional destination for people from all over the city, bringing an unforeseen haven used by circa 10,000 daily users to the center of São Paulo.

Eleventh floor, SESC 24 de Maio

Eighth floor, SESC 24 de Maio

Exterior view

Terrace and swimming pool, SESC 24 de Maio

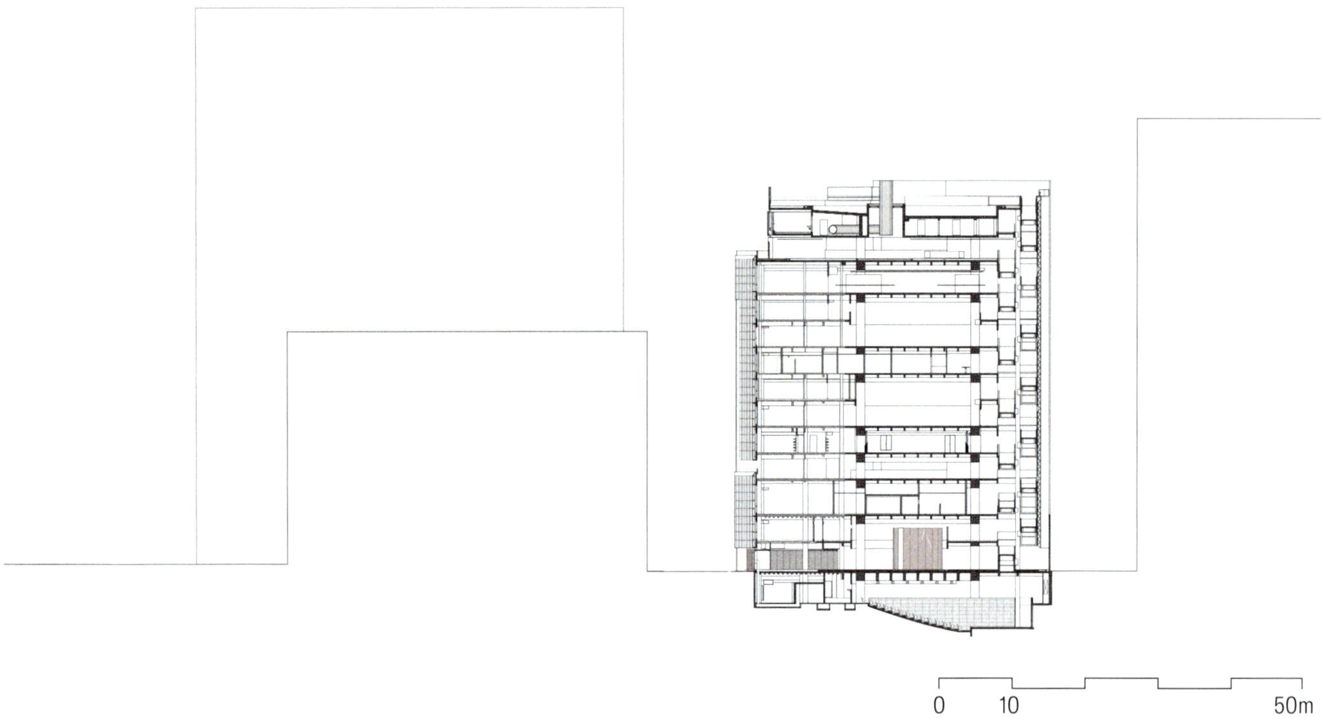

Section 1:1,000
© Guilherme Pianca, Gabriel Sepe and team

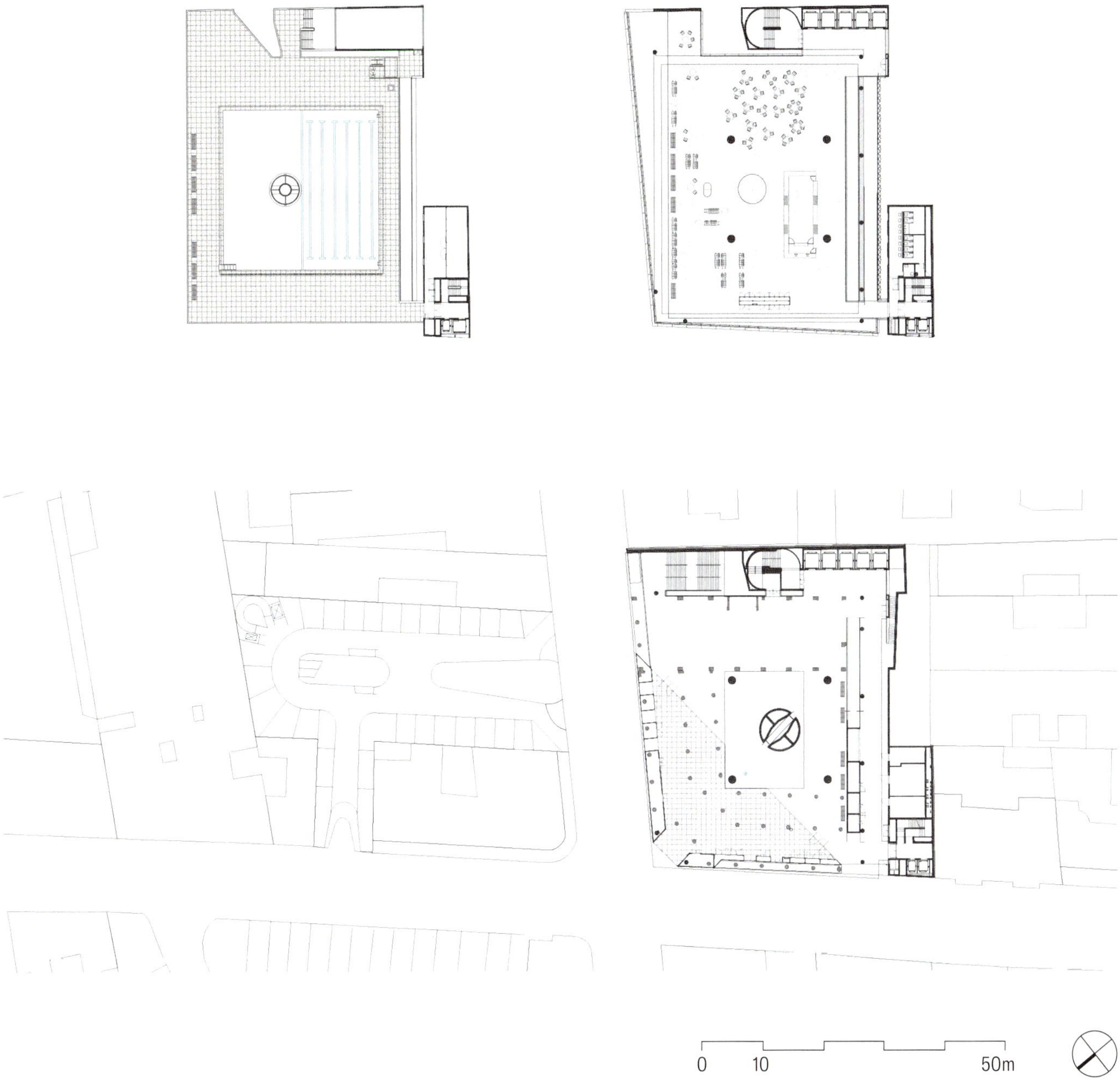

Floor plans 1:1,000
© Guilherme Pianca, Gabriel Sepe and team

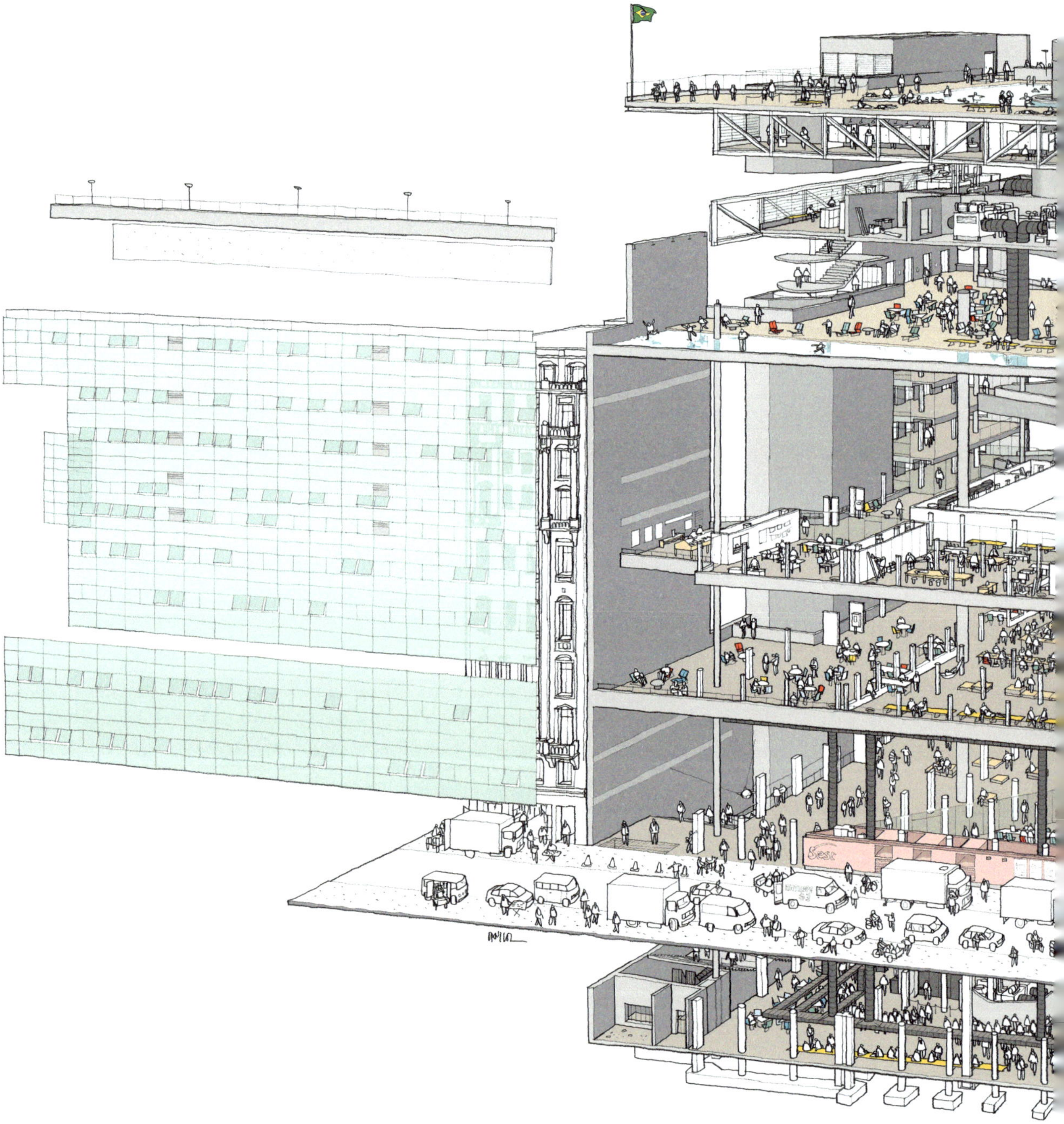

Exploded perspective drawing
© Danilo Zamboni

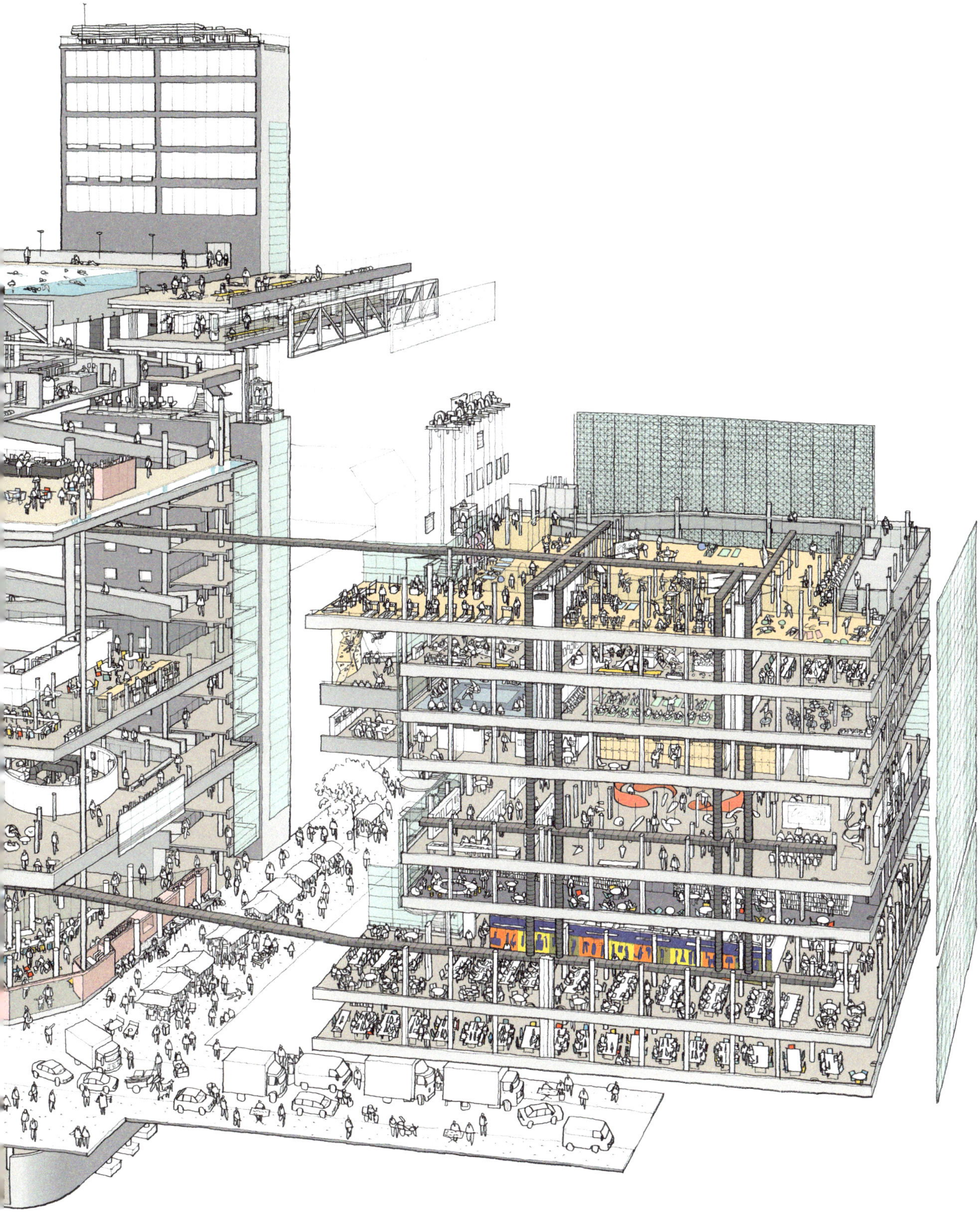

MASP (Museum of Art of São Paulo)

Name: Museu de Arte de São Paulo Assis Chateaubriand (MASP)

Address: Av. Paulista, 1578

Year of project: 1957-1968

Architect: Lina Bo Bardi

Engineer: José Carlos de Figueiredo Ferraz

Client/who commissioned: Francisco de Assis Chateaubriand, founder and patron, Pietro Maria Bardi (Art Director)

Type of institution: Private Art Museum (non-profit institution)

Hours: Tue., 10 am - 8 pm; Wed. - Sun., 10 am - 6 pm; Mondays closed; free ground floor always open.

Number of daily visitors: 3,500, more on Thursday when the museum is free.

Project: Lina Bo Bardi, 1957 - 1968. The museum was founded by Assis Chateaubriand in 1947 and was located in an old building in downtown. Assis Chateaubriand was owner of Diários Associados, the largest media conglomerate in Latin America, which at its golden times had more than one hundred newspapers, radio and TV stations, magazines, and a telegraphic agency. In 1951, where today is the museum, was built the pavilion for the 1st São Paulo Art Biennial, designed by Luis Saia and Eduardo Kneese de Mello, conceived by Ciccillo Matarazzo. To start MASP construction, the land was provided by the city administration and conceived works financed with municipal funds. In 1957 Lina Bo Bardi presented the first version of the project to the municipal authorities (public works), works started in 1959, but until 1964 the works were taken in a slow rhythm (between 1960 and 1964 Lina Bo Bardi was living in Bahia). Part of the structure was just painted in red in 1990. In 2018 the museum was visited by 502,642 people.

Program: museum collection gallery, temporary exhibition gallery, administration, lower temporary exhibition galleries, foyer, two theaters (374 seats and 80 seats), restaurant, café, store, library, and archive

Area: 11,000 m^2

Exterior view of MASP at Avenida Paulista

René
TERAPIA

Dedicated in 1968, and although it is a museum, the Museu de Arte de São Paulo Assis Chateaubriand (MASP) represents the big multi-programmatic dimension with two floors of exhibition galleries stacked over an open space that is very flexible (on an activity-to-activity basis). A sunken auditorium, restaurant, and another exhibition area, among other programs are located under the plaza. This is possible due to a drop in the level of the city towards the back of the plaza. Thus, the plaza is really the roof of the program underneath it, allowing for natural light at the sides and the back. The open space is created by the void between the above- and below-ground elements and connects to Avenida Paulista, putting an open-space/street strategy at play. Moreover, by lifting the galleries and "liberating" the ground space, the view to the Trianon Park was left unobstructed and the plaza was made available, also offering striking views to the city below. The MASP is the usual meeting point for protesters and manifestations on the left, from which marchers might then proceed to other parts of the city.

Different uses under the Museum of Art of São Paulo:

Playground Exhibition by Nelson Leirner, 1969
© Instituto Bardi

View of the open span, 1970s
© Acervo do Centro de Pesquisa do MASP/ Photo: Luiz Hossaka

Flea Market, 1970s
© Acervo do Centro de Pesquisa do MASP

"Diretas Já" Impeachment Protest at MASP's open span, 1992
© Instituto Bardi

Back view of MASP, Northeast façade

View of the open span

View from the street

View of the main exhibition gallery at MASP

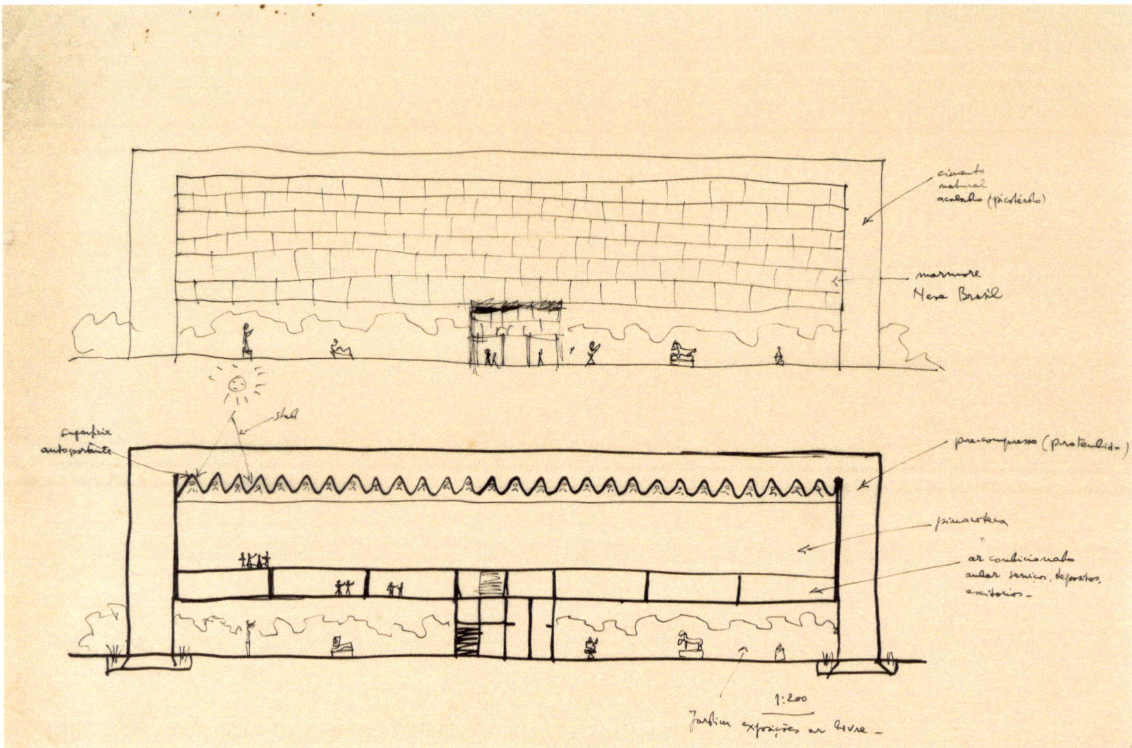

Preliminary sketch of the structure
© FAUUSP Library

Lina Bo Bardi, Installation of Piolin Circus on the Museum of Art of São Paulo, 1972
Watercolor, ballpoint, and felt tip pen on cardboard 32.1 x 47.0 cm © Instituto Bardi / Photo: Henrique Luz

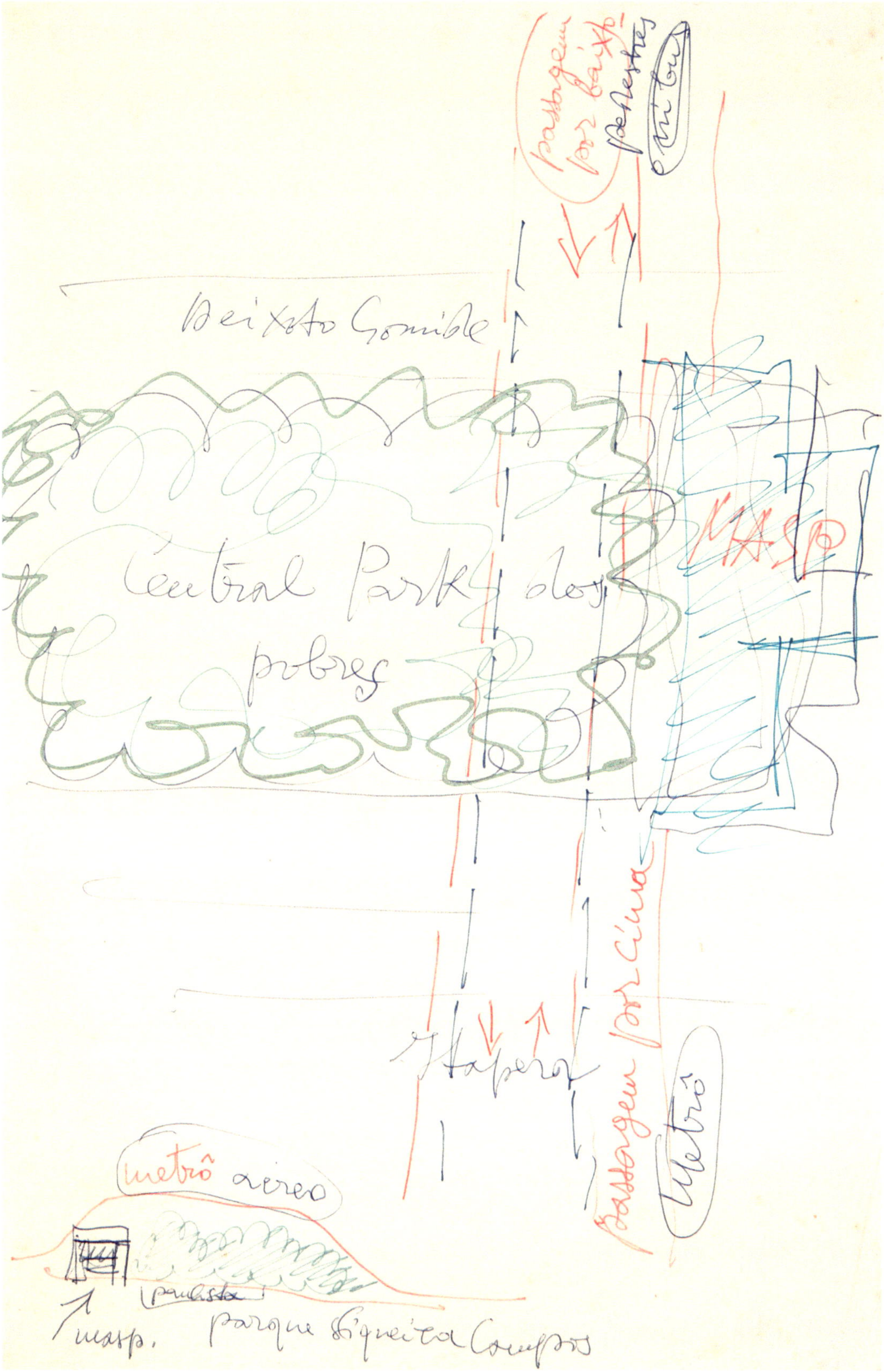

Lina Bo Bardi, study for the integration of the Museum of Art of São Paulo to the Trianon Park,
Ballpoint and felt tip pen on offset paper 31.5 x 21.4 cm © Instituto Bardi / Photo: Henrique Luz

Lina Bo Bardi, preliminary study - playground sculptures for the Belvedere, 1968, Nankin and watercolor, 56.3 x 76.5 cm

LBo.
4/5/'68

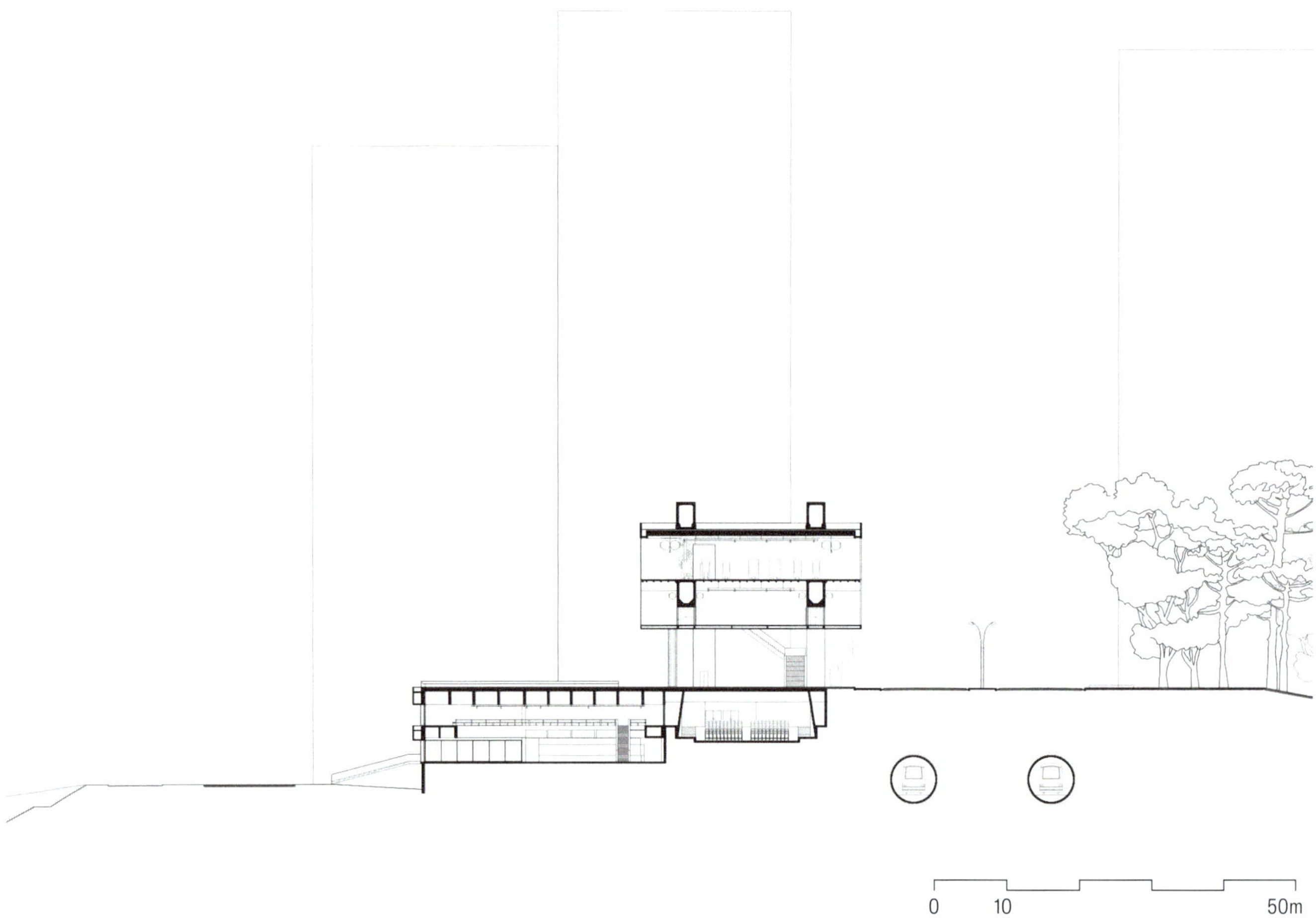

Section 1:1,000
© Guilherme Pianca, Gabriel Sepe and team

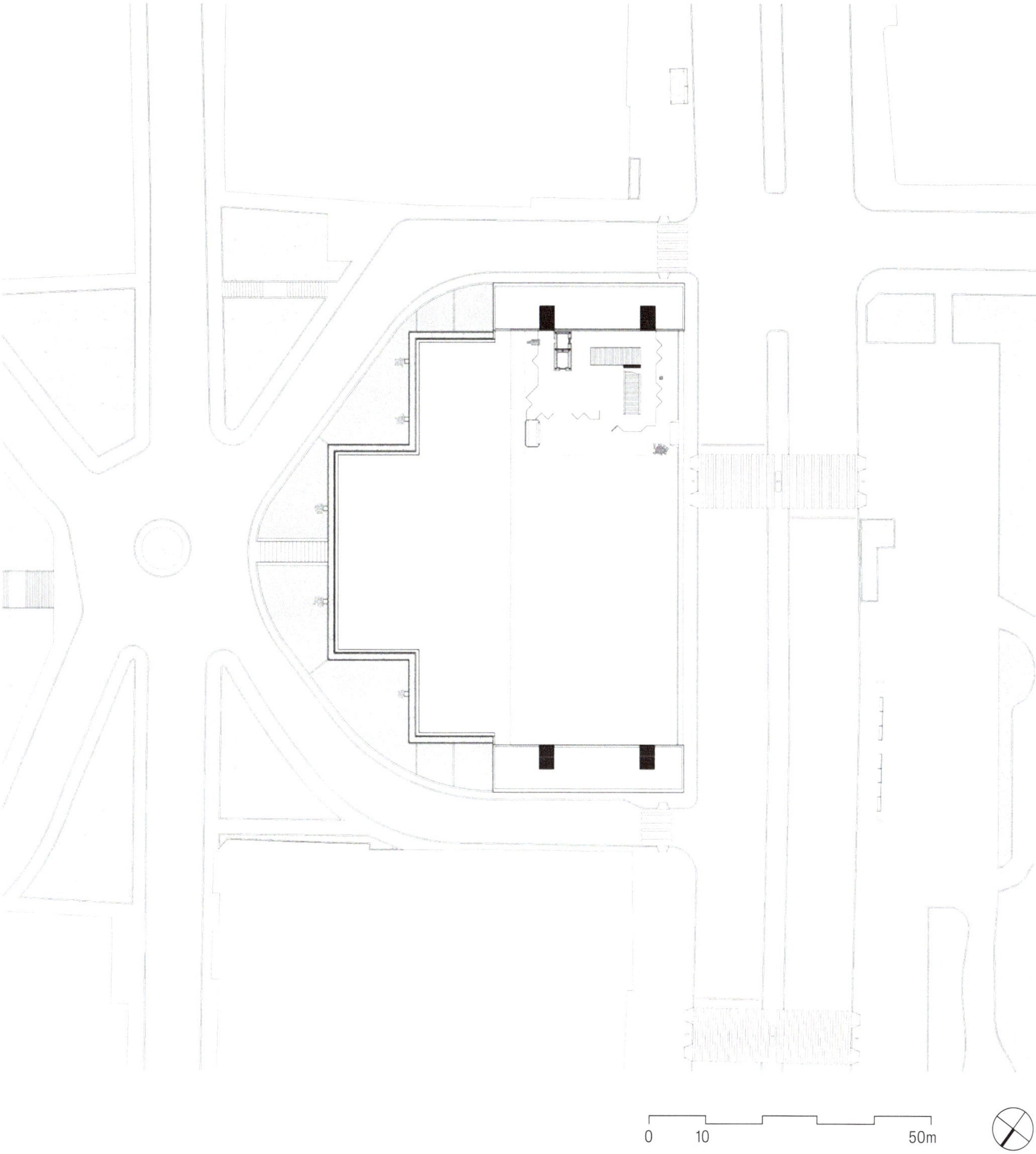

Floor plan 1:1,000
© Guilherme Pianca, Gabriel Sepe and team

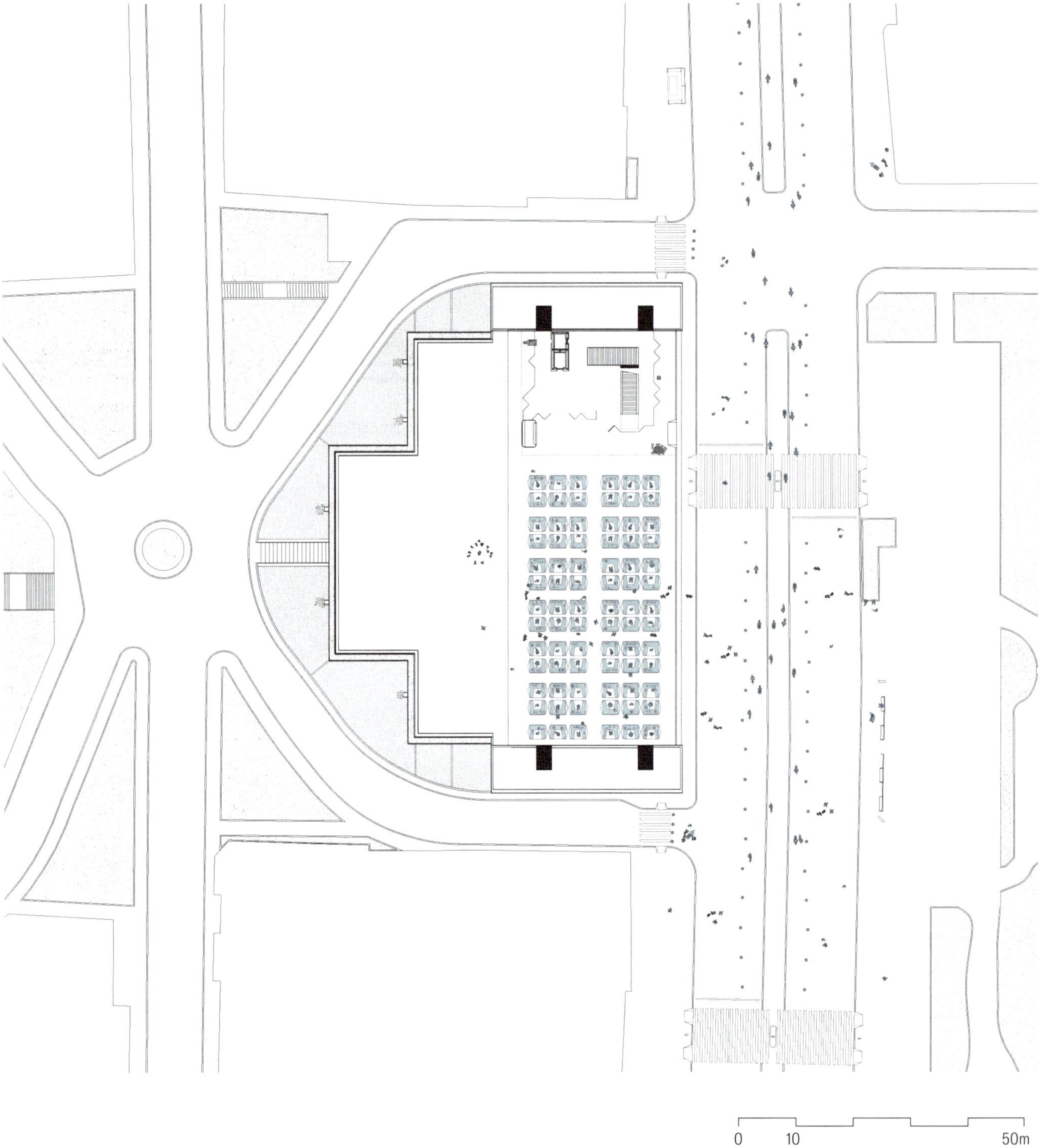

Floor plan - fair 1:1,000
© Guilherme Pianca, Gabriel Sepe and team

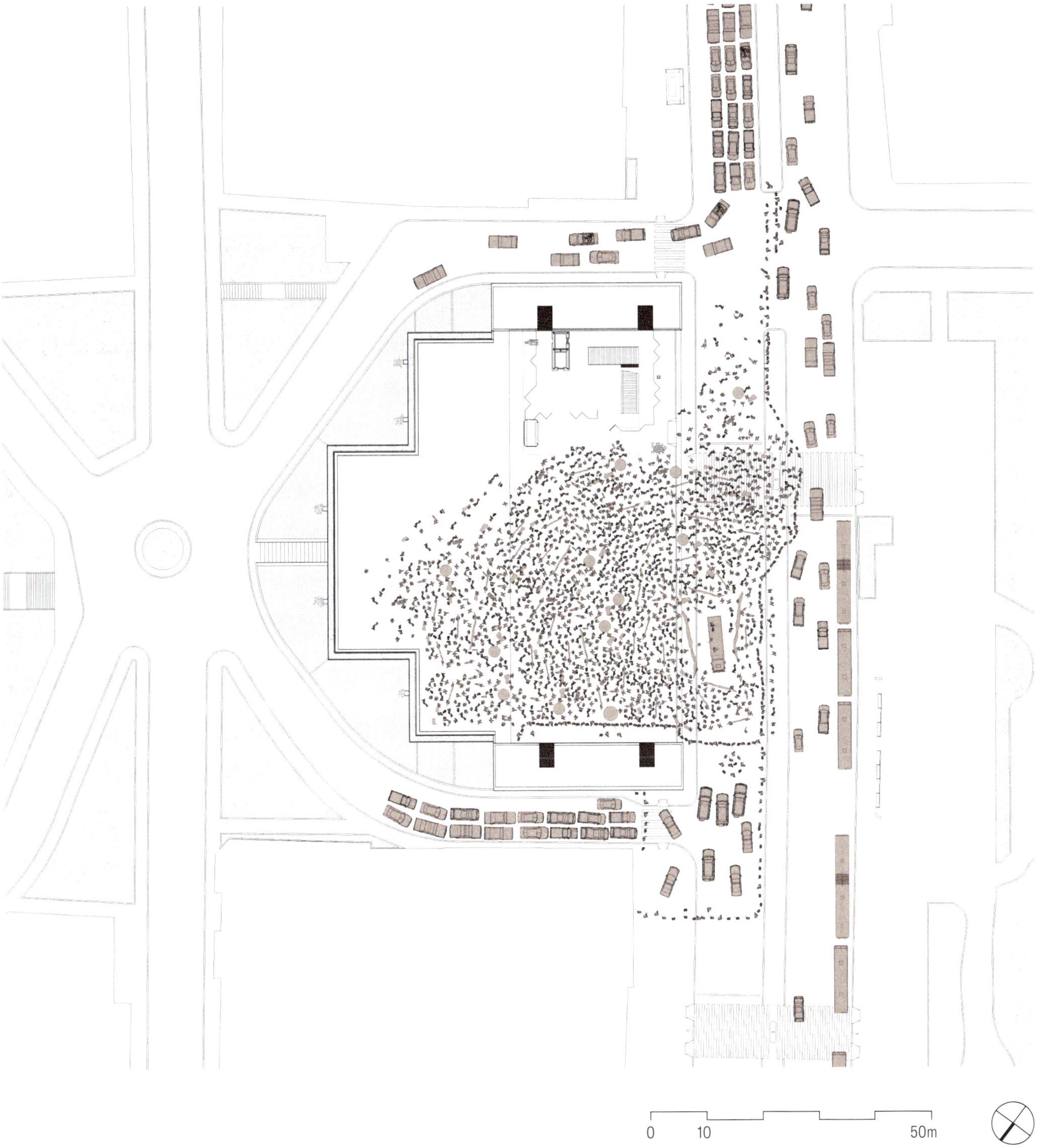

Ground floor plan - protest 1:1,000
© Guilherme Pianca, Gabriel Sepe and team

Exploded perspective drawing
© Danilo Zamboni

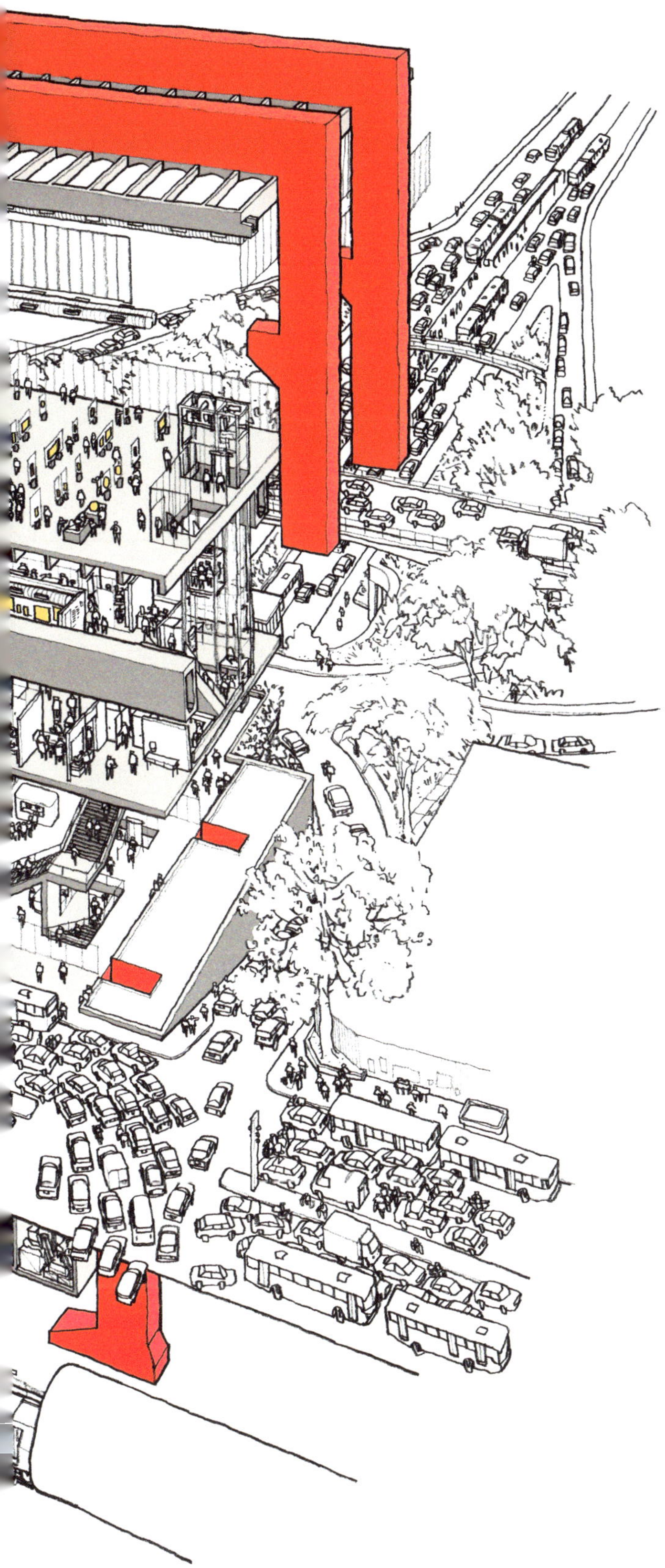

THE GROUND AS PROJECT

ANA LUIZA NOBRE*

"Brazil is an illegally taken land of six million square kilometers, chopped up at Tordesillas."
Oswald de Andrade, 1928

* This text is connected with an ongoing research project by the author ("Tanto chão: Inquérito à arquitetura contemporânea em Portugal"), which is funded by the *CNPq/Conselho Nacional de Desenvolvimento Científico e Tecnológico.*

The Portuguese architect Alexandre Alves Costa once defined Brazilian architecture as "a horizontal line hovering above the ground."[1] Despite being partial, this definition highlights a rich lineage of contemporary architecture in a country in which lifted buildings, inspired by Le Corbusier's *pilotis*, became more common from the 1930s on than anywhere else in the world, ultimately culminating in the *Superquadras* of Brasília. Well before Lúcio Costa's first sketches for the new capital city (1957), however, native stilt buildings and hammocks already expressed the effort to lift the structure above the ground. Because the terrain was unstable (being subject to landslides, silting, floods, and deluges) or simply non-existent (due to permanent high water), the ground was often associated with both a rough and frightening nature, to be kept at safe distance.

To understand Brazilian architecture's relationship with the ground, therefore, one must keep in mind its environment, characterized by high temperatures, humidity, strong smells, heavy rainfalls, wild animals, insects, and a kind of vegetation that literally hounds you, penetrates and overruns everything.

In one of the most enduring touchstones of Brazilian social science (*Raízes do Brasil*, 1936[2]), Sérgio Buarque de Holanda points out the difference between traditional agriculture and land exploration practices introduced in Brazil by sugar cane cultivation. According to the author, the frequent use of indigenous techniques, such as slash-and-burn, instead of the agricultural techniques mastered in Europe, can be explained, among other factors, both by the difficulties faced by the plow in an impenetrable vegetation and by Brazil's abundant land. Land to be used wastefully, even destructively, instead of protected. That is to say, within a logic more akin to ore mining than to cultivation.

This interpretation helps in understanding the so-called "scorched-earth culture" that is still largely practiced in Brazil today.[3] Here, too, lie the roots of the gap between architecture and geology which keeps causing so many serious accidents. And yet the relationship between construction and ground shown by a particular stream of Brazilian architecture (one that is most pronounced in São Paulo) echoes a long history of land conflicts whose origin lies in a line drawn on the other side of the Atlantic, even before Portuguese ships reached the Brazilian coast: an abstract line that regulated land ownership rights on a continent which at that time had neither a name, nor a shape, nor an end.

It should be noted that the demarcation of indigenous land is guaranteed by the Brazilian federal constitution since 1988. However, not always the law is actually enforced. There are currently 462 indigenous territories, which make up 12 percent of

View of the open span of Museum of Art of São Paulo

Flea Market at the open span

Visitors of Museum of Art of São Paulo

Photomontage of the possibility of a "closed" span © Ciro Miguel and Bruna Canepa

the land mass of Brazil, but appropriate regulations are only provided for 8 percent of these territories.[4] In many cases, as in the village of Pico do Jaraguá (located in the São Paulo metropolitan area), indigenous peoples are being pushed into areas that are far from corresponding to their cultural requirements. These displacements violate one of their cultural key principles: men belong to land, rather than land belong to men. It is no coincidence that both the escalation of the problems connected with the demarcation of indigenous territories[5] and the pressure applied by the constant territorial expansion of agribusiness have been named as determining factors in the rising suicide rate among the indigenous population, which is now three times higher than the national average.[6]

This rather schematic frame helps to understand why MASP/Museu de Arte de São Paulo (Lina Bo Bardi, 1961-68) would become such an unavoidable landmark, both in technical-architectural and political-symbolic terms. In Brazil, suspended buildings are intimately connected with a kind of modern experience that reached its apex and limit in the architecture of Oscar Niemeyer. By lifting the building from the ground one would ultimately guarantee a degree of autonomy and purity that echos a radically modern freedom —even if paradoxically anchored in a classical ideal.

But what can be seen as a characteristic feature of São Paulo's contemporary architecture since MASP (almost to the point of becoming a formula, actually), is a political-ideological attitude that tends to build a link between "ground" (in Portuguese meaning also "ground floor," *rés-do-chão*) and "public space" (*res-publica*). Or, more precisely, between architectural procedures of ground liberation and a critical posture towards the extremely perverse conditions of urban development in Brazil. Major projects designed in São Paulo over the last four decades follow this tradition. The main reference is almost always Lina Bo Bardi's design for MASP, where a plateau at Avenida Paulista level preserves the horizon of the viewpoint and creates a platform where the various facets of *res publica* become tangible. At the same time, this feature splits the museological program in two: the exhibition halls are raised whereas secondary spaces are lowered and consequently hidden from the eyes of those on the Avenida. The two counteractive forces of raising and lowering, therefore, work together and complement each other, rather than canceling each other out. An attentive observation of São Paulo's topography and city history serves as the orientation for the design. The result is a ground plane independent from the building's mass, and at the same time protected by it. An area of metropolitan dimensions, which creates a critical public and civic space in the nerve center of Brazil's largest city.

Before MASP, the raising of buildings off the ground had indeed been practiced in some earlier masterpieces of Brazilian architecture: not only the Brazilian Ministry of Education and Culture (designed in 1936 by Lúcio Costa, Oscar Niemeyer, Affonso Eduardo Reidy, Carlos Leão, Jorge Machado Moreira, and Ernani Vasconcellos, with Le Corbusier as consultant) and the Museu de Arte Moderna (Affonso Eduardo Reidy, 1953) in Rio de Janeiro; but also the Parque do Ibirapuera complex in São Paulo (Oscar Niemeyer, 1951-54). But MASP does mark a turning point in the relationship with the ground with its so-called *vão livre* (open span): a space free of intermediary structural supports, free of restrictions, free of the very notion of property, and free of the repressive power that architecture embodies. Free, ultimately, in terms of its exceptional urban availability. In doing so, it sets itself apart from the heritage of Le Corbusier's *pilotis*, which is basically rooted in a dual intention: to free the horizon from urban congestion and to create a penetrable ground floor in opposition to a long urban tradition represented by what he called the "street-corridor." MASP is basically the architectural expression of a concept of public space which remains inseparably connected in Brazil with a political struggle for urban reform, democracy, and civil rights: a public space that is ultimately understood as common ground, open and available to all people, all uses, and the full diversity of urban life.

Of course, raising buildings is not enough to create public space. Some of São Paulo's most remarkable public spaces are either partially or entirely below ground, such as the city's first subway stations, designed in the 1960s and 1970s by Marcelo Fragelli and team (São Bento, Sé, and Liberdade stations, among others) and the Luz railway/subway station (2002-04), one of the last projects of João Walter Toscano. There is also the embankment-like Centro Cultural São Paulo (CCSP) by Eurico Prado Lopes and Luiz Benedito de Castro Telles (1976-82), which turned a scarcely noticed area into one of the city's most vital spaces during the military dictatorship (1964-1985). Also of importance here is the building for the University of São Paulo's School of Architecture and Urban Planning, FAUUSP (1961-69), by João Vilanova Artigas and Carlos Cascaldi, where the building anchorage, together with its large covered square, integrates a series of social, environmental, and urban development challenges. These works remind us that every public space is also a political space. As such, they encompass a debate on territories, boundaries, and limitations that is profoundly architectural. Or better still—they stand as projects committed to the ground on which we try to find our balance everyday.

1 Alexandre Alves Costa, "Lembrando Lúcio Costa," in: Unidade, Porto: FAUP, volume 6, 1998 colon: 73-76.

2 Sérgio Buarque de Holanda, *Raízes do Brasil* (Rio de Janeiro: José Olympio, 1986).

3 Popular expression that condenses a series of destructive practices of different areas, associated in particular with "territorial adjustment" and various types of deforestation. The goal is to produce building, farming, and pasture land. In 2017 alone, for example, more than 200,000 fires were counted in Brazil, with about half of these in the Amazon Rainforest, in areas where soybean cultivation is on the rise. See http://www.inpe.br/queimadas/portal

4 "Bolsonaro transfere para a Agricultura a demarcação de terras indígenas e quilombolas," (*O Globo*, 02/01/2019, accessed March 3, 2019, https://g1.globo.com/politica/noticia/2019/01/02/bolsonaro-transfere-para-a-agricultura-as-atribuicoes-sobre-demarcacao-de-terras-indigenas-e-quilombolas.ghtml (accessed on March 3, 2019).

5 President Michel Temer (2016-19) did not conclude the demarcation of a single indigenous territory. His successor Jair Bolsonaro announced, right from his election campaign, his intention to reconsider all previous demarcation of indigenous territories in order to allow for commercial operations. After his election, the new president handed over the issue to an industrial agribusiness advocate.

6 "Taxa de suicídio entre indígenas é três vezes maior que a média nacional," *O Globo*, 09/21/2017 , accessed March 3, 2019, https://oglobo.globo.com/sociedade/saude/taxa-de-suicidio-entre-indigenas-tres-vezes-maior-que-media-nacional-21850401

THE PARK AND THE SLAB: IBIRAPUERA'S MARQUISE, BY OSCAR NIEMEYER

VANESSA GROSSMAN

One might say that, among the great works of modern architecture, there are seldom public spaces that are more intensely and spontaneously appropriated by the masses than Ibirapuera Park's Marquise [marquee], the covered pathway that graces the São Paulo urban park designed by Oscar Niemeyer with five collaborators: Hélio Uchôa, Zenon Lotufo, Eduardo Kneese de Mello, Gauss Estelita, and Carlos Lemos.[1] The popularity, in the best sense of the term, of this form of interval defined by the horizontal projection of a light and sinuous concrete roof, seems to overcome all the obstacles—in terms of accessibility—that could compromise its use.

This large 600-meter-long concrete slab was originally conceived as a connecting link for a larger architectural complex that was inaugurated in 1954 on the 400th anniversary of São Paulo. This original project consisted of three large, themed exhibition pavilions. Its main access would have been through a monumental entrance plaza, bordered by an art museum and an auditorium. Although the slab was conceived as a covered pathway, it has sufficiently generous dimensions to allow it to accommodate collective activities on its own, with horizontal spans ranging from 6 m at its extremities to 75 m in its central parts.

The "Marquise," as it is known, is part of one of the largest urban parks in South America, located in one of the wealthiest and most central neighborhoods of the largest metropolis in this part of the continent, yet difficult to access for the less-privileged population, which lives quite far away. In fact, the sexagenarian Marquise is not the only attraction in the park for the masses from the so-called "periphery," who cross the city from one end to another in search of leisure, culture, sports, and well-being. Ibirapuera Park as a whole is one of the few green collective facilities in São Paulo; however, the Marquise is the true agora of the park and, potentially, of the city as a whole. Under the slab, the most diverse representatives of one of the richest national urban cultures congregate: people of distinct classes, genders, ethnicities, creeds, and age groups, among which a strong young presence is evident.[2]

However, it is not only from a quantitative point of view—in terms of the number of users—that the Marquise stands out, but above all, from a qualitative perspective. The Marquise has the characteristic of creating a sort of Rio-de-Janeiro-style beach atmosphere, something intimate yet simultaneously collective, increased by the uniqueness of São Paulo's urbanity when the space underneath it becomes, mainly on weekends, both a stage and an auditorium for the most varied manifestations emanating from São Paulo residents at ease: not by wearing swimming trunks and bikinis as at a real beach, but instead by supporting the most

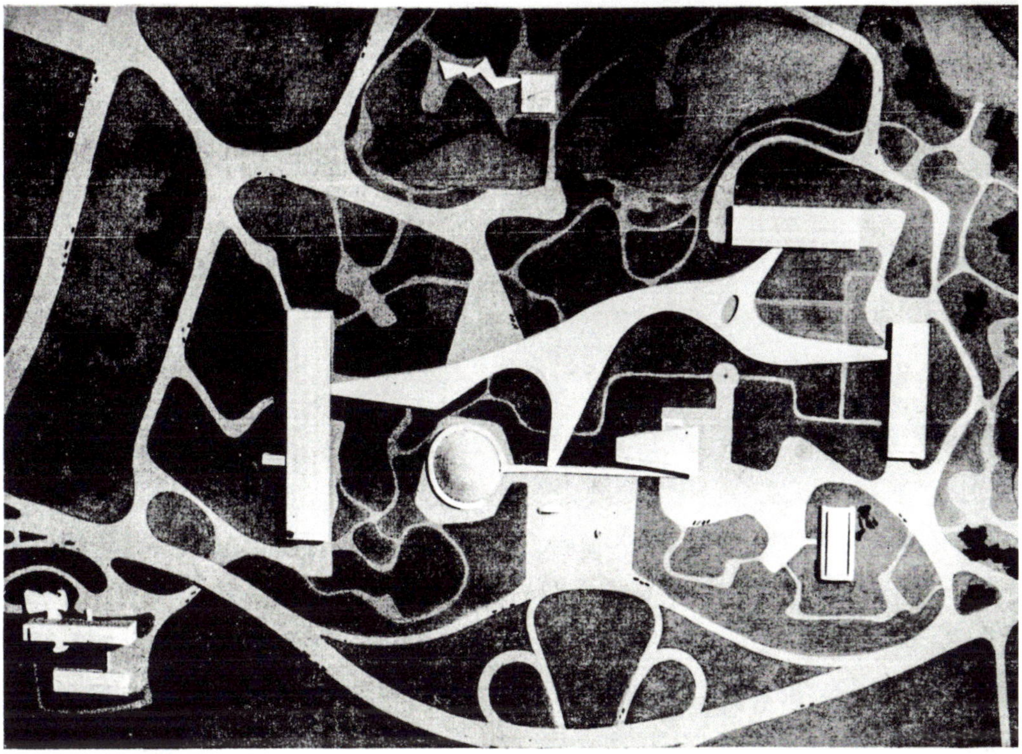

Fotos da "maquette": Pode-se observar a importância do Auditório no equilíbrio e harmonia do conjunto. As extremidades da seta apontam para o Palácio das Artes, que devia completar o grupo, ligando-se, ainda, ao Auditório (de forma triangular), em frente.

21

Oscar Niemeyer, Photographs of the scale model of the original project for Conjunto Ibirapuera, São Paulo (1951), published in *Módulo*, no. 1, March 1955, p.21.

diverse commercial, cultural, and urban sports devices. The Marquise is home to street vendors; roller-skaters, skateboarders, and cyclists, both beginners and professionals; children's games; unscheduled shows of hip hop, funk, capoeira, zouk, and other dances and artistic performances; congregations of young "metal" teenagers, people from the queer scene and other urban movements; as well as pets and a countless number of pigeons. There, popular urban culture meets that which is considered erudite or official, from the moment that its most ordinary users bump into the specialized public for the many exhibitions held in the pavilions connected by the Marquise. On every weekend and public holiday, the Marquise transforms into a big living area.

This pronounced attendance compensates, in Niemeyer's work as a whole, for the alleged failure in this regard of some of the collective spaces that the Rio de Janeiro architect conceived, which are often the targets of criticism. From the esplanades of Brasília to the Latin America Memorial in São Paulo, many of these spaces have been harshly judged by critics for the sparse number of visitors, thus having their uses, or even civic functions, compromised. As a result of historical destiny, the "structure" of Brasília's public spaces is still today interpreted as having been designed by the architect in order to "facilitate" the action of the military, and thus frustrate the assembly of the masses.[3]

The logic behind the unbridled and juxtaposed appropriation of the Marquise—as if the space under its shade legitimately belonged to each individual there—can be attributed to the combination of two entities that seem to be in a symbiotic relationship: the park and the concrete slab. The first, a program; the second, an architectural element to be programmed. One is rare, while the other is common in São Paulo. While the so-called "Jardins" neighborhoods, which were urbanized in São Paulo by the English firm Companhia City and founded in 1912, are the privilege of the very few, the banks of its rivers with their fauna and flora that once lent themselves to leisure and sports, were transformed almost a century ago into highways. In São Paulo, due to the lack of outdoor spaces dedicated to leisure and sports—such as beaches, forests, parks, and other natural or built-up green areas—this role is often fulfilled by concrete roof slabs. If shopping malls are the main indoor destination for Paulistanos of all classes and ages, the reinforced concrete slab is perhaps the most striking leisure device punctuating the horizon of the city's endless periphery. The flat slab, embodying one of Le Corbusier's "Five Points of Architecture" manifesto—the roof garden—is the cheapest form of rooftop for housing on the periphery.[4] Programmed at will, these slabs are often home to clotheslines, inflatable swimming pools, and improvised barbecues. Parties are often organized there and, especially in São Paulo, squadrons of children, young people, or even adults come together to fly kites, enhancing their few square meters, in veritable battles of slab-against-slab.

However, it would be implausible to dispense with the role of architecture in the popularity of the Marquise, where leisure is conquered under the slab. While the floor is the exact projection of this meandering white floating plane, demarcating a full horizontality, the 106 columns that support it give rhythm to this great "living room" dictating focal points of density for the activities that reverberate in the altercation between work and free time in the city. This structure is also reinforced by the eight V-shaped pillars located at its four ends, giving it a variable ceiling height between 3 m and 4.25 m, a form which is "curved and steep," as described by the builders at the time of its inception.[5] The ensemble is marked by tension between the geometric rigor of the implantation and shape of the pavilions—with trapezoidal, rectangular, or circular forms—and the free sinuosity of the Marquise that connects them. For its design, Niemeyer continued to explore the plastic possibilities of concrete he already forged in Pampulha, Belo Horizonte in the previous decade, a characteristic that the critic Mário de Andrade defined as the "Escola Carioca" —or Rio de Janeiro School—in 1944.[6] Spreading over the park like liquid concrete, this extensive

View of Ibirapuera's Marquise in the park

Lina Bo Bardi, *Bahia no Ibirapuera* exhibition, São Paulo, 1959 / Watercolor, ballpoint, graphite, china ink and metallic ink, on cardboard 50.5 x 70.3 cm
© Instituto Bardi / Photo: Henrique Luz

Street vendor under the Marquise

People gathering at Marquise

winding slab was to play, in Niemeyer's project for Ibirapuera Park, the "ordering role" that in Pampulha was embodied by the lake, which made the Marquise a kind of "concrete reflecting pool."[7] However, in Ibirapuera Park, the Marquise took the forefront of Niemeyer's project. Despite the formal expressiveness attributed to each of the pavilions in Pampulha, the Marquise became more than mere infrastructure, it became a superstructure.[8]

With the square and auditorium removed from the original project in the construction stage by the public authorities, for years the "entrance" of the Marquise was left incomplete, which led Niemeyer to consider that the "bold Marquise seems to be something unfinished (and, indeed, it is), or barely started: it comes out of some random point, strayed."[9] This unfinished effect was also emphasized by stands that were erected under the Marquise, which compromised the desired "panoramic amplitude" and "lightness."[10] By the same logic, what began in 1959 as a temporary exhibition pavilion designed by Lina Bo Bardi would end up becoming, since 1968, the permanent headquarters of the Museum of Modern Art of São Paulo (MAM). When she redesigned the MAM in the 1980s, this amplitude was still compromised "instead of freeing the Marquise to reconstitute Niemeyer's original design."[11] Despite the architect's *mea culpa*, the slab span would never be fully free. It was perhaps the persistence of this "unfinished" effect, producing constant tension between the original "ordering role" and a disorderly function, that condemned the pristine modernism of the Marquise as a space of informality, where everything seems possible for its users, even the passage from anonymity to fame.

There was one last controversial gesture on Niemeyer's part to reorder the Ibirapuera architectural project. When he was commissioned to resume the auditorium project, he proposed that a part of the Marquise would be demolished to create the formerly suppressed square in the area surrounding the new construction, which was completed in 2002. Despite the intention of the architect, who was the very author of the original project, the demolition was halted thanks to the intervention of the city's cultural property protection agencies.[12] In 2015, the year prior to the Park's architectural project being made an official national heritage site, the design of the square was taken over by Paulo Mendes da Rocha. This architect intends to implement it on the site currently occupied by the parking lot, which would thus become the main point of entry to the park, favoring walking or public transport. The intention is to ensure accessibility for users.

However, not even the pendency of the square seems to compromise the accessibility of the Marquise, which is now tangible even via Internet. It has become the main destination for *rolezinhos*, meetings of young people from the periphery, organized on social media, which have been banned from shopping malls. Framed by the white of the tortuous slab, with the green background of the park, the organizers of the events—the so-called "influencers"—materialize moments of fame by gathering thousands of followers, who flock there in spite of any material difficulties, some of these meetings culminating in tumult and violence but others in a mere search for photos and hugs.

1 I am thankful to the Oscar Niemeyer Foundation for granting me access to documents, and to Ciro Miguel for his assistance in my research and for his role as reader.

2 Ana Estela de Souza Pinto, "Rolezinhos do beijo lotam marquise do Ibirapuera com até 20 mil jovens," *Folha de São Paulo*, Feb. 5, 2017 accessed March 15, 2019, https://www1.folha.uol.com.br/cotidiano/2017/02/1855091-rolezinhos-do-beijo-lotam-marquise-do-ibirapuera-com-ate-20-mil-garotos.shtml

3 Cf. "Brasília by Rem Koolhaas," in *Revista Centro Aug. 2011, accessed April 2, 2019*, http://revistacentro.org/index.php/koolhaasen/

4 Cf. "Cultura da laje nas periferias." *Profissão repórter*. Episode aired Sep. 27, 2011.

5 Ruth Verde Zein, "A Marquise do Ibirapuera," *AU Magazine, no. 226*, Jan. 2012, accessed April 2, 2019, http://au17.pini.com.br/arquitetura-urbanismo/226/artigo275965-2.aspx.

6 Mario de Andrade, "Brazil Builds (1944)," in *Depoimento de uma geração, ed. Alberto Xavierr* (São Paulo: Cosac & Naify, 2003), 179.

7 Paulo César Garcez Marins, "O Parque Ibirapuera e a construção da identidade paulista," *Anais do Museu Paulista - História e Cultura Material*, São Paulo, vol. 6-7, 1998-1999 colon : 26.

8 This protagonism, guaranteed by the use it would achieve, was further intensified by the non-interference of landscaping in its immediate surroundings. It seems that this was Niemeyer's plan, which culminated in the elimination of the original Ibirapuera landscaping project, attributed, in 1951, to landscape architect Roberto Burle Marx; c (cf.). Fernanda Araújo Curi, "Burle Marx e o Parque Ibirapuera: quatro décadas de descompasso (1953-1993)," *Anais do Museu Paulista*, São Paulo: Nova Série, vol. 25, no. 3, Sep-Dec 2017 colon : 103-138; c (cf.) Fernanda Araújo Curi, "Ibirapuera, metáfora urbana. O público/ privado em São Paulo, 1954-2017," 2018. Thesis (Doctorate in History and Fundamentals of Architecture and Urbanism) - Faculty of Architecture and Urbanism.

9 Oscar Niemeyer, "Mutilado o conjunto do Parque," *Module*, no. 1, Mar. 1955 colon : 18.

10 Niemeyer, 1955: 20; c. Oscar Niemeyer, *Minha arquitetura*, (Rio de Janeiro: Revan, 2000), 31.

11 Cf. Mara Gama, "Um prédio polêmico," *Folha de São Paulo*, Jul. 2014, 1998, accessed March 15, 2019, https://www1.folha.uol.com.br/fsp/especial/fj14079811.htm

12 Cf. Benedito Lima de Toledo, "A polêmica sobre a Marquise do Ibirapuera," *Folha de São Paulo*, Dec. 18, 2005, accessed March 15, 2019 https://www1.folha.uol.com.br/fsp/cotidian/ff1812200512.htm

OPEN SPACES

Ibirapuera's Marquise

CEAGESP-MLP (Free Market Pavilion)

Praça das Artes

Minhocão (Urban Highway Presidente João Goulart)

The first example, Oscar Niemeyer's Marquise at the Ibirapuera Park, finished in 1954, is both an exception and exceptional structure in São Paulo. This canopy, or roofed sidewalk (although it is inside a park and not by a street), varies in width and is able to accommodate sports and leisure activities of different types, while also connecting a series of buildings. The next three examples in this category comprise open spaces in communication with the sidewalk/street that are contained within buildings. The first example is the space under the MASP, which has the capacity to host different types of events and activities, one at a time, as we illustrate in our visual survey The Companhia de Entrepostos e Armazéns Gerais de São Paulo's (CEAGESP) main market is a linear covered plaza, like Marquise, at the limit of being out-of-scale and completely at-scale, a space that serves as different types of markets and that some days of the week is open all day and night. Brasil Arquitectura's open spaces at the Praça das Artes Building, which is part of the facilities of São Paulo's Municipal Theatre, is a passage between streets, a covered and open plaza, and a rehearsal space, among other things. Finally, despite its polemical status, and the discussions about demolishing it or turning it into a park (it was described by one academic as a "cancer" in the city that had to be removed), the Via Elevada Presidente João Goulart, commonly known as Minhocão, is an elevated expressway from the early 1970s that has been closed to vehicular traffic on Sundays for some decades, and has been transformed of late because of its intense use into a vibrant 3.5-kilometer-long park-like space. This odd example expands the understanding of open space and opens a discussion on the temporary use of streets as parks, a makeover that happens with traffic cones and security personnel.

Ibirapuera's Marquise

Name: Marquise do Parque do Ibirapuera

Address: Complexo Viário Ayrton Senna - Vila Mariana

Year of project: 1951-1954

Architect: Oscar Niemeyer

Engineer: Joaquim Cardozo

Client/who commissioned: São Paulo's 4th centenary Commission (Lucas Nogueira Garcez, São Paulo State governor and Ciccillo Matarazzo, Commission director)

Type of institution: Public Park

Hours: Tue. - Sun., 5 am - midnight

Number of visitors: The park has over 14 million visitors a year.

Project: Oscar Niemeyer, 1951 - 1954. Ibirapuera Park was conceived as the stage for celebrations of São Paulo's 4th centenary celebrated in 1954. Conception by Ciccillo Matarazzo first team (Rino Levi, Oswaldo Bratke, Eduardo Kneese de Melo, Ícaro de Castro Mello, Roberto Cerqueira Cezar, Carlos Brasil Lodi, Carlos Alberto Gomes Cardim Filho and Alfredo Giglio) in 1951. Ciccillo Matarazzo was the nephew of the richest man in Brazil, a powerful industry magnate, the Italian-Brazilian Count Francisco Matarazzo. First Niemeyer project version from 1952 already foresee the Marquise connecting the pavilions (team: Zenon Lotufo, Eduardo Kneese de Mello e Hélio Cavalcanti, Gauss Estelita and Carlos Lemos). The last Marquise project version is dated from February 1953.

Program: marquise connecting other park pavilions (now museums)

Area: 28.000 m^2

View of the Ibirapuera's Marquise on a weekend day

Dedicated in 1954, the construction of the canopy structure was completed in 120 days. With a perimeter of about 1,700 m and an area of 28,000 m^2, its width varies from 6 m at the ends to 75 m in the central part, the distance between columns varies from 12 m to 28 m, and in its central part the distance on the diagonal between two columns can reach 44 m. In addition to the eight V-pillars located at its four ends, it is supported by 106 circular columns with a constant diameter of 50 cm—despite the variety of spans and loads, ranging from 75 to 275 tons per column. Quite slender, the shelter in a ribbed slab with "lost coffers" has longitudinal beams with a height of 80 cm and transverse beams of variable height, reaching 25 cm in thickness at the edge. The shelter's height is variable, from 3 m to 4.25 m. This detailed description of the structure is useful for understanding that one of the striking characteristics of the Marquise is its scale, and the scale of the buildings that it connects. Closer to the tradition of a pavilion—if one sticks to the facts—the Marquise is, in essence, a promenade that has two toilets, a restaurant, and also "houses" the Museu de Arte Moderna (MAM), designed by Lina Bo Bardi in 1982; the São Paulo Biennale Pavilion; the Afro-Brazilian Museum; the Brazilian Cultures Pavilion; Oca (temporary exhibition space); and an auditorium. If seen in photographs, particularly from an air view, it is a highly formal project, but from within, it is a playground, a covered open space in a public park, and a flexible space. Its main program is the absence of program, and its current uses range among multiple sports activities, dancing, rapping crews, strolling, et al. while also hosting informal gatherings of people drinking and other such activities.

View of the Marquise in the early morning

Roller skaters in the Marquise

Buildings done for São Paulo's 4th centenary celebrated in 1954, published in *Arquitetura e engenharia*, no. 27, October 1953, p. 22.

Aerial view of the construction site of Ibirapueira's Marquise, published in Acrópole, no. 185, February 1954, p.216.

Young people gathering at Marquise

V-shaped pillars located at one of the four ends

Ground floor plan 1:2,000
© Guilherme Pianca, Gabriel Sepe and team

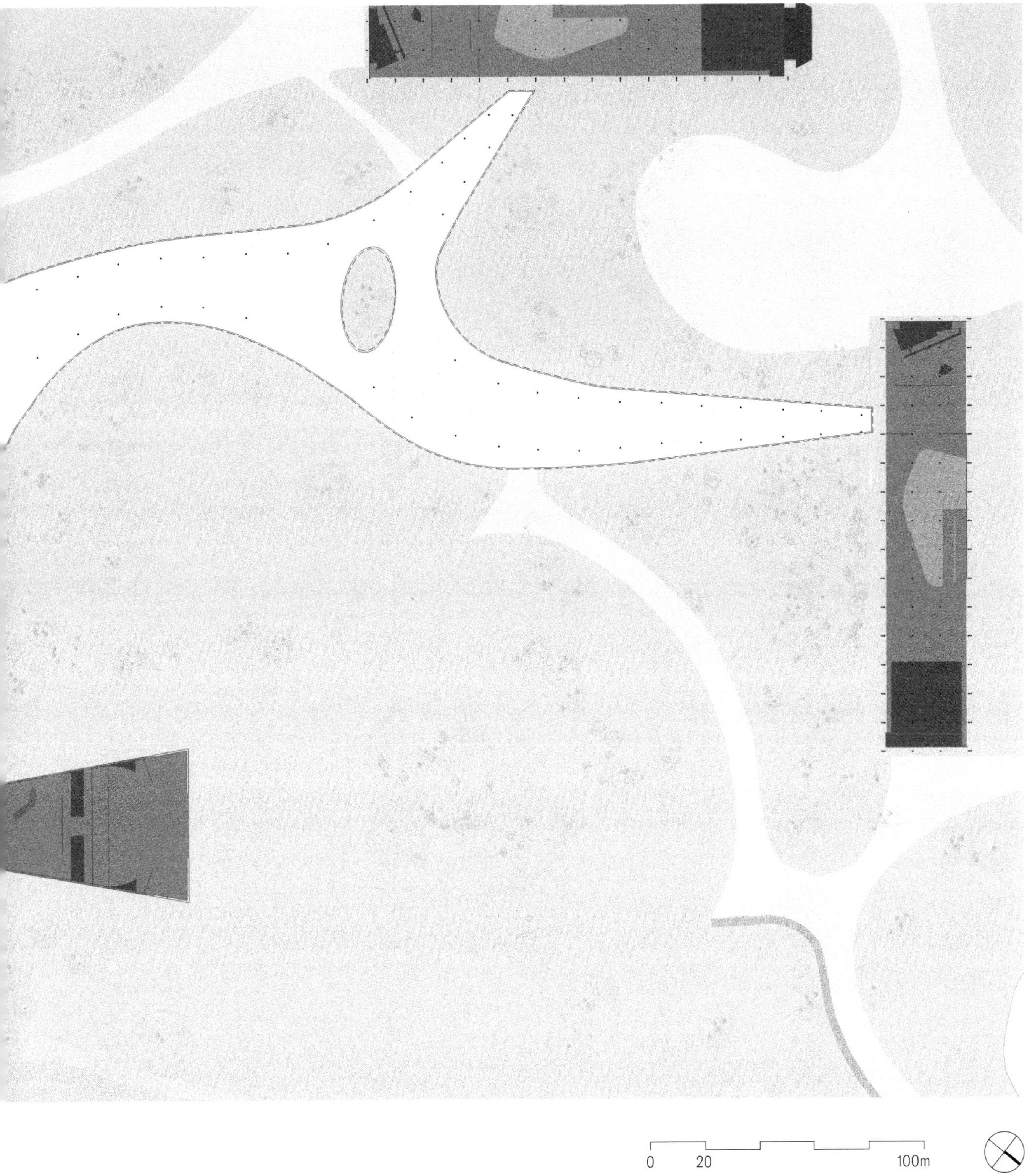
0
20
100m

CEAGESP-MLP (Free Market Pavilion)

Name: Mercado Livre do Produtor (MLP) at CEAGESP (Companhia de Entrepostos e Armazéns Gerais de São Paulo); ETSP (Entreposto Terminal de São Paulo)

Address: Av. Dr. Gastão Vidigal, 1946

Year of project: 1962-1974

Engineer: José Carlos de Figueiredo Ferraz engineering office / 1962-1964 (first phase and also the whole ETSP, "wholesale market unit," masterplan) / 1974 (MLP second phase conclusion). Until 1997, the company CEAGESP was owned by São Paulo State, now it's Federal.

Client/who commissioned: São Paulo State administration

Type of institution: Federal state owned company (Ministry of Agriculture, Livestock and Food Supply)

Hours: MLP open for wholesale (vegetables): Mon. and Thu. from 6 am to 8 pm; Tue. from 11:30 am to 9 pm; Wed. from 6 am to 9 pm; Fri. from 11:30 am to 10 pm; Sat. from 2 pm to 9 pm; Sun. closed. MLP open for retail: Tue and Fri. from 0 am to 8:30 am (flowers, plants, vases, garden material); Sat. from 7 am to midday; Sun. from 7 am to 1:30 pm

Program: sale of vegetables and flowers, wholesale and retail

Number of daily visitors: 50,000 people (the whole complex)

Project: A producer free market pavilion (MLP) for vegetables and flowers, covered open area with WC facilities and temporary tents of food and drink sale for buyers, sellers, and stevedores.

Program: 17 fruit pavilions, 6 vegetable pavilions, 5 onion and potato pavilions, 9 sundry products pavilions, 1 pumpkin pavilion, 3 fish pavilions, 2 pavilions for the general grain warehouse, parking lots, square for open retail market, buildings for security, inspection, maintenance, archives, banks, offices, administration, CEAGESP directorship, auditorium, clock tower. 50,000 people and 12,000 vehicles circulate daily in the whole complex.

Area: 450 m. long, covering 45,500 m^2 (MLP, "producer free market" pavilion), ETSP total area: 700,000 m^2 (271,000 m^2 built area)

View of the MLP - producer free market pavilion for vegetables and flowers

Takoish

With its last phase dedicated in 1974, this vast market space alternates between being a daily wholesale market from Monday to Saturday and a twice-a-week plant-and-flower market at night. The changeover of the space is part of what makes it attractive. Since things are mounted and dismounted on a daily basis, the quality of the space and its infrastructural features dominate the scene. The climate and the program allow for a completely open structure that is dynamic in its use and expands the notion of this category of "open space."

Interior view of the producer free market pavilion

View of the structure from the ground

Ground floor plan 1:2,000
© Guilherme Pianca, Gabriel Sepe and team

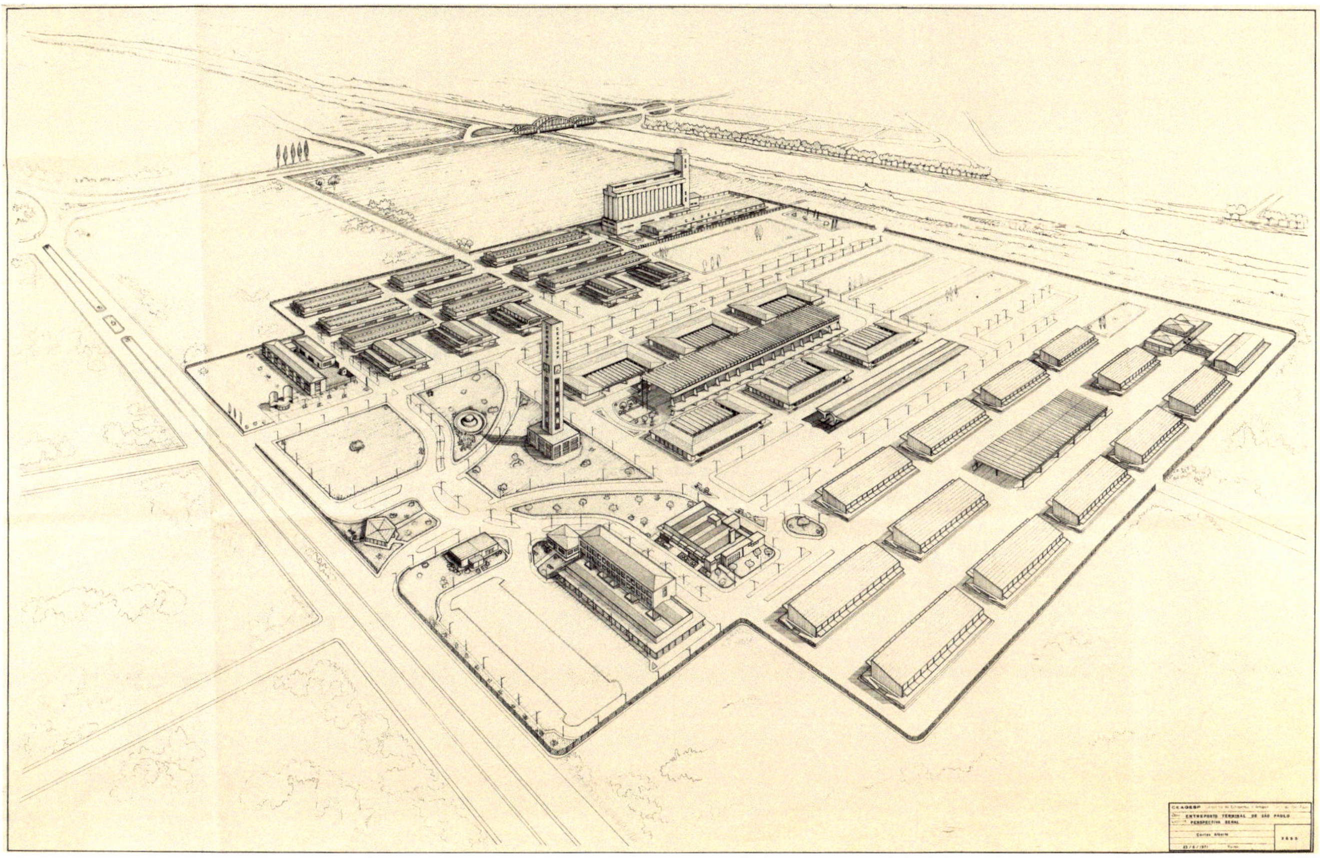

Bird's eye view of the CEAGESP complex
© FAUUSP Library

Praça das Artes

Name: Praça das Artes

Address: Praça das Artes, Avenida São João, 281

Year of Project: 2006-2012; 2017-2019.

Architect: Francisco Fanucci, Marcelo Ferraz e Luciana Dornellas (Brasil Arquitetura) with Marcos Cartum (Secretaria Municipal de Cultura - São Paulo Culture Authority)

Engineer: F. T. Oyamada Engenheiros Associados

Client/who commissioned: Theatro Municipal de São Paulo (City Culture Authority)

Type of institution: Municipal Theater annex

Hours: Mon.- Sat., 7 am - 10 pm

Number of daily visitors: Over 200 employees and 1,500 enrolled students use the buildings, there is no available data for the number of users of the open space

Project: Francisco Fanucci, Marcelo Ferraz e Luciana Dornellas (Brasil Arquitetura) with Marcos Cartum (Secretaria Municipal de Cultura - São Paulo Culture Authority), 2006-2012. A last stage, a broad square, was recently inaugurated, connecting the complex with the Vale do Anhangabaú Park. The project also consists of the restoration of the old musical conservatory (Conservatório Dramático Musical, 1909) with its auditorium for 400 people (Sala do Conservatório)

Program: As the Municipal Theater annex, the building houses the Orquestra Sinfônica Municipal (Symphonic City Orchestra) and the Orquestra Experimental de Repertório (Experimental Orchestra), Corais Lírico e Paulistano (Lyric Choir and City Choir), Balé da Cidade (City Ballet), Quarteto de Cordas (City String Quartet). Escolas Municipal de Música (City Music School, with 39 rooms, 700 students and 78 professors) Escola Municipal de Dança (City Dance School, with 10 rooms, 840 students and 30 professors), Museu do Teatro (Theater Museum), Centro de Documentação Artística (Artistic Documentation Center), restaurant, administration, underground parking, free ground floor square.

Area: 28,500 m^2

View of Praça das Artes from the street

With the last stage dedicated in 2019 Brasil Arquitetura's open spaces at the Praça das Artes Building are also a passage between streets, offering quiet spots to rest in the shade and large open spaces for group rehearsals of dancers and musicians. Performances also take place there. The administration considers controlling the flux of pedestrians through the building to be a critical issue, but it is precisely this activity that makes this building participate with the city—its open condition. The building itself was designed to meet several demands that the historic building of the Municipal Theater could no longer meet, thus externalizing the administration of the Municipal Theater Foundation and the Odeon Institute (manager of the Municipal Theater complex), and housing the facilities of the municipal dance and music schools, as well as the rehearsals and the administrative offices of the artistic bodies (City of São Paulo Ballet, Experimental Repertory Orchestra, Municipal Symphony Orchestra, Lyric Choir, Paulistano Choir, and String Quartet). There is also an exhibition hall and a concert hall in the former building of the Musical Dramatic Conservatory, a historic building that is part of the complex. The square itself (Praça) brings out into the open and into communication with the street the energy of all of these groups in rehearsals and performances, thus making culture available to more people and in a myriad of formats.

View of Praça das Artes from Avenida São João

Interior view of Praça das Artes

Ground floor plan 1:2,000
© Guilherme Pianca, Gabriel Sepe and team

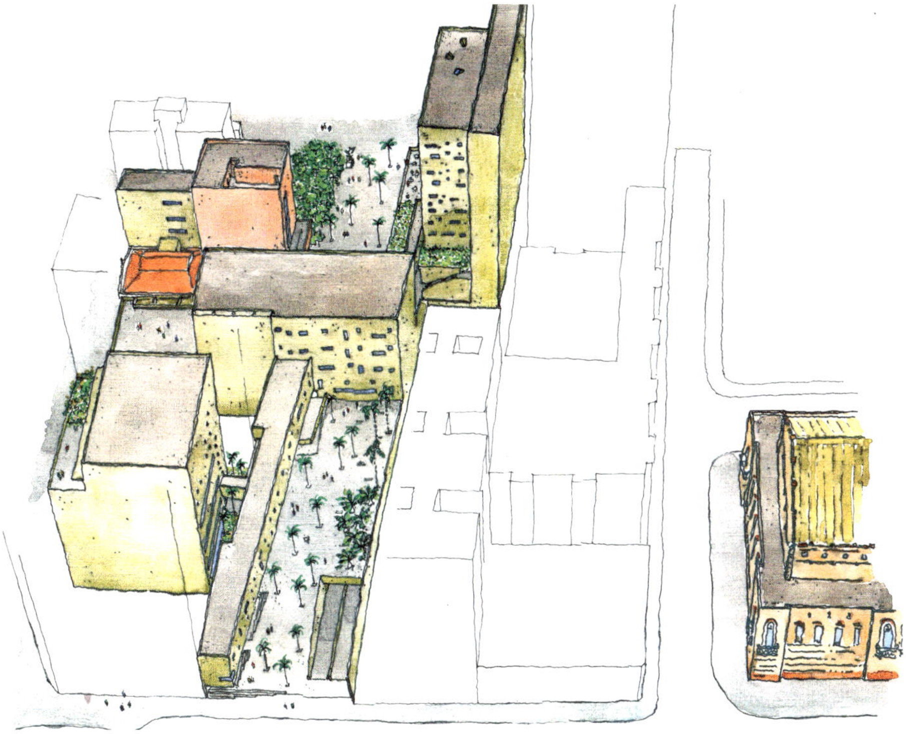

Sketches for Praça das Artes
© Brasil Arquitetura

Minhocão (Urban Highway Presidente João Goulart)

Name: Elevado Presidente João Goulart (Minhocão), previously Elevado Presidente Costa e Silva

Address: Connecting Praça Roosevelt to Largo Padre Péricles (East-West connection, crossing part of São Paulo's central area)

Year of project: 1969-1970

Engineer: Hidroservice (company)

Client/who commissioned: city administration

Type of institution: public road infrastructure

Hours: vehicles use the elevated road from 6:30 am to 9:30 pm (Mon. to Fri.), 6:30 am to 3:00 pm on Saturdays, and closed for vehicles on Sundays.

Number of weekend visitors: 10,000

Project: built and designed in 14 months under the management of the mayor Paulo Maluf, who was not democratically elected but designated by then president General Costa e Silva, member of the military dictatorship established by the military coup of 1964. It was built by the construction company Hidroservice that worked with a team of 3,100 workers, technicians and engineers, between 1969 and January of 1971. Built in reinforced and prestressed concrete.

Program: elevated two-way vehicle lane

Area: around 63,000 m^2

View of Minhocão on Sundays

DEVAGAR
CURVA

Dedicated in 1971, this elevated two-way vehicle lane in each direction with 3.5 km long and 15 to 22 m wide, is elevated 5.5 m above street level. Every day around 70,000 vehicles use the elevated road, carrying 80,000 people, from 6:30 am to 9:30 pm (Mon. to Fri.), 6:30 am to 3:00 pm on Saturdays, and closed for vehicles on Sundays. During night time and weekends Minhocão is occupied by people and works as a "dry-park", a place for meetings, sports, picnics, parties, concerts, theater presentations, informal commerce, et al. especially on Sundays.

On February 21, 2019, the Minhocão Park official project was presented by the new mayor Bruno Covas. The project was designed by the architect and former mayor of Curitiba Jaime Lerner and refers to a first part of the park, 900 meters between Roosevelt Square and Largo do Arouche. The transformation of the elevated road in a park was foreseen in a law sanctioned by former mayor Fernando Haddad (Workers' Party) in 2016, based on the 2014 São Paulo master plan, that already foresaw the gradual deactivation of the use of the highway by vehicles. The future park however is polemical and has many detractors, including academics, urbanists, and community leaders. At the heart of the polemic is the fact that maintaining the concrete structure which has for years been responsible of the decay of part of central São Paulo, and promoting this new park as an equivalent to New York's Highline might be misleading, particularly because there was no public survey, plebiscite or high level discussion around the decision.

The inclusion of Minhocão opens a discussion of what is/can be open space in a megacity, and reflects on a phenomenon that has been popular to São Paulo's citizens.

View of Minhocão from the ground

View of Minhocão open to pedestrians on a Sunday

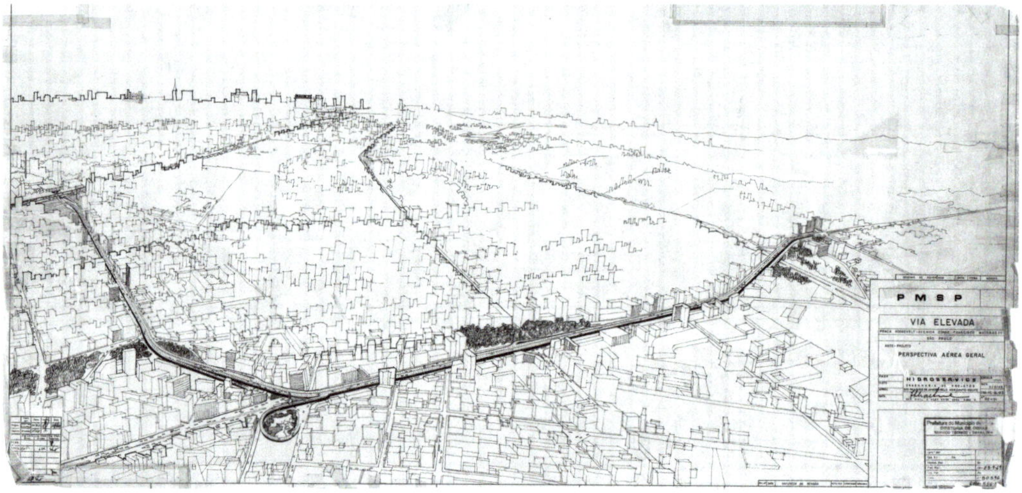

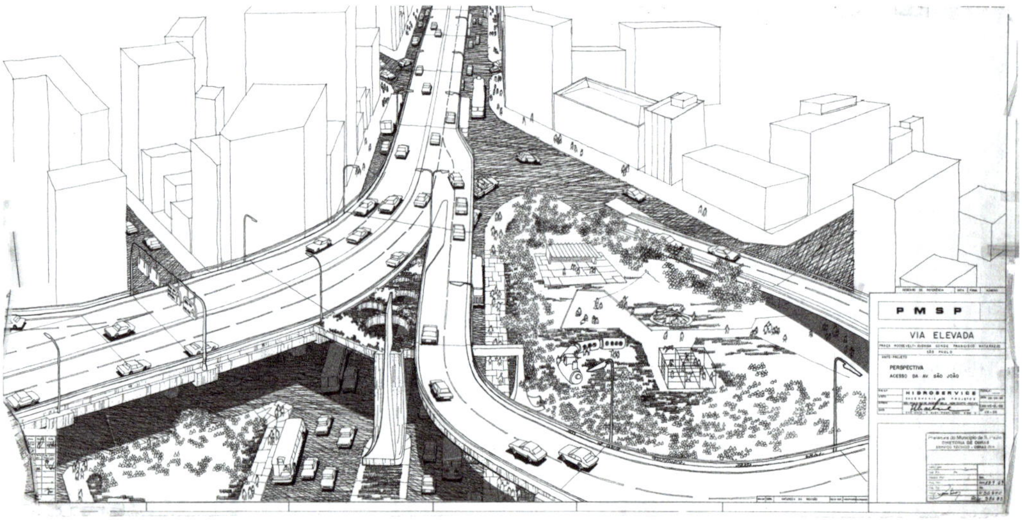

Bird's eye views of the project

View of Minhocão on a Sunday

Floor plan of part of Minhocão (area around Praça Marechal Deodoro) on a Sunday 1:2,000
© Guilhereme Pianca and Gabriel Sepe

0
20
100m

ARCHITECTURE, COMMON SPACE, AND EXCEPTION

JOSÉ TAVARES CORREIA DE LIRA

"Le Brésil n'a pas de peuple,"[1] the French physiologist Louis Couty declared in 1881, shortly before slavery was abolished in Brazil: along with the 500,000 "masters" then dominating the country and two-and-a-half million "useless" slaves and natives, there were some six million Brazilians who merely "vegetated" hand-to-mouth in the country's hinterland and cities—in such a way that no more than three million people would eventually attain the status of free, productive citizens. Couty's brutal slogan reverberated for many years to come—in Brazil itself as well in the rest of the world. In 1906, almost twenty years after the abolition of slavery and at a time when Brazil had already become a republic, the law professor, folklorist, and historian of literature Sílvio Romero quoted Couty's declaration on the occasion of Euclides da Cunha's nomination as a Member of the Academia Brasileira de Letras. Referring to the French physiologist, he emphasized that the nation's worthless elite could not effectively lead the country.[2] This gloomy forecast is perhaps no longer comprehensible today, but the image of a country without citizens, without a middle class, and without an effective ruling class, per the European model, did permeate a great deal of the social thinking in Brazil well into the twentieth century.

It should be noted here that this idea of citizenship was based on racial prejudice and legal constraints, typical of an ethnocentric intelligentsia raised on evolutionism, both in Brazil and elsewhere. This idea of citizenship generally assumes an informed morally enlightened electorate, whether cosmopolitan bourgeois or organized working class. In European societies, the validity of such a conception may be relative, but in Brazil, where the effects of the genocide inflicted on indigenous groups, of multi-secular slavery, as well as of the country's patriarchalism are felt to this very day, much of that which we call a citizen or the "public" imposes on the lower strata of society various kinds of inequality, violence, and exclusion.

Even in a city like São Paulo, which by the mid-twentieth century had developed into a major symbol of the country's modernization, it was difficult to overcome such national atavisms and all their atrocious side effects. Florestan Fernandes, one of the fathers of Brazilian developmental sociology, wrote a wonderful essay on the nascent metropolis in 1959.[3] According to him, the increased competition among São Paulo's population did help to improve the spatial distribution of social activities (even among the working class), but a truly urban material basis had not yet been created. The patrimonialistic order was indeed gradually disintegrating with the advance of the impersonal, but the insistence on handling collective affairs as someone's own private affairs showed how prevalent the legacy of colonialism truly was. So, if material progress had created conditions that

Ibirapuera Park's Marquise
© Nelson Kon

Avenida Paulista in the 1950s. Collage of Conjunto Nacional Competition, Architect David Libeskind © Arquivo Casa da Arquitectura – Centro Português de Arquitectura

Minhocão open to pedestrians on Sundays

Terrace and swimming pool, SESC 24 de Maio

were conducive to a class society and democratic processes, this same progress also promoted the illusion that life in São Paulo would proceed under similar conditions to those in large European or US cities. Conversely, the tumultuous and intermittent character of the city's urban growth was reducing the dynamic influence of tensions on the performance of local institutions and on the often quite narrow life patterns. Such inconsistencies were manifest in the malfunctioning of the transportation system; security, healthcare, and social assistance services; energy, sewage, and water supply infrastructures; and other public facilities there.

Despite the perceptive diagnosis of the paradoxical conditions reigning in São Paulo, Fernandes's difficulties in overcoming the binary oppositions of modern/archaic and civilized/popular can be collated with two contemporary urban processes —the creation of the Ibirapuera Park and the transformation of Avenida Paulista into a vigorous metropolitan centrality. The park, constructed between 1951 and 1953 at the behest of the industrialist Ciccillo Matarazzo, was intended to provide the framework for the spectacular celebrations of the 400th anniversary of the city's foundation. The park's magnificent architectural complex was designed by Oscar Niemeyer to serve as venues for the São Paulo Art Biennial and for future industrial fairs requiring a monumental site. Even if the enterprise's distinguished institutional program, the park's location within socially exclusive garden-neighborhoods, and the still inadequate public transportation links are quite relevant to any discussion, the increasing popularity of the Ibirapuera Park in recent decades must still be emphasized. This popularity applies in particular to the Marquise, a large roofed area in the park, whose typologically unclassifiable form has always evaded any attempt to define its precise program.

The Avenida Paulista, which was opened in 1891 as a residential area for some of the wealthiest families, developed rather swiftly into a key locus for the local bourgeois to display their means and tastes. Since the 1950s, when the 2,700-meter-long straight-as-an-arrow boulevard began to see its splendid mansions rapidly replaced by skyscrapers, the avenue developed into the city's most important financial district and a major focus for real-estate speculation. Far from the tsunamis of informal building, land-use irregularity, and environmental destruction which took hold on the city's periphery, this new centrality seemed to document the urban "logic of disorder" in an underdeveloped country in an exemplary way, halfway between the search for normativity and the rationalization of the exception.[4] Not by chance, in recent decades, as the avenue began losing its former global relevance, an impressive number of new cultural facilities have emerged around the Avenida Paulista, which, together with the subway's number 2 line which began running in 1991, and the banning of cars on Sundays and holidays since 2015, have generated quite visible changes in the area, attracting a totally new population.

And therefore, both in Ibirapuera Park and on the Avenida Paulista, each originally conceived as elite spaces, we have been seeing a real urban metamorphosis, similar to that which one may find in the beach areas of the Brazilian coastal cities. In fact, in cities like Rio de Janeiro and Recife, urban beaches, a typical residential address for the local elites, have long been attractive as leisure sites for people of the most diverse ethnic-social origins. In São Paulo, a form of "city beach" seems to be emerging in Ibirapuera, on the Avenida Paulista, and to a certain degree on the Minhocão urban expressway as well. On the one hand, these "city beaches" denounce real separations, but they also encompass micro-political territorial pressures vis-à-vis the formal dynamics of the country's democratic new beginnings since the 1980s.

And indeed, structures such as the Marquise in Ibirapuera Park; the external staircase on the Gazeta building; the free span under the MASP; the malls in the Conjunto Nacional; the open spaces at the Centro Cultural São Paulo (CCSP); and, of course, the little alleys, patios, crosswalks, and ramps of the SESC Pompéia and the SESC 24 de Maio exhibit

Jules Martins, Avenida Paulista inauguration day, 8 December 1891
© Public domain / Museu Paulista (USP) Collection

Guilherme Gaensly, Avenida Paulista in 1902
© Public Domain / Biblioteca Nacional

Avenida Paulista in the 1970s
© Arquivo Casa da Arquitectura – Centro Português de Arquitectura

Avenida Paulista on a Movimento dos Trabalhadores Sem Teto (Movement of Workers without a Roof-MTST) protest December 31, 2018

an architecture whose virtues include openness to the indefinite, unstable, and disturbing aspects of metropolitan life. In all these projects, the ability to implement these urban qualities is remarkable, utilizing the borders between outside and inside, the connections between building and city, the elements of circulation, and the most auspicious spaces for official and unofficial gatherings and for collective events.

Examples here include the enormous increase in the kinds of public flows and situations that were triggered by the equally seductive and enigmatic design of Niemeyer's Marquise in Ibirapuera Park, and the magnetic attraction exercised by MASP's belvedere, designed by Lina Bo Bardi. This big public square on Avenida Paulista challenges both the huge concrete walls that enclose it, the density and verticality of the adjacent skyscrapers, and the coveted local land values in order to allow the most diverse performance genres of popular, peripheral, activist, and youth cultures to blossom on it. Another compelling example is, of course, the absorption of the city's topography into the interplay of terraces, stairs, ramps, and patios that Eurico Prado Lopes and Luiz Telles developed for the CCSP. The sociocultural requirements of huge contingents of students and members of the most diverse urban "tribes," with their own identity rituals, are met here day-in-and-day-out. Also, quite powerful are the social interactions that happen in the SESC Pompéia and the SESC 24 de Maio, designed by Bo Bardi and Paulo Mendes da Rocha/MMBB respectively. The obvious differences between the two do not belie the pronounced urban commitment of each building, which both tackle the relations between the project, a complex institutional program, and the spatial experience, opening up each building to its potential uses and users, while interacting with the context and selectively reflecting its values.

All these projects have not only proven themselves capable of repositioning architectural modernism in Brazil—they have also developed some of the most inspiring design hypotheses for contemporary public buildings. And this not only in parts of the world, like Brazil, where highly modern ventures had to adjust to profound social dilemmas, but also at the global poles of architectural canonization. All of these projects, in their own ways, promote a shifting of the disciplinary agenda towards confronting the object as a component of a broader territorial organization, which is at the same time capable of compacting certain moral economies of the urban crowds, both functionally and erotically.[5] These economies seem to be as uncertain as they are engulfing, as fleeting as they are numerous, out of order, and ready to put all things to the test.[6]

Like a few other major examples of architectural experiments in São Paulo, these projects are balanced on the narrow ridge of the extraordinary. And they suggest possibilities for articulating the common space without withdrawing from the frictions, dissolution, and reconstruction processes which are peculiar to every big city. These buildings are truly exceptional in the face of a most anomic urban process, and yet they function in the city like a detail in a painting: entirely unnoticed sometimes, and nevertheless capable of giving the whole scene a purpose. They are like a place of refuge for the joys and hazards of social life, operating like an anti-production machine or a device for residual social productions, not always controllable, because they are transformative, quicksand-like, desiring, exuberant, deviant—not unlike Mario de Andrade's fictional hero, Macunaíma—and also very similar to those that could be heard in the Warburgh-style Samba theme created by the Mangueira Samba School at the carnival performance in Rio de Janeiro last March: an "história pra ninar gente grande" (lullaby story for adults) made as a "story of deleted verses," whose heroes were not preserved in "framed portraits," but rather full of "Marias, Mahins, Marielles, malês" and numerous other characters "out of the picture."[7] Perhaps here, in their pleading for presence, in their ability to let in the ghosts of civilization, lies the key to understanding such an architecture's undisputed public efficiency.

1 Translated from French: "Brazil is a country without a people." Louis Couty, *L'Esclavage au Brésil*, (Paris: Librairie de Guillaumin et Cie, 1881), 87.

2 Sílvio Romero, *Discurso pronunciado aos 18 de dezembro de 1906, por ocasião da recepção do Dr. Euclides da Cunha*, (Porto: Chardron de Lello & Irmão, 1910).

3 Florestan Fernandes, "O homem e a cidade-metrópole," in *Mudanças Sociais no Brasil*, (São Paulo: Difusão Européia do Livro, 1960), 266-283.

4 Luxion Kowarick and Vinicius Caldeira Brant, *São Paulo 1975: crescimento e pobreza*, (São Paulo: Loyola, 1976); Francisco de Oliveira, "A economia brasileira: crítica à razão dualista," in *Estudos Cebrap*, n. 2, 1972; idem, "O Estado e a exceção – ou o Estado de exceção?" in *Revista Brasileira de Estudos Urbanos e Regionais*, vol. 5, n. 1, May 2003 colon : 9-14.

5 E. P. Thompson, "A economia moral da multidão inglesa no século XVIII," in: *Costumes em comum* (São Paulo: Companhia das Letras, 2008) , colon : 150-202.

6 Caetano Veloso, "Fora da Ordem," in *Circuladô*, CD, 1991.

7 Mangueira Samba School's song refers to the strength of ordinary men and women and their leading roles in various moments in Brazil, in the past and the present. Luisa Mahin was an early-nineteenth-century revolutionary female slave in Bahia, and Marielle Silva was a black lesbian activist and a brave city councilor elected in 2016, brutally killed in Rio in March 2018. Cf. Danilo Firmino, Deivid Domênico, Mamá, Márcio Bola, Ronie Oliveira, Tomaz Miranda, História pra ninar gente grande. Rio de Janeiro: Estação Primeira da Mangueira, 2019.

IN FAVOR OF (RARE) AESTHETIC CONTACT WITH THE STREET IN PRESENT-DAY SÃO PAULO

FRAYA FREHSE

What contribution do specific multifunctional buildings on display in the exhibition, the ones with incisive architectural signatures—covered walkways, museums, cultural centers, a market, an educational center, a building— offer to the everyday life of the inhabitants of São Paulo today? My answer is based on a sociological perspective which is sensitive to the historicity of the rules of a symbolic nature that guide the relations that pedestrians, by means of their bodies, daily (re) produce with each other and/or with material/ symbolic goods in empirically existing streets and squares—in short, on the street. Beyond their varying structures, forms, functions, and scales, the selected projects share one common incentive for their users—if not also for their non-users: all of them are encouraged to make aesthetic contact of an architectural nature with the street, as an urban space which is both physical-material and social. As this contact, which is based on architectural representations of what is "beautiful" in relation to the street, is uncommon in present-day São Paulo, the unique contribution of these buildings is precisely to stimulate this kind of contact.

Assuming that space is produced by the body relations of human beings in places,[1] the street has a physical and social materiality which is also historically generated by social interactions that can be named "contact" in Erving Goffman's terms.[2] A set of verbal and non-verbal signs and exchanges interfere in the production of the street as space. These signs, which integrate the "body idiom" of those who interact,[3] operate every time two or more individuals are in a physically— or symbolically— intermediated co-presence.[4] From this methodological point of view, it is conceptually revealing to contemplate the architectural infrastructures on display in light of the socio-cultural history of pedestrians' patterns of body contact with the street in São Paulo. If, as we will see below, (i) now that these projects have been accomplished, they have become places which are aesthetically charged with an architecture favorable to physical and symbolic contact with the street, then a synthetic historical retrospective will show (ii) the exceptionality of this design emphasis in São Paulo and (iii) its unique contribution to the daily lives of at least the users of the works at stake.

(i) The architecture of the buildings on display and the street

The physical appearance of these buildings connotes in three distinct ways that their architects have elevated the street to a privileged object of aesthetic architectural treatment. On the one hand, the projects give absolute priority to the scale of the pedestrian freed from automobiles. It is no wonder that most of the projects do not include parking lots. On the other hand, they are full of architectural devices which amplify the physical or, at least, visual contact that the buildings' users

View of IMS from Avenida Paulista

View of the pedestrian street at SESC

View of the ground floor of Conjunto Nacional

View of the ground floor of Praça das Artes

can make with the surrounding streets and squares: regarding physical contact, I think of free spans and staircases; in relation to visual contact, I mean terraces, ramps, and large windows.

Finally, some works also further metaphorical contact between their users and the street. It is not only the toponymy in the interiors that refers explicitly to "squares" and, in one case, to the "sidewalk." The furniture is also functionally analogous to that of streets and public places in São Paulo—although with significant differences. I recall, for example, carefully stylized signs for users, instead of those that in a poor physical state of preservation and scrambling various typographies are intended for pedestrians in the city. There is also no shortage of physical body supports for users, which carry unmistakable authorial designs, quite different from the relatively few park benches that persist in São Paulo.

If all these resources are evidence of the respective projects' purpose of keeping their users in constant physical or, at least, symbolic contact with the physical and social street through the mediation of architectural aesthetics, what may this emphasis reveal about the collaboration of the buildings with the everyday life of the inhabitants of São Paulo? After all, projects for multifunctional spaces with a physical and metaphorical focus on the street are by no means exclusive to this city. In search of an answer, there is nothing like a bit of history.

(ii) On the historicity of the patterns of body contact with the street in São Paulo

Legally "public" streets and squares, that is, places accessible by law to the greatest number of human types, have existed for less than one third of São Paulo's 465 years.[5] Until the official abolition of African slavery (1888), everyday life in the street in the still rural city of almost 64,000 inhabitants was avoided by those people whose high social status enabled them to dispense with the need to physically pass through or stay therein on a regular basis.[6] The figure of the passer-by only slowly gained social consistency in streets and squares which were daily crowded with pedestrians typically involved in manual labor and in the sociability linked to it: slaves legally subject to daily curfews, and the so-called freedmen and free men, people who were economically and, above all, socially poor.

Evidently, a lot has changed since then, and the circulation of passers-by and particularly of vehicles currently is a powerful pattern of bodily use of the street in the city. Powerful, but not hegemonic. After all, one rule of body behavior from the times of slavery—the regular physical permanence of pedestrians on the street for economic and sociability purposes—remains current. Streets and squares, subjected almost without interruption to policies in favor of automobiles, bustle with an immense diversity of pedestrians who do not pass amid the traffic of humans and machines: street vendors, artists, and craftsmen, preachers and beggars, the self-proclaimed street dwellers. Whether their motivations lie in economic or social factors is not up for discussion here; the fact is that 131 years after becoming legally accessible to all, the street is a space of reference for the daily life of *non-passers-by*.[7]

In light of this retrospective synthesis, the exceptionality of the buildings on display becomes evident. Their authors' privileged design concern is directed to a space that is historically marginal in social terms. Moreover, one of the profoundly current social contradictions of the street in São Paulo is also of a historic nature. Despite all the political-administrative and socioeconomic pressure in favor of mobility —as a quality deemed so decisive in today's globalized world— the historically long-standing immobility of the urban poor often prevails on the streets of São Paulo.

It is true that these circumstances do not fully explain why the streets and public squares that prevail in the city today are largely devoid of any aesthetic refinement in any way analogous to that of the architectural infrastructures under consideration. But they do allow us to recognize that the peculiarity of this design emphasis is also due to a sociocultural history which, by way of the bodies of pedestrians, is (re)produced on the street day by day – and (re)produces it in turn.

(iii) The rarity of the exhibited works' contribution

From this perspective, it is not surprising that the buildings in focus enhance a type of contact which is rare in current-day São Paulo: *at least* their users are encouraged to aesthetically interact with the street either inside the buildings or physically from therein. Which is practically like saying: through the mediation of architectural aesthetics, these users and also non-users are stimulated to make physical or at least symbolic contact with the sociocultural difference and social inequality that this space, like no other in the city, has borne for centuries. The situation is probably bothersome, but it can also delight the users facing non-passers-by who are (potentially) copresent in or around these places of architectural beauty. Indeed, in São Paulo such aesthetic refinement prevails in places of private access.

Therefore, it is possible to clarify, at last, why my argument refers to at least the users of the works being exhibited. These are the people who physically prevail therein. Despite the presence of free spans and free admission for most of the functional activities in these places, non-passers-by in general do not use them: from what I have observed during the opening hours of these respective infrastructures, non-passers-by predominantly remain either on the streets and squares of the neighborhood or in the architectural limits indicating entrances — which, by the way, are frequently monitored by security guards. As to why this is the case, the data I collected on the body contact of non-passers-by with other architectural infrastructures in downtown São Paulo in 2013 and 2014 are suggestive. They indicate that the buildings are enchanting through their architectural beauty, but also bothersome due to the embarrassment that non-passers-by may experience in the face of their users' gazes, dress, gestures, postures, and emotional expression—in short, their body idiom.

Nonetheless, the works also offer non-passers-by the rare aesthetic contact highlighted here. After all, by translating all this sociocultural history of body contact with the street into cement, stone, and glass, the works materially express, both for users and non-users, how the social contradictions implicit in the body contact of the inhabitants of São Paulo with the street present themselves in a precise temporal moment: exactly when this same street is subjected to the architect's aesthetic sensitivity.

1 Fraya Frehse, "Relational Space through Historically Relational Time – in the Bodies of São Paulo's Pedestrians", *Current Sociology*, vol. 65, n. 4, 2017 colon: 511–532.

2 Erving Goffman, "The Interaction Order: American Sociological Association, 1982 Presidential Address," *American Sociological Review*, vol. 48, n. 1 colon : 6.

3 Erving Goffman, *Behavior in Public Places*, (New York: The Free Press/Collier-Macmillan, 1963) 33.

4 Erving Goffman, "The Interaction Order: American Sociological Association, 1982 Presidential Address," *American Sociological Review*, vol. 48, n. 1, 1982 colon : 6.

5 Lyn Lofland, *A World of Strangers*, (Prospect Heights: Waveland Press), 19; Fraya Frehse, *Ô da Rua!* (São Paulo: Edusp, 2011), *passim*.

6 Fraya Frehse, *O Tempo das Ruas na São Paulo de Fins do Império*, (São Paulo: Edusp, 2005); Fraya Frehse, *Ô da Rua!* (São Paulo: Edusp, 2011).

7 Fraya Frehse, "On Regressive-Progressive Rhythmanalysis," in *Perspectives on Henri Lefebvre*, eds., Jenny Bauer and Robert Fischer, (Berlin/Boston: De Gruyter 2018), 107.

AVENIDA PAULISTA

IMS Paulista (Moreira Salles Institute)

Gazeta Building

Conjunto Nacional Building

FIESP Cultural Center

São Paulo's 2.8-kilometer-long Avenida Paulista is a paradigmatic example of how, in certain cities, beyond monuments, memorials, or buildings, an avenue can be understood as an ultimate memory repository. The Paulista was inaugurated in 1891, becoming the most coveted address in São Paulo as coffee barons lined it with their mansions. However, since the 1950s it has undergone a process of verticalization and all but one of the original mansions have been replaced by high-rises.

Paulista perpetuates its significance on a daily basis as it is activated by the transit of pedestrians and various types of vehicles, as well as through the use of the buildings that flank it. In parallel, Paulista is the ultimate site for protests and demonstrations in the city, and this is where its political significance appears, generating its multilayered protagonism in the city and country's history. The Paulista has had the capacity to provide a stage for voices that are not usually heard in the city. Since the 1990s, and particularly since 2013 through several waves of protests, the volume of marching crowds has increased incrementally. The last major manifestations happened during the 2018 presidential campaign. What enhances Paulista's historical role is that it is also a place of celebrations, including Carnaval, the largest LGBT Pride parade in the world, the São Silvestre run, and a series of other events that take place on a yearly basis.

One quite important detail is that, since 2015, Paulista has been closed to vehicular traffic every Sunday, becoming an urban park and thus mitigating the lack of open space in the city. The overnight gyms, stages, markets, etc. provide an unprecedented urban scene. One of the main characteristics of Paulista, both in its everyday life as well as in its singular moments, is that several of the buildings that flank it either multiply vertically or stretch horizontally the public space of the sidewalk and avenue through calculated architectural strategies. (Think of the plaza under the MASP building or the galleries under the Conjunto Nacional building.) The recently opened roof terrace at the SESC Paulista building on the avenue, with its elevated platform on the 17th floor that offers a central view of the avenue, is the latest illustration of this phenomenon.

p. 142-143 Avenida Paulista on a weekday
p. 144-145 Avenida Paulista on a Sunday
p. 146-147 Avenida Paulista during a protest

R. Pamplona
40
DOMINGO 7-16h
ÔNIBUS

24h
SP SÃO PAULO
Onofre
CVS pharmacy

2200
R. Haddock Lobo
Augusta
Safra
DAS 22H DE
27/01 AS
04H DE
28/01

Estacionamento
Shopping
Rua Luis Coelho, 91
25°C

MAIS CONVENIÊNCIA:
Santander
SHOPPING CENTER 3
POVO SEM MEDO
DO
CAPÃO

Itaú
McDonald's

Avenida Paulista as space for New Year's celebration, 2018
© picture alliance/ZUMA Press/ Photo: Dario Oliveira

Avenida Paulista as space for the Parade of LGBT Pride, 2018
© picture alliance / NurPhoto / Photo: FotoRua

Avenida Paulista as space for manifestation, 2018
© picture alliance / NurPhoto / Photo: FotoRua

Avenida Paulista as space for the São Silvestre Road Race, 2016
© picture alliance / NurPhoto / Photo: FotoRua © picture alliance / dpa / Photo: Fernando Bizerra Jr.

IMS Paulista (Moreira Salles Institute)

Name: Instituto Moreira Salles (IMS) Paulista

Address: Avenida Paulista, 2424

Year of Project: 2011-2017

Architect: Andrade Morettin Arquitetos

Engineer: Ycon Engenharia / GOP / Yopanan Rebello

Client/who commissioned: Instituto Moreira Salles

Type of institution: private institution

Hours: Tue. to Sun., 10 am – 8 pm; Thu., 10 am - 10 pm; closed Mon.

Number of daily visitors: In 2018 the peaks were 3,000 daily visitors and 76,000 monthly visitors.

Project: Andrade Morettin Arquitetos (Vinicius Andrade e Marcelo Morettin), closed private contest in 2011 commissioned by IMS, private cultural institution from the Moreira Salles family, financed by the fortune of the patriarch (banker, diplomat and ex-minister, Walther Moreira Salles) and Unibanco bank. Five other important architects participated in the competition: Angelo Bucci (spbr), Arquitetos Associados, Bernardes + Jacobsen, Marcio Kogan (Studio MK27) e Una Arquitetos. Works started in 2013 and were completed in 2017. During its first year of operation it was visited by 827.426 people.

Program: free ground floor square and restaurant; library, media library, studying room and administration; "elevated square, belvedere" with café, book store, and ticket office; cinema/theater with 132 seats, three exhibition galleries (total 1,200 m^2), three classrooms.

Area: 8,662 m^2

Exterior view of Moreira Salles Institute (IMS)

CACAU
NÃO!

Dedicated in 2017, the Instituto Moreira Salles (IMS) building is in many ways a foreign building in Avenida Paulista and in Brazil at large, due to the choice of materials and some of the formal moves, like having an envelope that is not related directly to the inner programs in the upper floors, or the opening in the terrace façade that does not cover the whole of the façade but stops short in front of the staircase. This resistance to the Paulista School allowed the architects to understand and interpret some of the typical architectural moves in Avenida Paulista, the strategies that allow buildings to communicate building with the Avenue. The free space on the first floor is in dialogue with the space under the MASP, with Conjunto Nacional, and a series of other buildings, and the elevated square allows for views to the avenue and the back of the lot. These moves both amplify horizontally and multiply vertically the open space of the street inside the building. The cultural program is free, and the library is open to all. The elevated terrace that divides the library and theatre from the museum in the upper floors, a detached continuation of the sidewalk, goes so far as to use what used to be the same pavement treatment.

View from the elevated plaza looking down at Paulista Avenue

View of the cafe and bookstore at the elevated plaza

View from the ground floor towards Avenida Paulista

View from the elevated plaza looking down at Paulista Avenue

View from the ground floor towards Avenida Paulista

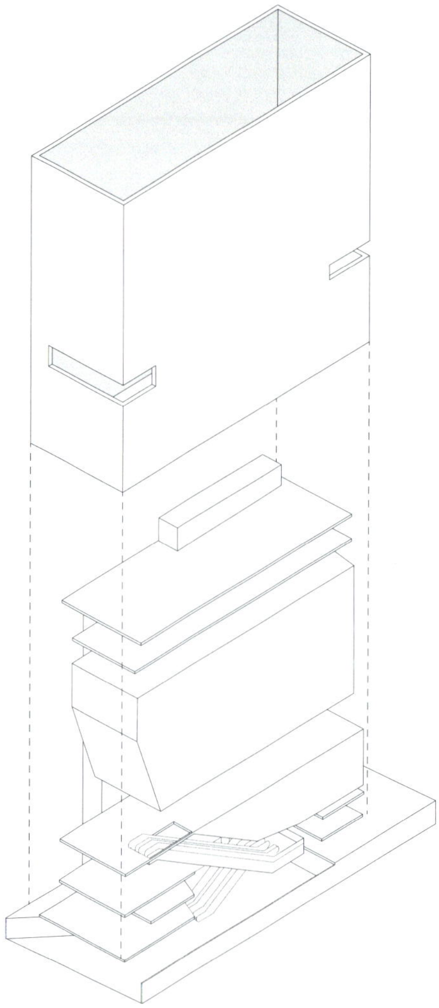

Axonometric drawing
© Andrade e Morettin

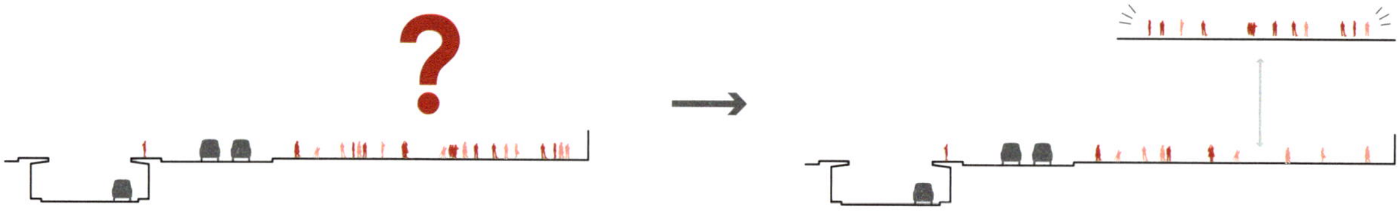

Diagram of the strategy of the project
© Andrade e Morettin

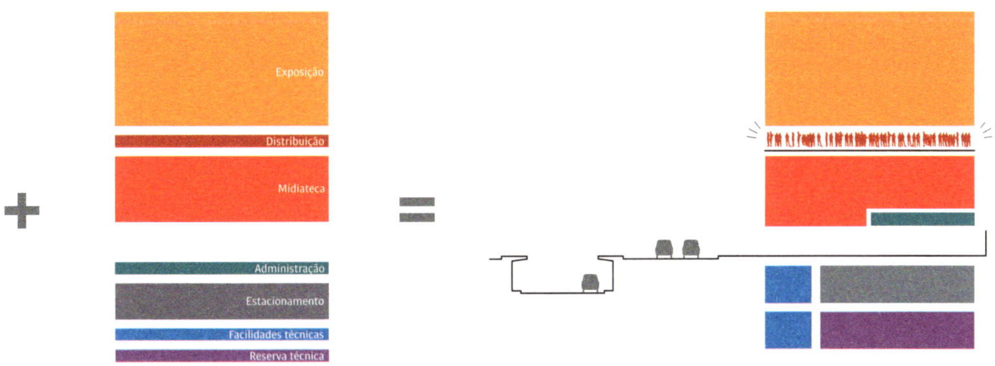
Exposição
Distribuição
Midiateca
Administração
Estacionamento
Facilidades técnicas
Reserva técnica

Gazeta Building

Name: Edifício Gazeta

Address: Avenida Paulista, 900

Year of Project: 1958-1966

Engineer: José Carlos de Figueiredo Ferraz

Client/who commissioned: Fundação Cásper Líbero

Type of institution: private media conglomerate

Hours: Mo.-Fri. 8 am-10:30 pm; Sat. 8am–2 pm

Program: the stair is the open entrance to the big hall, connecting the busy avenue to the building (it houses Cásper Líbero Foundation, a private high school, a private university, radio studios and a important alternative)

Number of daily visitors: 20,000

Project: José Carlos de Figueiredo Ferraz, 1958 – 1966, the stair is the open entrance to the big hall, connecting Avenida Paulista to the building

Program: it houses Cásper Líbero Foundation, a private high school, a private university, radio studios, et al.

Area: 68,000 m^2

Exterior view of Gazeta from Avenida Paulista

TV GAZETA
RÁDIO GAZETA AM-FM
Uber
Juntos
19:10

Dedicated in 1966, the Gazeta building hosts several different programs: a foundation, a radio station, a university, a school, and they all share the facilities. The monumental stairs providing access to the Gazeta represent one of the architectural "moves" in Avenida Paulista for expanding public space from the sidewalk into the interior of buildings. The stairs end in an elevated-plaza-like lobby with public seating, which relates to another of the "Paulista strategies" that is present in several other buildings along the avenue, with the difference that this one is recessed from the façade because of the stairs. The procession from the building to the street is quite dramatic: the depth of the plaza/lobby is exaggerated, and then one descends to the city via the monumental stairs which are at the scale of the avenue but not of the sidewalk. People use the stairs heavily as a meeting spot, a place to rest, or simply somewhere to look at Avenida Paulista from a higher standpoint.

Side view of the stairs of the building

View of the model and construction, 1958
© Arquivo Público do Estado de São Paulo

Interior view of the hall

View of the stairs

Conjunto Nacional Building

Name: Conjunto Nacional

Address: Avenida Paulista, 2073

Year of project: 1954-1962

Architect: David Libeskind

Engineer: Hans Eger

Client/who commissioned: José Tjurs

Type of institution: private housing and commercial development

Hours: commercial ground floor: Mon. - Fri., 6 am - 10 pm; Sat. - Sun., 10 am - 10 pm. commercial and office tower: Mon. - Fri., 7 am - 10 pm; Sat., 7 am - 7 pm.

Number of daily visitors: around 35,000

Project: David Libeskind, Hans Eger design and execution of the geodesic dome, 1954 (commission and project), 1956 (partial conclusion of the "horizontal base"), 1958 (base conclusion), 1962 (tower conclusion). The project was commissioned by the businessman in the hospitality industry, José Tjurs, who bought in 1952 the whole block previously occupied by a high-end villa (as the whole Avenue).

Program: mixed use with commercial center (offices), shopping mall, housing. Ground floor and other floors of the "horizontal volume" (61,354 m^2) with around 60 stores including one of the most important São Paulo's book store (Livraria Cultura), one theater and two cinemas. The 25-floor tower is divided in three parts: Horsa I, 24,237m^2, with 562 small and medium-sized establishments (offices, clinics, computer companies, etc.); in Horsa II, 23,682,074 m^2, with 107 larger ventures, such as multinational companies, consulates and law firms. In the housing part (Edifício Guayupiá) there are 47 apartments from 180 to 890 m^2. 5,000 residents and people working in the building plus 30,000 daily users and visitors.

Area: block (ground floor with large sidewalks) 14,600 m^2, total built area around 150,000 m^2.

Exterior view of Conjunto Nacional

Av. Paulista

Dedicated in 1962, strictly speaking, Conjunto Nacional's low-rise building is a commercial gallery, but due to its location in the city and the qualities of the open spaces it offers, it is more than that. It is a meeting point, a haven in Avenida Paulista, a place to rest and avoid the heat and the rain. Originally, the Portuguese-style floor treatment matched the sidewalk design of the avenue, which reinforced the idea that the sidewalk entered and was widened and multiplied inside of a private commercial gallery. Here the strategy of stretching public space into a building finds a prime example. Architect Paulo Mendes da Rocha is known for criticizing Avenida Paulista as a confused avenue, a place where the footprints of former mansions were extruded and became high rises, thus quite often inadequate in area for their height. However, he always highlights Conjunto Nacional as the only appropriate building on the avenue, and celebrates the way it connects to the city.

Interior view of Conjunto Nacional

Interior view of the upper gallery

Interior view of the ground floor

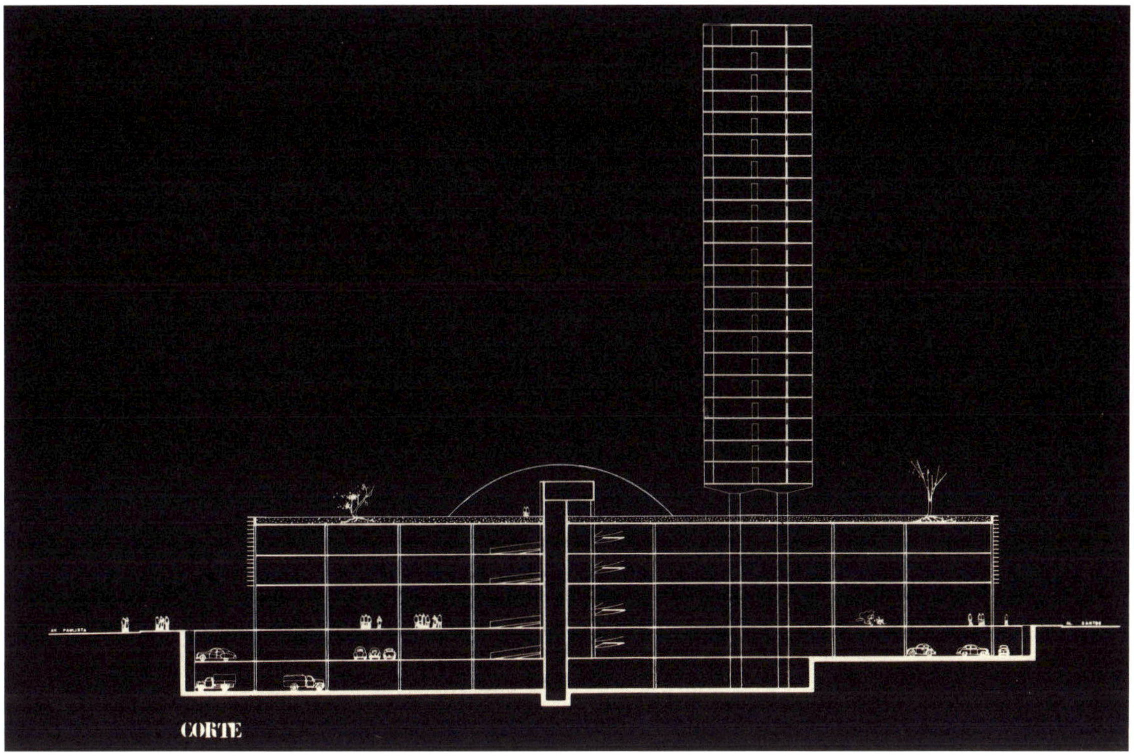

Transverse section
© Arquivo Casa da Arquitectura – Centro Português de Arquitectura

Sketch of Conjunto Nacional's ground floor, Architect David Libeskind
© Arquivo Casa da Arquitectura – Centro Português de Arquitectura

FIESP Cultural Center

Name: Centro Cultural Federação das Indústrias do Estado de São Paulo (FIESP) and SESI-SENAI-CIESP-IRS building

Address: Avenida Paulista, 1313

Year of Project: 1969 - 1979; 1996 - 1998

Architect: Rino Levi Arquitetos and Paulo Mendes da Rocha + MMBB

Engineer: Jorge Zaven Kurkdjian

Client/who commissioned: Federação das Indústrias do Estado de São Paulo

Type of institution: private institution (Federation of Industries)

Hours: Cultural center, Tue. - Sat., 10 am - 10 pm; Sun., 10 am - 8 pm. Café, Tue. - Sat., 10 am - 7 pm; Sun., 10 am - 8 pm. Offices, Mon. - Fri., 6:30 am - 8 pm (for workers, not for the cultural center visitors)

Number of daily visitors: 3,000 weekdays and 6,000 weekends.

Project: Rino Levi Arquitetos, 1969-1979, ground floor renovation (cultural center), Paulo Mendes da Rocha + MMBB (Angelo Bucci, Fernando de Mello Franco, Marta Moreira, Milton Braga), 1996-1998.

Program: Reception hall, bookstore, café, Burle Marx garden, art gallery (1,000 m^2), photo gallery (about 300 m^2), exhibition gallery (about 1,000 m^2), foyer, theater (450 seats), mezzanine and terrace on the sidewalk (now closed for cultural center users).

Area: cultural center 5,000 m^2

Exterior view of FIESP

FIESP
CIESP
SESI

Dedicated in 1998, the Centro Cultural FIESP is an intervention on a Rino Levi building from the 1970s by Paulo Mendes da Rocha and MMBB Arquitetos, which at the time included Marta Moreira, Milton Braga, Fernando Mello Franco (who are still partners), and Angelo Bucci (who went on to found spbr Arquitetos). The split first-floor spaces where they intervened existed in the original project, but the redesign of the program, which came to include a gallery, a theater, and a book store, among other program elements, required a structural intervention that gives the space its character (white I-beams and other metal elements). These split levels, offering the possibility of going to open programs on a half-sunken level and on a half-elevated one, multiplies the single-level open space and accommodates multiple cultural and leisure-related programs.

For a while, the bookstore and the cultural spaces became a meeting point for alternative youth cultures and LGBT groups, particularly the comic bookstore that used to exist inside, but the political turn in Brazil and the standpoint of the host institution curtailed this diversity. Recently, this building, including the stage that is installed in front of it, has become a meeting point for protesters on the right, and the building administration went so far as to commission a large sculpture of a yellow duck some years ago that became a symbol of the fight against corruption and high taxes, a symbol that was mobilized in the period leading up to the impeachment of former president Dilma Rousseff (which eventually took place in August 2016).

A highlight of the building is that once one reaches the end of the plot in the back, the open part of the program of the building leads to a landscape and mural design by Roberto Burle Marx.

Side view from Avenida Paulista

Exterior view with Avenida Paulista on the background

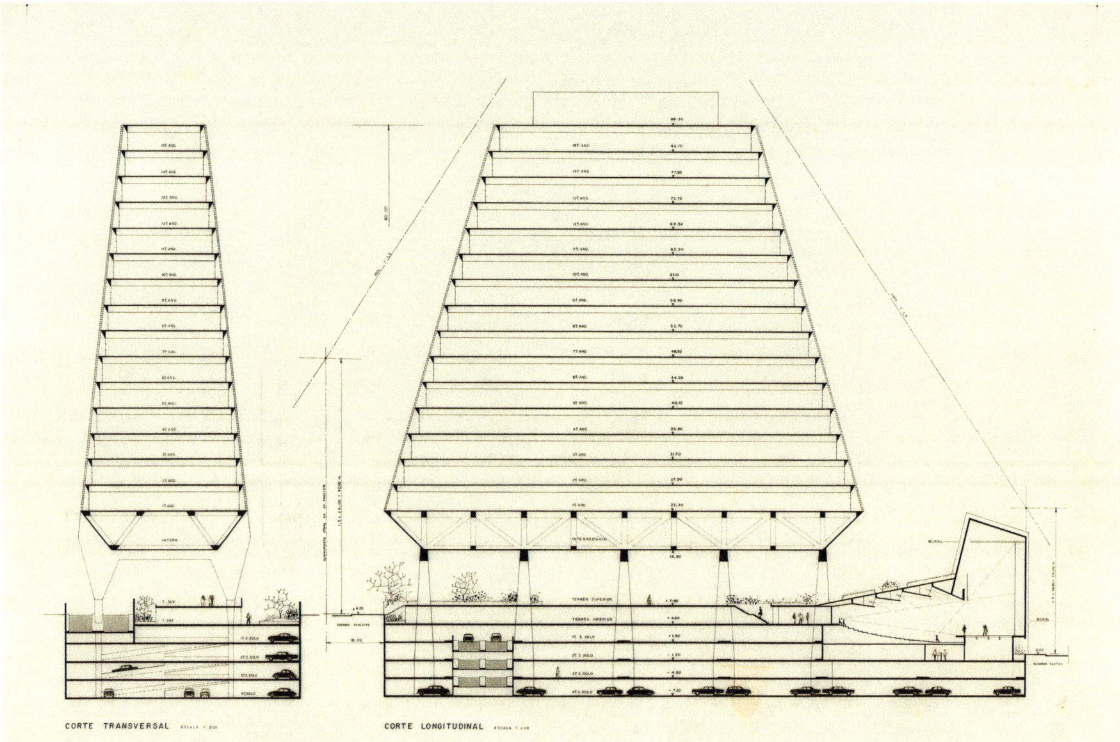

Sections, architect Rino Levi
© FAUUSP Library

View of FIESP Cultural Center

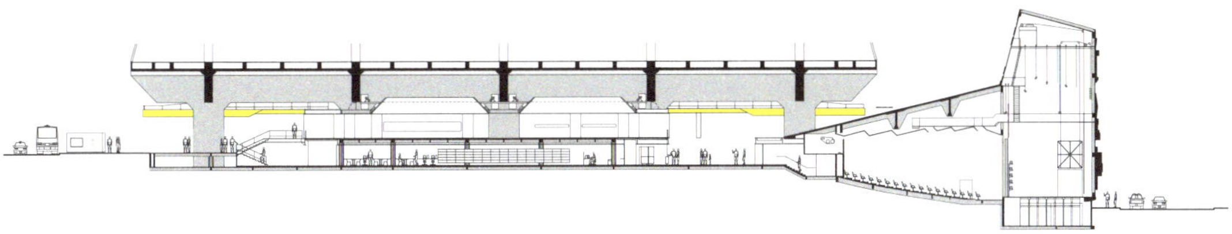

Section of the Cultural Center, Architects Paulo Mendes da Rocha and MMBB
© MMBB Arquitetos

View of the entrance of FIESP Cultural Center

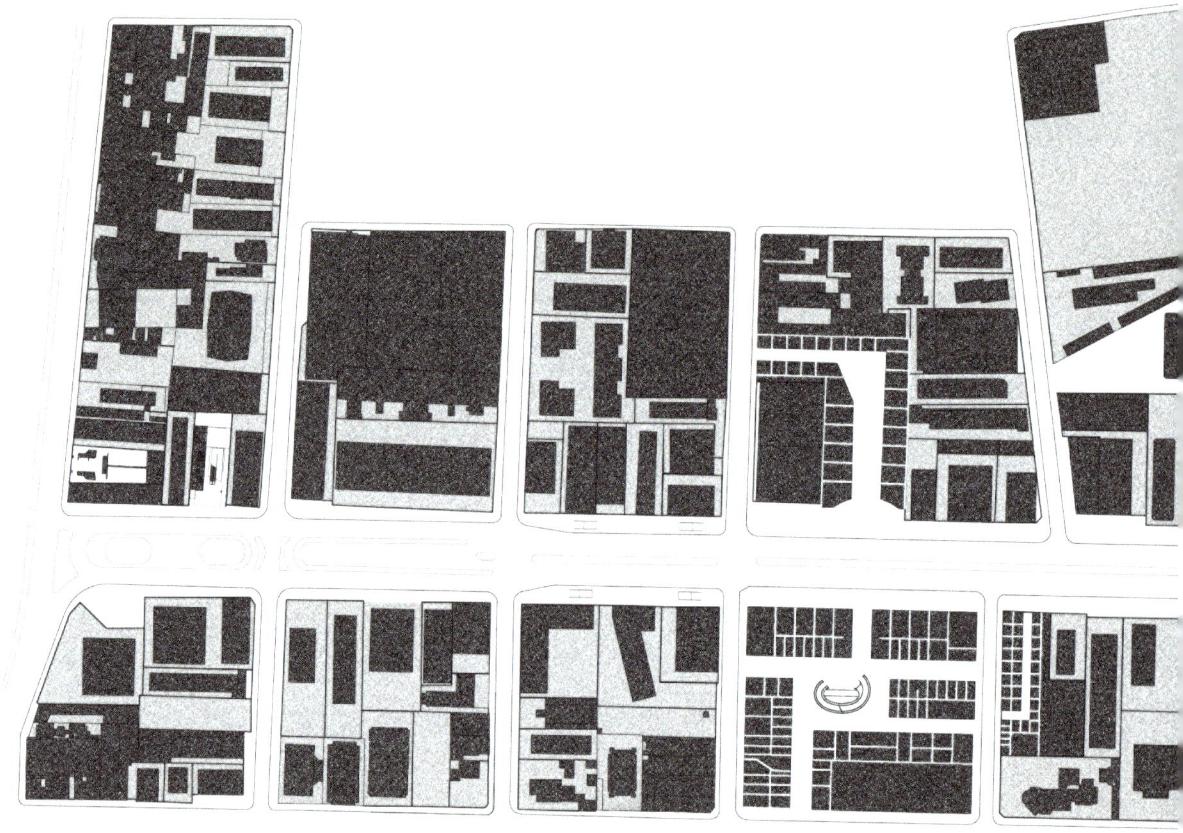

Ground floor plan (first stretch of Avenida Paulista) 1:4,000
© Guilherme Pianca, Gabriel Sepe and team

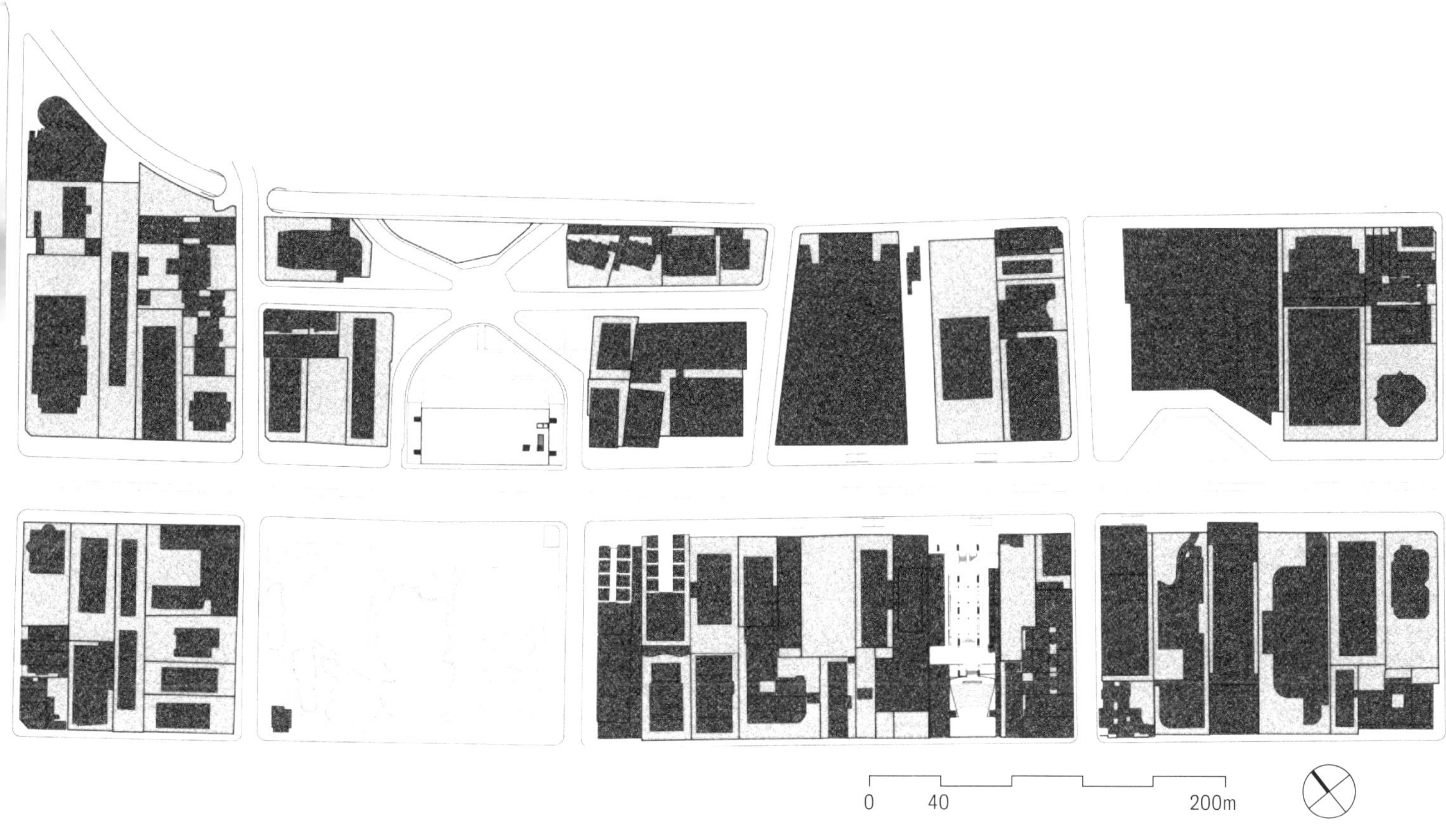
0
40
200m

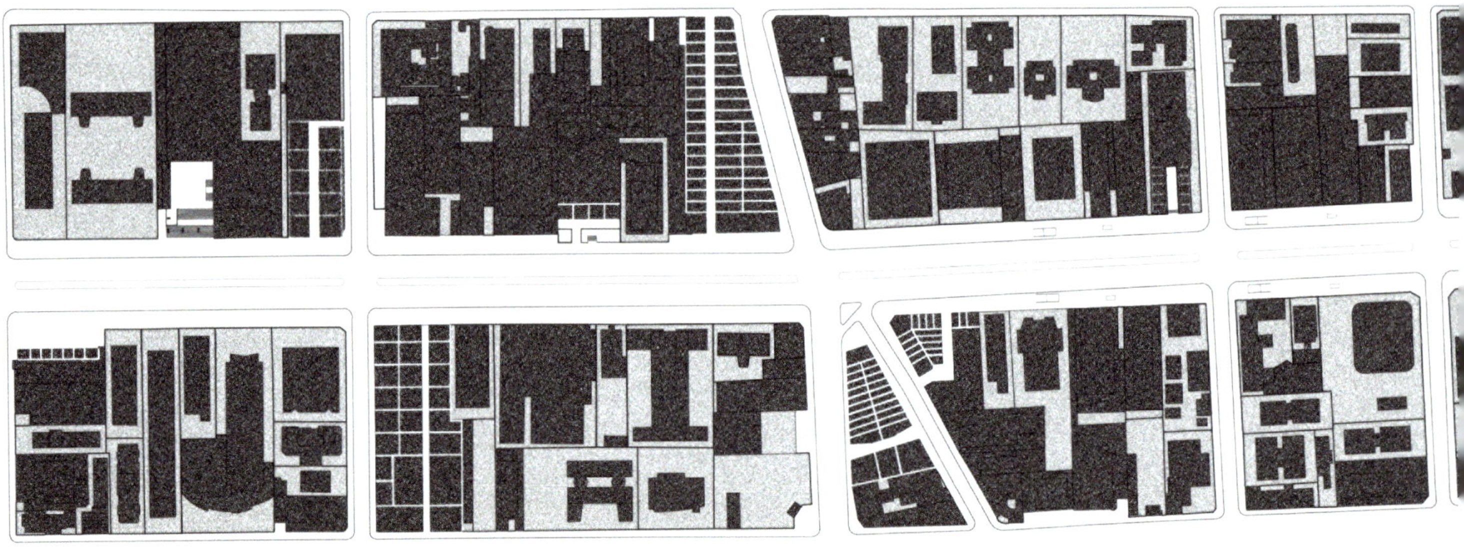

Ground floor plan (second stretch of Avenida Paulista) 1:4,000
© Guilherme Pianca, Gabriel Sepe and team

0
40
200m

#bike

Trianon-Masp

INTERVIEW

Paulo Mendes da Rocha and Marta Moreira in conversation with Enrique Walker

São Paulo, December 17, 2018

Enrique Walker: SESC 24 de Maio opened last year. I had the chance to visit it two days ago, and was extremely impressed. It is an exceptional building: a dynamic open structure, a vibrant urban space, a social condenser of sorts. I would like to devote this conversation to it, and trace a brief history of the project. To that end, I would suggest that we examine it in terms of the circumstances of the brief, the design problem and the design strategy you formulated at the outset, and, in particular, the concepts you formulated during its materialization. I understand that the project developed over a long period of time . . .

Paulo Mendes da Rocha: Fundamentally, you can say that this project belongs to the SESC because it reinforces the mission of this association of employers, which is to support employees in the commerce and services sector. The SESC does this in various ways, with a program that involves culture and entertainment to attract this population of workers and their families. The SESC also builds libraries and theaters, as well as sports courts and swimming pools—and since not every city in Brazil faces the sea, pools are very important to the interior of the country. This mission allows one to see the existence of a project before it actually materializes. The project of the SESC is something in the air.

Another important factor in this project is the idea of transforming a building, something we call "occupation." In contemporary cities, this operation is carried out every day by every citizen. This idea of occupying buildings for new purposes is a very interesting one, and it is not novel. However, in today's dense and already vertical contemporary cities, this process takes place faster and with more energy than before. But what is happening today is not really extraordinary: what is extraordinary, however, is our awareness of the process. Therefore, the influence of this issue, of the change in how a building is used, is due to this new awareness within each of us that we are agents in this process. Deep down, one can conclude that we are the city, not the buildings.

EW: Let's start with the site, which was actually an existing building . . .

PMdR: We must remember that the SESC decided to create another one of its institutions, this time in the heart of the city.

Marta Moreira: SESC 24 de Maio is just one hundred meters from the Teatro Municipal. It is in a very important historic area.

EW: And this new SESC in an existing building in the city center would still include all their usual culture and leisure programs . . .

PMdR: Strictly speaking, the SESC does not repeat the same programs for its buildings. Depending on the location, certain items of the program might not fit. For example, there was no pool in the initial program for SESC 24 de Maio. There was no space in the building they bought. I, as the architect, inserted the pool.

EW: The tension between the large-scale programs and an existing—and arguably inadequate—building to house those programs is precisely what interested me about the project as a design problem . . .

PMdR: When the SESC invited me to work on the project, they had already bought the site. If I had not wanted to do the project for whatever reason, they would have hired another architect. What is curious is that when Marta and I went to see the site for the first time, along with some representatives from the SESC, I already knew the existing building, which had once been a Mesbla department store that also sold cars. Moreover, in 1945 or 1946, my father had bought a Chrysler DeSoto there. I must have been seventeen or eighteen years old. My father took me, we got the car, and I drove it out. And now, in the same place, the SESC wanted me to design its new project. Nobody knew that I knew the place.

Let me tell you something about my process: I'm not sure if I'm right, but the impression I have is that I don't design projects the way you think I do, little by little, as a work in progress. I design the whole project at once. I see everything. It is obvious that some details are not conceived right away, but the idea of the project is—to the extent that I realized that there was a plot of land next to the SESC site, facing Rua Dom José de Barros. This property was odd because of its width: seven meters at the front and twenty meters at the back. The small existing building there had a for-sale sign which read "Caixa Econômica Federal" [a Brazilian state-owned bank that is the largest mortgage lender in the country]. This bank repossesses assets that were given as guarantees for loans. Therefore, when the sign says, "For Sale, Caixa Econômica," it means that you will be buying from the bank, a very straightforward process.

So, when I saw this sign, I immediately knew it would be possible to build, with a certain grace, all the programs that the SESC wanted, as long as the support facilities—the things disrupting the floorplan—were put on the side, in an annex on this additional lot, with direct access to the street. What do I mean by support? Staff changing rooms, large refrigeration units for the food area, and all the sanitary facilities.

The site was a rectangle. But you can see it as a square of forty meters by forty meters: not exactly, but close enough to seem like a perfect square, with an annex on one side measuring seven by twenty, a little vessel separated by three meters. Well, what did we do? We put up a building on the side lot, with all the support facilities, and a few small bridges that link to and supply the main building.

For the circulation from one space to another in the main building, the flow was intended to parallel the experience of walking around the city itself. That's the origin of the idea of developing a ramp that would be continuous, from the ground all the way to the top. As you walk, you come across a library, or a dance room, all the elements of the SESC program. Therefore, this continuum is a kind of imagined and projected idea,

Ground floor, SESC 24 de Maio

Third floor, SESC 24 de Maio

constructed materially as a continuation of urban space itself. Because that energy, like an unexpected topography, is what a building is all about. It's a transformation of nature itself into a place.

Another thing that struck me during the first visit to the site, at this moment when one can see everything at once, was the realization that the building had a very ordinary structure, one that was vulgar, or even ugly, because the building had been refurbished so many times.

EW: In fact, the existing building was actually two buildings; that is, two different structural systems with small modules and low floor-to-ceiling heights, seemingly at odds with the program . . .

PMdR: But with an accidental and marvelous piece of fortune: in the center, at the intersection of the diagonals of that forty-by-forty-meter square, was a void, also square, measuring fourteen by fourteen meters.

EW: The void existed . . .

PMdR: It existed! It existed! This empty space was the origin of everything!

EW: In other words, the original building, together with its earlier extension, was a U-shaped building . . .

MM: Exactly.

PMdR: That empty space made me see that I could place four columns, just four columns, one in each corner of this fourteen-by-fourteen-meter square, extending even below street level, to create a void, which would become a theater. The theater could then be connected to the street and therefore independent. And this independence means everything to the theater. Then, the SESC can close and the theater can stay open until two in the morning.

Another thing I realized right from the start that the SESC hadn't put in the program—but that I could introduce—was a swimming pool. This realization was based on a critical observation of societal behavior, a political vision of one issue of being in a city like São Paulo, so densely vertical and densely populated. Owning a swimming pool is possible only for the very rich, because they buy up the top floors of buildings and make a so-called "duplex" with a rooftop pool. In other words, the average workers, the shopkeepers, the people at the counter, the people who work hard, would very much like to have such pools on the roofs of their buildings. I soon saw that with the four columns I could insert a structure completely independent of the existing building itself. I could put the theater down there, the pool up there, and better than that: by infilling the void bounded by the four new columns, on one floor or another, I could make a very interesting duplex space, with a fourteen-by-fourteen-meter double-height core, and a kind of balcony and mezzanine, excellent for a dance hall, for a library, for a restaurant. But I kept everything I envisioned to myself!

We went out on the street again. I don't remember exactly who was there, except for Danilo Miranda, the director of the SESC. I said, "Look, Danilo, do you see the sign there? 'Caixa Econômica Federal.' With your legal advice, and with Caixa Econômica, you can buy it over the phone. Properties in general often have big problems with inheritances, that sort of thing. But not with Caixa Econômica. If you buy the land next door, I will do it. If not, then I will not."

Ground floor and ramp, SESC 24 de Maio

EW: The strategy was to free the site from all services, and in turn to program the central void with all the large-scale programs and the perimeter with all the small-scale programs. The ramp would connect all levels as a public street cutting through from the ground to the roof . . .

PMdR: The ramp introduces to the building, to some extent, the virtue of the occupation of a territory. What is more, especially in this case, the distribution of loads, with independence, on the four columns that are one meter in diameter . . .

MM: 1,2 meters . . .

PMdR: 1,2 meters in diameter is necessary to support the load of the pool. The pool is very interesting, and it is not a small pool: the dimensions are twenty-five by twenty-five meters. And the beach around it averages ten meters wide. Therefore, the pool is a place that many people can frequent at the same time, in the center of the city of São Paulo. I find that very interesting.

EW: The strip separating the existing building and the other adjacent site—where you placed the vertical circulation, elevators and stairs, plus some terraces—also existed . . .

PMdR: It existed!

MM: It existed. But it existed as an element of vertical circulation. The existing building was a U shape, as you have noticed. It formed the corner of Dom José de Barros and 24 de Maio. An addition, which dated back to the 1970s, closed the U, and this space that you are referring to is an empty space formed with the building next door. The vertical circulation of that building was a little off the street. All that was demolished too. Then there was that space formed with the building next door, and then came what you just described. Sometimes we reach the limit of the lot with terraces or with the building itself, and sometimes we don't.

EW: So you just demolished that strip, plus the building on the adjacent site you previously referred to . . .

MM: No. Also, in the area with the ramp, we demolished the vertical circulation of the original building, which was part of the existing U-shaped building. That is, we demolished a dome in the center covering the first floor and a mezzanine. So we demolished all the vertical circulation, as well as the entire façade.

EW: In other words, you decided to demolish very little. You said to the client that you would accept the commission only if they bought the adjacent site, whose building you would demolish. And this would allow you, in turn, to keep most of the existing building on the main site . . .

PMdR: That's what I said to the client. And I left. Two or three days passed, then Danilo called me. He told me: "We've bought the plot of land next door." Then I signed the contract, we sent proposals, and we entered the partnership with Marta and MMBB to develop the project.

EW: So the main design operation was to build an independent building within the existing building, with double-height floors aligned with the existing building every other story, to locate all large-scale programs—the theater, the culture and leisure spaces, the pool . . .

PMdR: It's not that! That's a wonderful consequence. The fundamental parts are the four columns which enable the excavation of the theater and support the load of the swimming pool. You see, a cubic meter of water weighs a metric ton. So how much does this twenty-five-by-twenty-five-meter pool weigh? It is supported by the four columns, not the old building. It is also difficult to make four columns of that height because of the bracing issue. That's the big problem, more than the load itself, because the foundations are relatively straightforward and support of a vertical load is one of the virtues of reinforced concrete. The existing building was useless for bracing; therefore, on each floor, there is a connection between the columns . . .

MM: What Paulo is describing is that sometimes, from floor to floor, when there is a double-height space, there is a beam that connects those four columns. And then, on some levels, there is the floor slab. That's the connection Paulo is referring to that braces the whole structure.

PMdR: If it were just the four columns at that height, it wouldn't work. It's braced on every floor, so it's a tower! Because an architect doesn't imagine something and then think about how he's going to build it later on. He imagines it along with the construction, as any novelist, for example, writes with words, and doesn't go and look for them later.

EW: In fact, the tower is detached from the existing building, and the so-called vessel for services on the adjacent site. What appears to be one building is actually a series of four or five different structures . . . Let's turn to the program. To what extent was the program defined, and to what extent was it actually redefined as the project developed, according to the limitations and opportunities instigated by the building?

PMdR: The program was defined . . .

MM: But it was only defined to a certain extent . . .

PMdR: But there's always an interpretation. We discussed some details of the solution that we presented with the SESC, but basically it is their program that is being carried out . . .

MM: There are a few things that had to adapt to the building dimensions, like the sports court. It was impossible to make a regulation court in that building, even though the SESC generally follows the official requirements. Paulo just described the pool, and it was an invention to put it on the roof. If it didn't go there, it would probably have been impossible to put a pool in the building. Dance, for example, is a program typically offered by the SESC but usually doesn't have that much emphasis. Here, it takes on great importance, because the city center is a place that is traditionally linked to music. So, the program underwent some minor changes or accommodations due to being in that location.

EW: You also decided the way in which the other programs would stack, their sequence . . .

MM: Yes, we did. Including how to link the programs.

EW: And, most importantly, as you mentioned, you also decided to add a pool to the program, and to put it on the roof . . .

PMdR: Put the pool on the roof? I wanted the pool to be in the sun! If it's not on top, it doesn't get sun!

EW: Yes, but it was actually a decision . . .

PMdR: The pool chooses its place, not the architect! A sunny, open pool, despite the winter, is completely different from a closed, heated pool. My image is Copacabana, Leblon, Ipanema! I was born in Espírito Santo. It's a beach. Sea! Sun! A swimming pool is not an artificial thing, a heated bathtub, or something unhygienic. So the pool could only go there. The pool's in charge, not the architect! And so goes the whole program . . . It is clear that the project then had developments and details. Would you like to hear something interesting about the layout of the building? Eating near the pool is forbidden for hygiene reasons. But everyone likes to eat a little something and go back to the water. You get hungry, you feel like it! You get thirsty, you drink something, fruit juice, especially in Brazil. I'm talking about my childhood, my youth. If you're at the beach, in Copacabana, for example, it's common for you to leave the beach, cross the street and buy something right there, in small establishments and counters with snack bars or restaurants, facing the beach. You eat a little something and go back to the beach. So, I figured I needed to make a place with a big snack bar on the water's edge, but not next to the main pool, somewhere the people could wear their swim clothes, dripping wet. So I created a space on the eleventh floor, two floors below the pool level, even with a small reflecting pool. It's nice to see the children bobbing around in that water. But the water was there mostly to create a climate, an environment. The people are still at the beach, as if they were on the sand and have crossed the street to buy a snack. As the main pool needs a spillway for the overflow caused by waves that are produced by the movement of the bathers, I made it in the center. Since twenty-five by twenty-five meters is a lot, I made a three-meter-wide circle, if I'm not mistaken, more or less . . .

MM: Five-meter . . .

PMdR: Five! The water enters and then falls down to the snack-bar level. Therefore, you can have something to eat on the lower level and then go stand underneath the shower of pool water dropping from above: you remain in the same space. Especially if you go down the ramp, not the elevator, you are still on the beach. I multiplied by two, let's say, the area that was exposed to the sun. But our profession forces you to develop these strategies over time: the technical ability to multiply the grace of what was invented as part of the initial matrix.

MM: One thing I also find interesting is the availability of places where you can do various things. For example, the third floor is a living space, but many different activities take place there. Even the balcony has a high ceiling where presentations and things like that are held. So, these are places that can host a multitude of activities, whose uses are not predetermined.

EW: The building is activated, between the theater and the pool, by public spaces on the third and eleventh floor, in addition to the open ground floor, cutting diagonally across the site. You then decided the position of the other programs within the sequence . . .

MM: Yes, for example, the restaurant on the second floor is a very popular place. The fact that it is very close to the street was interesting, because it also establishes this direct relationship: the people who are working there are going to have lunch there. It's not much of a living space, so it's right there on the second floor. The administration area is on the first floor, so it's very visible. You see the people who are responsible for the functioning of the whole thing. They are not in a hidden place. Because usually administrative areas are relegated to the background. And that was a design decision: the association of certain program elements. For example, the close relationship between the restaurant and library levels: those eating lunch will relax for a while, pick up a newspaper . . .

EW: As you suggested, the existing building had little architectural value. Unlike, for example, FIESP and Pinacoteca, your previous cultural projects on existing buildings. Rather than design in conversation with an existing building, as was the case in those projects, you brought together the various parts, old and new, into a (difficult) whole . . .

PMdR: The existing building was said to have very little architectural value. But the greatest virtue of a building, for me, in today's cities, is its address. Therefore, the existing building had a fantastic virtue. For example, it was in a strategic place, between Praça da República and Praça do Patriarca, connected by the famous Viaduto do Chá.

EW: Yes, but the point was that you decided to keep, and design through, a building which was seemingly at odds with, or inadequate for, the program. That was quite a radical design decision. The floor-to-ceiling height of the original building must be about three meters and fifty centimeters . . .

MM: Three meters and seventy centimeters . . .

EW: Right. It would have probably been impossible to organize those large-scale programs without the double floor-to-ceiling height tower. The main design operation was to mobilize the void at the core, and, as you said, to free the site from all servant space by virtue of the adjacent site . . .

PMdR: Yes, that's right. That's what I saw. That's the condition I set: seeing that empty space and buying the building next door. So much so that after we signed the contract, the first thing we did was to call a specialist in soil mechanics to determine the viability of the design approach, based on the presumed load of the columns supporting the pool on top. Little by little, the possibility of this approach was confirmed, even though the soil conditions are very bad. Unfortunately, the construction of basements in the area has obstructed the natural drainage patterns, so the water table is very high. And indeed, the most serious issue facing the building was the construction of the foundations and the basement, given the unfortunate quality of that soil.

MM: There was water, right there.

EW: We have already discussed most design operations: the fourteen-by fourteen meter building within the building, the annex with all servant spaces, the organization of programs, the ramp cutting through them in section as a public street. Let's return to your earlier comment about conceiving the project at the very outset before you asked the client to buy the adjacent site . . .

PMdR: No. Not before they decided to buy. I conceived the project based on using the annex for all service facilities. If not, it wouldn't be possible.

EW: Exactly. You had already, by and large, formulated the project.

Eleventh floor, SESC 24 de Maio

Terrace, SESC 24 de Maio

PMdR: Every architect does this.

MM: Not always . . .

EW: Not many . . .

PMdR: But you notice. When they don't do it like this, you notice.

EW: The project then took about eight years to complete . . .

MM: Yes, but it remained very similar to his first drawing . . .

PMdR: The project didn't take ten years. Construction did.

EW: I am interested precisely in the tension between those two speeds: a precise formulation at the very outset (fast) and a negotiated resolution over a long time (slow). Which in my opinion allowed for the project to meet a difficult design problem, and also granted the building its open-ended and dynamic condition. Did the project undergo important changes during those eight years, or did it retain its original formulation?

MM: It completely followed the original formulation: the rooftop swimming pool, the theater connected to the street, the service building, and the ramp. The essential features were maintained from the very first moment.

EW: Were there any unexpected findings, or positive accidents, during the construction process?

PMdR: The fact that I didn't die . . .

MM: Well, I don't know what you call positive . . .

EW: The question was, actually, whether you considered the construction process simply the materialization of the initial concept, or the trigger for new concepts? Were there accidents you decided to use to your advantage?

PMdR: A lot of accidents!

MM: Yes, there were accidents. For example, during the construction work, many design changes were made. The installations, the shaft doors that we decided not to make, the electrical panels—all became apparent . . . The façades as originally designed were changed as well. As the project went on, they became more conventional. The building became more and more—I don't know—perhaps stripped is the right word.

PMdR: And it became apparent that the concept was able to incorporate all these changes to the appearances of things. Of course, you can't predict everything at once. This always happens in any very complex work or project. We kept the essence of the idea with the details, even as they evolved. But the initial idea can absorb these occasional circumstances. That's the virtue of a good initial idea.

EW: I would like to return to your earlier comment about the pool on the roof, which you said was based on a political vision, in order to discuss the ways in which the project—and architecture—operates politically (particularly given the inherent limitations of buildings as instrument: they are slow; they are expensive.) SESC 24 de Maio offers a glimpse into an alternative city, and an alternative life . . .

PMdR: Every project is a political statement. The project idea is one of projection, of the future. So the intention is to imagine what we should be, what we can be. Then the design is not simply a matter of architecture. I think any one of us can speak about any form of our existence, because you may not know exactly how to do a certain thing, but you may know exactly what you shouldn't do! Generally speaking, society throughout the world is exclusive, in principle. It always protects itself from free public action: these are the famous gated communities, the buildings with security. We made this building open to public use, as much as possible. And the SESC comes into that as well, which tells us something about the SESC's policies. So everything we do has a political value: there is a political essence in the idea of decision. And this new occupation of an existing building is part of a very interesting policy linked to the economy. You are better off reusing buildings rather than discarding them, demolishing them.

EW: In fact, the project diverted an existing building, it looked for potential in the actual. As the May '68 slogan read: *under the cobblestones, the beach . . .*

PMdR: Every construction, every action of ours has a value, a political essence, which must be read between the lines of what is there. That's what all architects want. All intellectuals. All human beings. They want their actions to have an intelligible political meaning. Therefore, in the work of art in general, and in architecture in particular, the first thing it entails is to seduce others so that they can see the dimension of what, despite the circumstances, we must do.

BIOGRAPHIES

Andres Lepik is director of the Architekturmuseum der TU München (TUM) and professor of the history of architecture and curatorial practice at TUM. He studied art history, graduating with a PhD on *Architectural Models in the Renaissance*. From 1994 he worked as Curator at Neue Nationalgalerie, Berlin where he presented the exhibitions *Renzo Piano* (2000), and: *Content. Rem Koolhaas and AMO/OMA* (2003). From 2007 to 2011 he was Curator at the Architecture and Design Department at The Museum of Modern Art, New York, presenting the exhibition *Small Scale, Big Change, New Architectures of Social Engagement* (2010). In 2011-12 he was Loeb-Fellow at the Graduate School of Design at Harvard University.

Daniel Talesnik is a curator at the Architekturmuseum der TU München (TUM) and assistant professor of the history of architecture and curatorial practice at TUM. He is a trained architect specializing in modern and contemporary architecture and urbanism, with a particular focus on architectural pedagogy and relationships between architecture and political ideologies. He was awarded a PhD by Columbia University in 2016 with the dissertation *The Itinerant Red Bauhaus, or the Third Emigration*. He has taught at Columbia University, the Illinois Institute of Technology, and the Universidad Católica of Chile.

Guilherme Wisnik is a professor at the Faculty of Architecture and Urbanism of the University of São Paulo (USP). A columnist for *Folha de S. Paulo* newspaper (2006-07 and 2016). Author and editor of several books, he has published essays in international magazines. He was the curator of art and architecture exhibitions including *Paulo Mendes da Rocha Occupation* (Itaú Cultural, 2018) and with Fernando Serapião, *Infinito Vão: 90 years of Brazilian Architecture Portugal* (2018). He was the General Curator of the 10th Biennial of Architecture of São Paulo (Institute of Architects of Brazil, 2013).

Renato Anelli is a full professor of the Institute of Architecture and Urbanism of the University of São Paulo (USP), researcher of CNPq and current Counselor of the Casa de Vidro - Instituto Lina Bo e PM Bardi. He is an architect and urbanist (FAU PUC Campinas, 1982), Master in history (IFCH UNICAMP, 1990) PHD in history of architecture (FAUUSP 1995). He has been a visiting professor at the Department of Art History and Archeology, Columbia University, New York (Fall, 2016, FAPESP). He currently develops partnerships with HafenCity Universität (Hamburg, Germany) and University of Texas in Austin (USA).

Ana Luiza Nobre is a professor at the Department of Architecture and Urbanism and the Graduate Program in Architecture at PUC-Rio, and researcher at CNPq. Architect (UFRJ), Master and PhD in social history of culture (PUC-Rio). She organized a book of interviews with Lucio Costa: *Encontros* (Azougue, 2010) and is one of the organizers of *Um Modo de Ser Moderno: Lucio Costa e a crítica contemporânea* (Cosac Naify, 2004). She was executive director of the House of Lucio Costa (2001-03), coordinator of Research and Education of the Instituto Moreira Salles (2014-6) and adjunct curator of the X Biennial of Architecture of São Paulo (with Guilherme Wisnik and Ligia Nobre in 2013).

Vanessa Grossman is an architect, a historian of architecture, and a curator working on architecture and urbanism's intersections with ideology, power and government policies, with a special interest in Brazilian and French modernism. After obtaining her PhD from Princeton University, she was selected postdoctoral researcher as one of first two fellows of the newly created Center for Advanced Studies in Architecture at ETH Zürich.

José Tavares Correia de Lira is a full professor of the Department of History of Architecture of the Faculty of Architecture and Urbanism of the University of São Paulo (FAUUSP). He graduated in architecture and urbanism and also philosophy. He has done postdoctoral research at Columbia University (2009) and the École Nationale Supérieure d'Architecture de Paris-Malaquais (2015). He directed the Center for Cultural Heritage of USP between 2010 and 2014. He teaches in undergraduate and graduate courses at FAUUSP, developing research history and criticism of architecture, modern and contemporary architecture in Brazil, city history, urbanism and social housing in Brazil.

Fraya Frehse is a professor at the Department of Sociology at the University of São Paulo (USP), *alumna* of the Alexander von Humboldt Foundation and visiting researcher of the Alexander von Humboldt Foundation of the Collaborative Research Centre "Re-Figuration of Spaces" of the Technische Universität Berlin (March–August 2019). She has experience in the areas of anthropology and sociology interfacing with history, with emphasis on urban studies.

Enrique Walker is an architect. He is associate professor at Columbia GSAPP, where he directed the Master of Science program in advanced architectural design from 2008 to 2018. He teaches the lecture course Metropolis, and runs the seminar course and guest lecture series Arguments. In addition to GSAPP, he has taught at the Princeton University School of Architecture, the Escuela Técnica Superior de Arquitectura de Madrid, the Barcelona Institute of Architecture, the Tokyo Institute of Technology, the Pratt Institute, and the Universidad de Chile.

BIBLIOGRAPHY

Andreoli, Elisabetta, and Adrian Forty. *Brazil's Modern Architecture.* New York and Berlin: Phaidon, 2004.

Anseloni, Carol. "Centro Cultural São Paulo: En tiempos de represión y desarrollo urbano," in *Registros (Mar del Plata)*, v. 14, 2018: 48-60

Artigas, Rosa. *Paulo Mendes da Rocha: Projects 1957-2007.* São Paulo: Cosac Naif, 2007.

Bastos, Maria Alice Junqueira, and Ruth Verde Zein. *Brasil: Arquiteturas após 1950.* São Paulo: Perspectiva, 2010.

Bauer, Jenny, and Robert Fischer. *Perspectives on Henri Lefebvre.* Berlin: De Gruyter, 2018.

Bechara, Renata Carneiro. *A atuação de Lina Bo Bardi na criação do SESC Pompeia (1977-1986).* Master thesis, São Carlos: Instituto de Arquitetura e Urbanismo USP, 2016.

Bergdoll, Barry, and Carlos Eduardo Comas. *Latin America in Construction: Architecture 1955–1980.* New York: Museum of Modern Art, 2015.

Bo Bardi, Lina. *Architecture Words: 12 Stones Against Diamonds.* London: Architecture Association Publications, 2014.

Bokov, Anna. "Soviet Workers' Clubs: Lessons from the Social Condensers," in *The Journal of Architecture,* 22:3, (2017) colon : 403-436.

Botey, Josep Ma. *Oscar Niemeyer.* Barcelona: Editorial Gustavo Gili, 1997.

Buarque de Holanda, Sergio. *Raízes do Brasil.* Rio de Janeiro: José Olympio, 1986.

Bucci, Angelo. São Paulo, *razões de arquitetura: da dissolução dos edifícios e de como atravessar paredes.* São Paulo: Romano Guerra, 2010.

- - -. *São Paulo, Reasons for Architecture: the Dissolution of Buildings and How to Pass Through Walls.* São Paulo: Romano Guerra, 2010.

- - - . *The Dissolution of Buildings.* New York: GSAPP Books, 2016.

Caffé, Carla. *Colecao Opera Urbana - Av. Paulista.* São Paulo: Sesc, 2009.

Camacho, Sol, and Gabriel Kozlowski et.al. *Muros de ar, Brazilian Pavilion 2018, Walls of air.* São Paulo: Bienale de São Paulo, 2018.

Cárdenas, Alexandra Silva. *Masp: estrutura, proporção, forma.* São Paulo: Editora Da Cidade, 2000.

Cavalcanti, Lauro. *When Brazil was modern, Guide to architecture 1928-1960.* New York: Princeton Press, 2003.

Correa, Felipe. *A Graphic Biography.* Austin: University of Texas Press, 2018.

Costa, Alexandre Alves."Lembrando Lúcio Costa," in, *Unidade.* Porto: FAUP, volume 6, 1998.

Couty, Louis. *L'Esclavage au Brésil.* Paris: Librairie de Guillaumin et Cie, 1881.

Curi, Fernanda Araujo. *Ibirapuera, metáfora urbana, O público/privado* em São Paulo, 1954-2017. São Paulo: Catálogo USP, 2018.

Delijaicov, Alexandre, and André Takiya. *Räume bilden. Formar espacos, espacos que formam. building spaces, spaces that build.* São Paulo: Servico de Tecnico de Biblioteca da Faculdade de Arquitetura e Urbanismo da USP, 2017.

França, Elizabeth, and Maria Braga, *A cidade informal no seculo 21,* São Paulo 2010.

Ferraz, Isa Grinspum. *Lina Bo Bardi Exhibition.* São Paulo: Edizioni Charta, Milan/ Instituto Lina Bo e P. M. Bardi, 1994.

Fernandes, Florestan. "O homem e a cidade-metrópole," in, *Mudanças Sociais no Brasil.* São Paulo: Difusão Européia do Livro, 1960 colon : 266-283.

- - - . *Mudanças Sociais no Brasil.* São Paulo: Difusão Européia do Livro, 1960.

Frehse, Fraya. *O Tempo das Ruas na São Paulo de Fins do Império.* São Paulo: Edusp, 2005.

- - - . *Ô da Rua!* São Paulo: Edusp, 2011.

- - - . "Relational Space through Historically Relational Time – in the Bodies of São Paulo's Pedestrians," in *Current Sociology,* vol. 65, n. 4, 2017.

- - - . "On Regressive-Progressive Rhythmanalysis." In *Perspectives on Henri Lefebvre, edited by Jenny Bauer and Robert Fischer, 107.* Berlin: De Gruyter 2018

- - - . "Burle Marx e o Parque Ibirapuera: quatro décadas de descompasso (1953–1993)," *Anais do Museu Paulista.* São Paulo: Nova Série, vol. 25, no. 3, Sep–Dec 2017.

Futagawa, Yukio, ed. *Oscar Niemeyer, Form & Space.* Tokyo: ADA edita, 2008.

Gallo, Antonella. *Lina Bo Bardi architetto.* Venezia: Marsilio Editorio, 2004.

Gravazzi, Matteo, and Tatiana Engelbrecht et.al. *Prédios de São Paulo para Crianças.* São Paulo: Gaps editora, 2018.

Goffman, Erving. *Behavior in Public Places.* New York: The Free Press/Collier-Macmillan. 1963.

- - - . "The Interaction Order: American Sociological Association, 1982 Presidential Address." *American Sociological Review,* vol. 48, n. 1, 1982.

Goodwin, Philip Lippincott. *Brazil Builds: Architecture New and Old 1652-1942 / Construção Brasileira: Arquitetura Moderna e Antiga 1652-1942.* New York: Museum of Modern Art, 1943.

Guerra, Abílio, ed. *Rino Levi: Arquitetura e cidade.* São Paulo: Romano Guerra Ed., 2001.

Hartmann, Sarah. *Monuments of Everyday Life: Interplays of City, Infrastructure and Architecture in São Paulo.* São Paulo: Jovis, 2019.

Heureux, Encore. *Infinite places: constructing buildings or places?.* Paris: B42, 2018.

de Holanda, Sérgio Buarque. *Raízes do Brasil.* Rio de Janeiro: José Olympio, 1986.

Instituto Lina Bo e P. M. Bardi. *Lina Bo Bardi.* São Paulo: Edizioni Charta, 1994.

Joffre, Dumazeidier, *Vers une civilization du loisir.* Paris: Ed. du Seuil, 1962.

Kimmel, Laurence, and Bruno Santa Cecilia et. al, *Architectural Guide Brazil.* Berlin: Dom publishers, 2013.

Kraft, Sabine, and Nikolaus Kuhnert et.al. Stadtarchitektur São Paulo. *Ausblick auf ein sociales Raumkonzept.* Aachen: ARCH+, 2008.

Klein, Richard, ed. *Le maisons de la culture en france.* Paris: Centre des monuments nationaux, 2017.

Kowarick, Luxion and Vinicius Caldeira Brant. *São Paulo 1975: crescimento e pobreza.* São Paulo: Loyola, 1976.

Koolhaas, Rem. "Brasília" Aug. 2011. Available in *Revista Centro,* http://revistacentro.org/index.php/koolhaasen/ (accessed Apr. 02, 2019)

- - - . *Delirious New York, A Retroactive Manifesto for Manhattan.* New York: Oxford University Press, 1994 (1978).

Le Corbusier, "Brazilian Corollary... Which Is Also Uruguayan." In *Drifts and Derivations: Experiences, Journeys and Morphologies.* Publications Department, Museo Nacional Centro de Arte Reina Sofia, Madrid, 2010.

Lefebvre, Henri. *Writings on Cities.* Hoboken: John Wiley and Sons Ltd, 1995.

- - - . *Das Recht auf Stadt.* Hamburg: Edition Nautilus, 2006.

Leite Rosa, Marcos. *Microplanning. Urban Creative Practices.* São Paulo, 2010.

Lepik, Andres, and Vera Simone Bader. *Lina Bo Bardi 100, Brasiliens alternativer Weg in die Moderne.* Ostfildern: Hatje Catz Verlag, 2014.

- - - . *Lina Bo Bardi 100,Brazil´s Alternative Path to Modernism.* Ostfildern: Hatje Catz Verlag, 2014.

Lima, Zeuler. *Lina Bo Bardi.* New Haven and London: Yale University Press, 2013.

Lira, José. O *visível e o invisível na arquitetura brasileira.* São Paulo: DBA, 2017.

Lofland, Lyn. *A World of Strangers. Prospect Heights.* Illinois: Waveland Press, 1985.

Lores, Raul Juste. *São Paulo nas Alturas.* São Paulo: Três Estrelas, 2017.

Niemeyer, Oscar. *Marquise e o projeto original do Parque Ibirapuera.* São Paulo: Imprensa Oficial, 2006.

- - - . "Mutilado o conjunto do Parque." In *Módulo,* no. 1, Mar. 1955.

- - - . *Minha arquitetura.* Rio de Janeiro: Revan, 2000.

Mc Guirk, Justin. *Edge city: Driving the periphery of São Paulo.* Moscow: Strelka Press, 2014.

Marins, Paulo César Garcez. "O Parque Ibirapuera e a construção da identidade paulista." *Anais do Museu Paulista - História e Cultura Material.* São Paulo, vol. 6-7, 1998-1999.

Mendes da Rocha, Paulo. "Genealogia da imaginação." In Rosa Artigas ed., *Paulo Mendes da Rocha: projetos 1957-1999.* São Paulo: Cosac Naify, 2000.

Mindlin, Henrique. *Modern Architecture in Brazil.* Rio de Janeiro and Amsterdam: Colibris Ed., 1956.

Montaner, Josep Ma., and Maria Isabel Villac. *Mendes da Rocha.* Barcelona: Gustavo Gili, 1996.

Murawski, Michał "Introduction: crystallising the social condenser." In *The Journal of Architecture* Volume 22, Issue 3 (2017): 372-386.

Musgrave, Lucy. "Civic Urbanism." In: *PNYX,* 53/2019 colon : .52-54.

de Oliveira, Francisco. "A economia brasileira: crítica à razão dualista." In *Estudos Cebrap,* n. 2, 1972.

- - - . Francisco. "O Estado e a exceção - ou o Estado de exceção?." In *Revista Brasileira de Estudos Urbanos e Regionais,* vol. 5, n.1, May 2003 colon : 9-14.

de Oliveira, Olivia, ed. 2G 23.24, Lina Bo Bardi, Barcelona, 2002. - - - . *Lina Bo Bardi, Obra Construida: Built Work.* Barcelona: Gustavo Gili, 2014.

- - - . ed. *2G* 23.24, Lina Bo Bardi. Barcelona: Gustavo Gili, 2002.

- - - . *Subtle Substances: The Architecture of Lina Bo Bardi.* São Paulo: Romano Guerra Editora Ltda, 2006.

Paul, Andreas, and Ingeborg Flagge. *Oscar Niemeyer, A Legend of Modernism.* Basel: Birkhäuser, 2003.

Pereira, Cristina Rodrigues, *Tres obras arquitectónicas y una ciudad en transformación: Estación de Subte São Bento, Centro Cultural São Paulo y SESC Fábrica Pompéia en la ciudad de San Pablo.* Master thesis, Buenos Aires: Universidad Torquato di Tella, 2015.

Pilis, Alexander. *All Things Considered.* São Paulo. Raleigh: Lulu Press, 2018.

Philippou, Styliane. *Oscar Niemeyer, Curves of Irreverence.* London: Yale University Press, 2008.

Puntoni, Álvaro, and Ciro Pirondi. *Vilanova Artigas.* São Paulo: Instituto Lina Bo e P. M. Bardi e Fundação Vilanova Artigas, 1997.

Salvaing, Matthieu. *Oscar Niemeyer.* Paris: Assouline, 2001.

Sampaio, Maria Ruth. *A Promoção Privada de Habitação Econômica e Arquitetura moderna 1930-1964.* São Paulo: Rima Editora, 2002.

Sánchez Llorens, Mara, and Manuel Fontán del Junco y María Toledo Gutiérrez. *Lina Bo Bardi: tupí or not tupí: Brasil 1946-1992.* Madrid: Editorial de Arte y Ciencia, 2018.

Serapião, Fernando. *Centro Cultural São Paulo: Espaço e Vida / Space and Life.* São Paulo: Editora Monolito, 2012.

Serapião, Fernando. "Concurso Moreira Salles/ SP." *Monolito 8.* São Paulo: Editora Monolito, 2012.

Spiro, Annette. *Paulo Mendes da Rocha: Works and Projects.* Zurich: Niggli, 2002.

Stanek, Łukasz. *Henri Lefebvre on Space: Architecture, Urban Research, and the Production of Theory.* Chicago: University of Minnesota Press, 2011.

Siza, Álvaro. "Entrevista com Álvaro Siza." In *Caramelo* n. 9. São Paulo: GFAU, 1997.

Stanek, Lukasz. *Henri Lefebvre on Space: Architecture, Urban Research, and the Production of Theory.* Minneapolis, MN : University of Minnesota Press, 2011 colon : 179-248.

Telles, Luiz. *CCSP- Centro Cultural São Paulo: um projeto revisitado.* São Paulo, 2002.

Thompson, Edward Palmer. *Costumes em comum.* São Paulo: Companhia das Letras, 2008.

Underwood, David. *Oscar Niemeyer and the Architecture of Brazil.* New York, 1994.

Vainer, André , and Marcelo Ferraz. Cidadela da Liberdade: *Lina Bo Bardi e o Sesc Pompeia.* São Paulo: Sesc, 2013.

Vaz Milheiro, Ana, and Ana Luiza Nobre et.al. *Coletivo: arquitetura paulista contemporânea.* São Paulo: Cosac Naify, 2006.

Wisnik, Guilherme, ed. 2G 54, *João Vilanova Artigas.* Barcelona: Gustavo Gili, 2010.

Wisnik, Guilherme, and Diego Matos. *Espacio en Obra: Cidade: Arte arquitetura.* São Paulo: Sesc São Paulo, 2018.

Xavier, Alberto, and Carlos Lemos et.al. *Arquitetura Moderna Paulistana.* São Paulo Ed. Pini, 1983.

Xavier, Alberto. *Depoimento de uma geração.* São Paulo: Cosac & Naify, 2003, p.179.

Zwoch, Felix (Ed.), *Stadtbauwelt,* Mexiko-Stadt und São Paulo, 36, September 2002.

Zein, Ruth Verde. "A Marquise do Ibirapuera." *AU Magazine, no. 226*, Jan. 2012.

ACKNOWLEDGEMENTS

First of all, we would like to thank Wolfgang A. Hermann, president of the Technical University of Munich (TUM), and the Architecture Faculty for their generous support of the Architekturmuseum over many years. There have been several essential collaborators in the whole exhibition process whom we would like to thank personally for their help and engagement: the photographer Ciro Miguel, who offered assistance and provided contacts; Sören Metz, our TUM liaison colleague in São Paulo who facilitated contacts and coordination; the student researcher João Bittar Fiammenghi, whose investigative capacity and commitment to the project have been invaluable; student assistant Pia Nürnberger, whose diligence helped move things forward; and Marcelo Della Giustina, who came on board as assistant editor for this catalogue and has been essential for its development and completion.

During the winter semester of 2018-19, we conducted a class at the TUM on social condensers, and we would like to thank the students in the class (Clara Pollak, Sutong Dong, Tomás Gonzalez, Anna Gonchar, Italia Cazar, Jakob Bahret, and Alesia Kasapi) for helping us think through some of the overarching problems and themes in this exhibition. On December 2018, we traveled to São Paulo and hosted a work session with local experts, coordinated by the head of cultural programming at the Goethe Insitut, Julian Fuchs. In addition to some of those involved in the production of the exhibition—the designer Kathryn Gilmore and the architects Mariana Vilela, Joao Bittar Fiahmengini, Danilo Zamoboni, Guilherme Pianca, and Pedro Kok—we also invited Renato Cymbalista, Marcos Rosa, Marta Moreira, and Angelo Bucci, all of whom ended up participating in the exhibition in one way or another. All of the contributing authors in the catalogue—Guilherme Wisnik, Renato Anelli, Ana Luiza Nobre, Vanessa Grossman, José Lira, Fraya Frehse, and Enrique Walker—have been supporters of the project and generously accepted our invitation to participate. Architect Alexandre Delijaicov also met with us to discuss the argument of the exhibition and offered advice and information. Mariana Lourenço helped us conduct surveys with the management of the studied buildings.

Alina Paias and Andres Nunes sent us their dissertations on protests in São Paulo and Avenida Paulista respectively, which have provided us with interesting points of view. Felipe Correa sent us his book *São Paulo, A Graphic Biography* (2018); James Graham from Columbia University's GSAPP sent us Angelo Bucci's *Dissolution of Buildings* (2015); and the Éditions du Patrimoine, Centre des monuments nationaux offered us the book *Les maisons de la culture en France* (2017); we thank them all.

Our colleague Anna Bokov allowed us to use an image of the Constructivist Social Condenser from one of her articles; Nelson Kon, Marco Antonio de Avila, and David Rego Jr. provided photographs for some articles; and Maíra Bühler, Paulo Pastorelo, and João Sodré lent us their documentary *Elevado 3.5* (2007). Gisele Ferreira de Britoat of the FAUUSP Library and the photographer Rafael Schmidt who documented originals there. We would also like to thank: Sol Camacho and Carolina Itami at the Instituto Bardi | Casa de Vidrio; Ana Filipe and Nuno Sampaio at the Casa de Arquitectura of Porto; and Nilton Laganà Junior and Sérgio Ricardo Unterkircher at the Departamento de Obras de Infraestrutura Urbana of the São Paulo Secretaria Municipal de Infraestrutura Urbana e Obras (SIURB).

On November 22–23, 2018, Daniel Talesnik participated in a symposium entitled *Leaving Traces / Living*

Politics in the City, organized by Carmen Popescu and Flavia Marcello on behalf of the GRIEF (the laboratory of research at ENSAB – Ecole Nationale Supérieure d'Architecture de Bretagne), the Rennes 2 University, the Centre for Urban Research at RMIT University, and the Centre for Design Innovation at Swinburne University. We want to thank the organizers and all participants for their feedback and questions; we hope they see some of the criticism reflected in this catalogue.

Numerous people helped our production team in their work: Pedro Kok, who taped interviews and shot video at Avenida Paulista, would like to thank his interviewees (Marta Moreira, Renato Cymbalista, Alexandre Delijaicov, Marcos Rosa, Marina Grinover, and Luis Loiola). Guilherme Pianca and Gabriel Sepe, who produced architectural drawings for the catalogue and exhibition, would like to thank their team members Gabriel Biselli, Luiz Solano, as well as Luiz Florence, for his help with Minhocão; for IMS, Andrade Morettin Arquitetos (Marcelo Morettin, Vinícius Andrade, Marcelo Maia Rosa, Renata Andrulis and Raphael Souza); for CEU, Alexandre Delijaicov e EDIF (Fernando Tavares, Ana Carolina Alves da Silva e Barbara Camucce); for Sesc 24 de Maio, MMBB (Marta Moreira, Milton Braga, Victor Pio and Gleuson Pinheiro) and Rafael Urano; for Sesc Pompeia, the FAUUSP Library; for Ibirapuera, the Museu da Cidade, Alvaro Razuk Arquitetura (Alvaro Razuk and Ligia Zilbersztejn); and for Praça das Artes, Brasil Arquitetura (Francisco Fanucci, Marcelo Ferraz, Luciana Dornellas and Cícero Ferraz).

Architect and illustrator Danilo Zamboni would like to thank Beatriz Cyrineo and Jurandy Valença and SIAA Arquitetos.

Photographer Ciro Miguel would like to thank Angelo Bucci, Sophie Piticco, João Paulo Miguel Cristina Miguel, Paula Tinoco, Daniela Moura Zanette (CEU Inacio Monteiro), Raisa Scandovieri (FIESP), Heloísa Pisani (SESC), Barbara Rodrigues (SESC), Cristina Tobias (SESC), Gabriela Valdanha de Araujo (MASP), Inacio Issamu Shibata (CEAGESP), Barbara Giacomet de Aguiar (IMS), Walter Tadeu Hardt (CCSP), Marisa Bueno (CCSP), Gibo Pinheiro (Gibolab), Urs Walther (SOSETH), and Lukas Matthys (SOSETH).

In collaboration with the exhibition, architect Mariana Vilela would like to thank Brunno Tolisani Resendes and Teo Butenas Santos.

At Park Books we would like to thank Muriel Blancho and Lisa Schons for their great support in the production of this book. We would like to thank John Wriedt and Carolina Alfaro de Carvalho for their editing advice and Charlotte Eckler for the proofreading.

We would like to express our deep gratitude to the whole team at Architekturmuseum der TUM for continuous support and advice: in particular the administrative staff members Martina Heinemann, Marlies Blasl, and Rike Menacher; for the local organization and execution of the exhibition architecture, Thomas Lohmaier, Andreas Bohmann, and Anton Heine; Thilo Schuster as Registrar. Many thanks to Anna-Maria Meister for translations for the exhibition and videos.

Great thanks go to our generous lenders: Instituto Bardi | Casa de Vidro, Museum of Art of São Paulo Collection, Museum of Art of São Paulo Research Center, Casa da Arquitectura Archive – Centro Português de Arquitectura, FAUUSP Library, and Secretaria Municipal de Infraestrutura Urbana e Obras (SIURB).

Andres Lepik and Daniel Talesnik

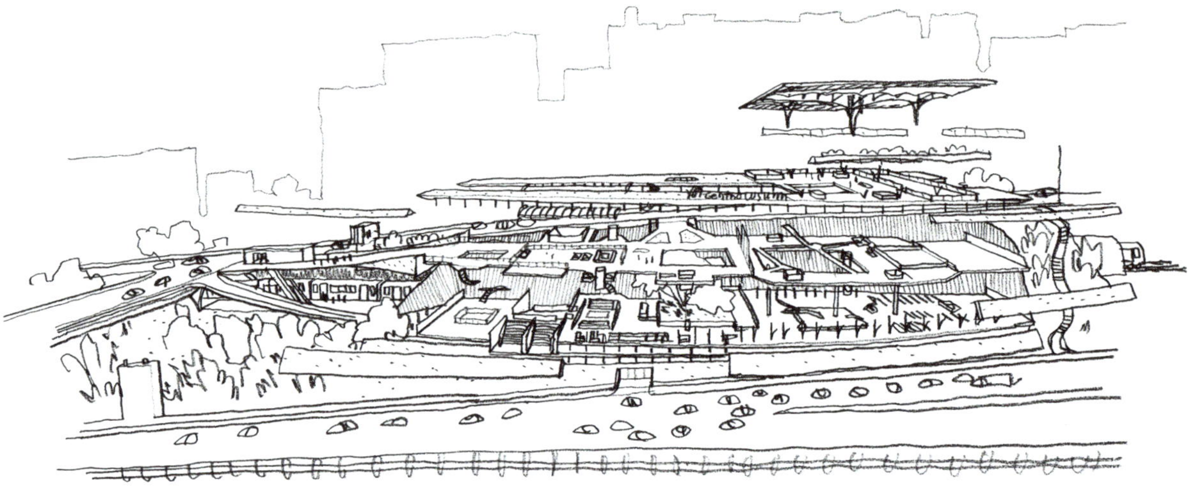

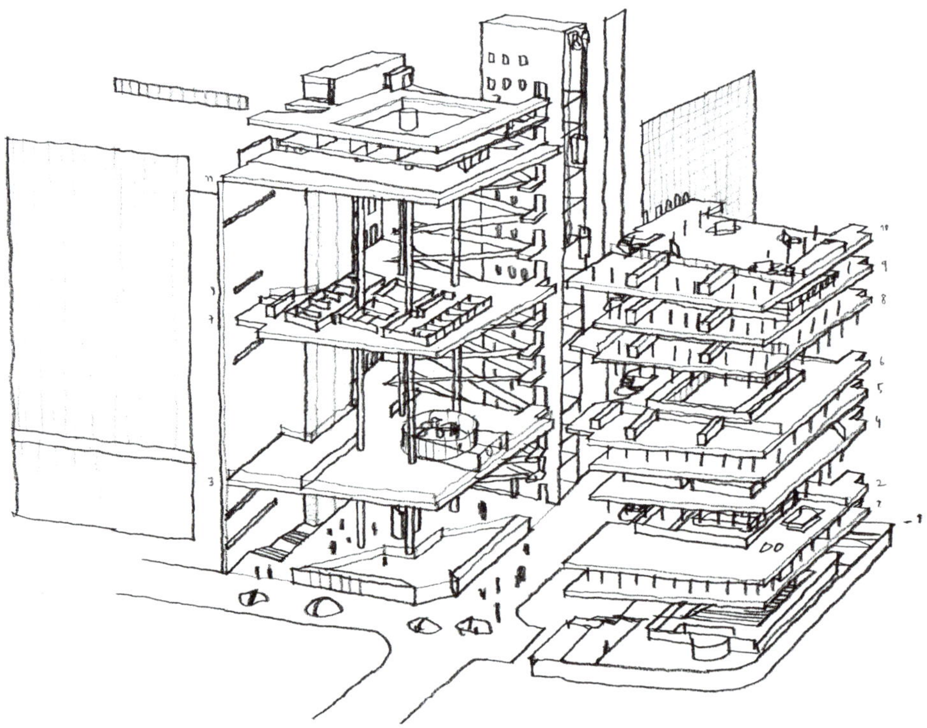

Drafts of the four commissioned drawings to Danilo Zamboni. Clockwise: exploded perspective drawings of CCSP, SESC Pompéia, CEU Inácio Monteiro, and SESC 24 de Maio.

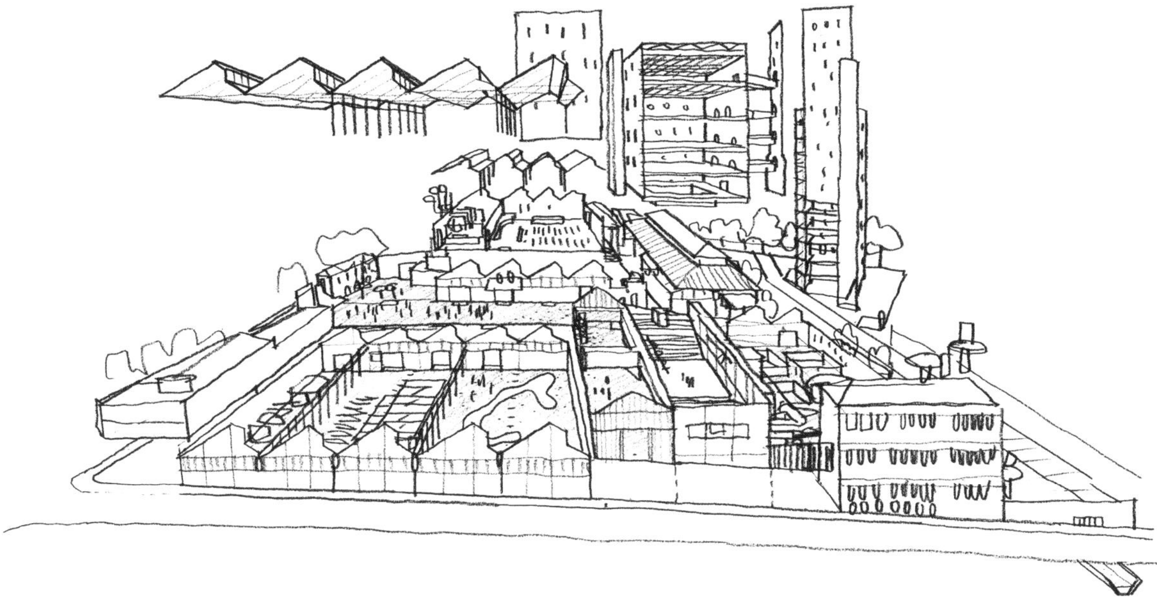

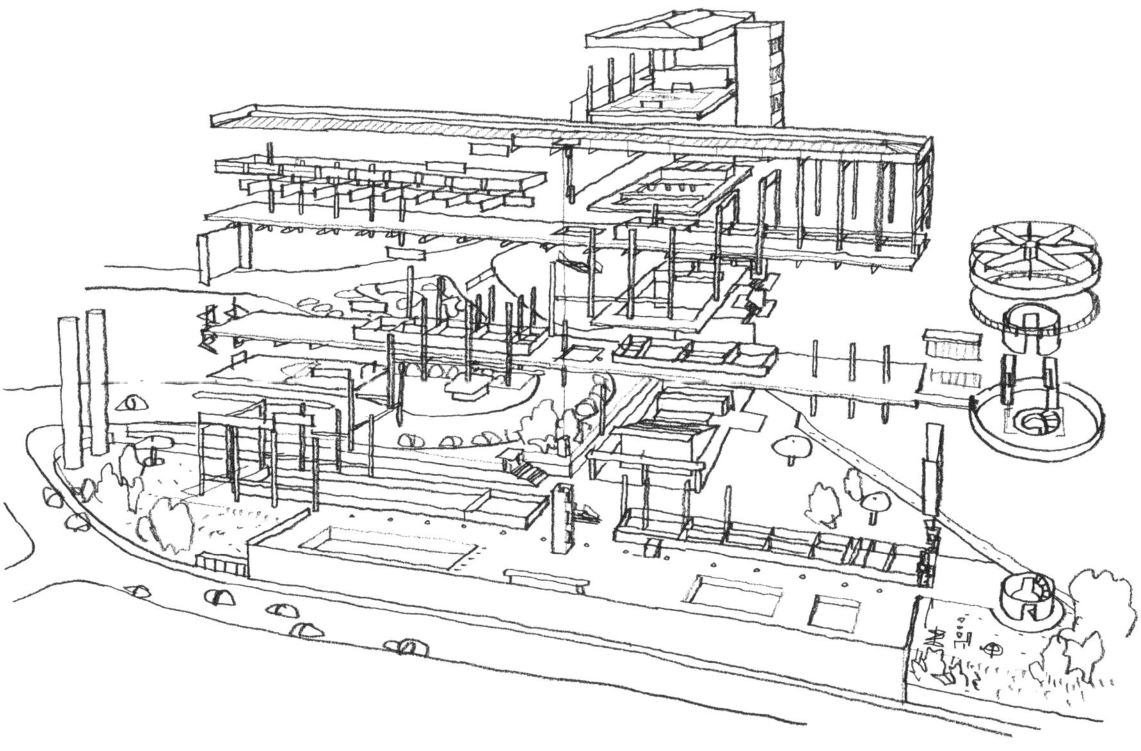

ANNEX

Essays in portuguese

Arquitetura como infraestrutura: o *desenho* político

Guilherme Wisnik

A arquitetura da chamada Escola Paulista embute em cada programa a noção modelar e ampla de infraestrutura, entendida como um conjunto de grandes equipamentos públicos que, implantados de forma sistêmica, organizam os fluxos e os serviços básicos da cidade. Assim, edifícios escolares, recreativos e mesmo residenciais, por exemplo, são, via de regra, concebidos como se fossem obras de infraestrutura urbana: terminais de transporte de massas, dotados de peças estruturais de grande porte, como pontes e viadutos. Daí a programática substituição de escadas por rampas, ou de janelas por claraboias, em muitas das residências paulistanas. Um exemplo notável é a Casa Mendes André (1966), de Vilanova Artigas. Duas grandes treliças suspensas, apoiadas em apenas quatro pilares, com grandes vãos e balanços, formando aquilo que o arquiteto considerava carinhosamente como uma viga habitável.[1]

Desdobrado a partir da engenharia, o ensino de arquitetura em São Paulo coloca a noção de técnica como a própria premissa da imaginação. "É impossível pensar em transformações formais se não se sabe como realizá-las", afirma Paulo Mendes da Rocha. Pois "raciocina-se com a engenhosidade possível, não se pensa com formas autônomas ou independentes de uma visão fabril delas mesmas"[2], completa. Nesse contexto, a Faculdade de Arquitetura e Urbanismo da Universidade de São Paulo (FAUUSP), com seu espaço físico desenhado por Vilanova Artigas, vem a afirmar-se como um ponto de convergência entre a excelência do conhecimento técnico, herdado da Escola Politécnica, e a forte tradição humanista da Faculdade de Filosofia, Ciências e Letras. Esse é o legado fundamental deixado por um grupo de importantes arquitetos e pensadores que tem Artigas, Paulo Mendes da Rocha e Flávio Motta como exemplos destacados. Projetado em 1961, o edifício da FAUUSP se define como uma caixa de concreto armado e aparente sem portas, dentro da qual os espaços fluidos, levemente defasados em meios-níveis e conectados por largas rampas, não são nunca corredores, e sim ambientes de encontro, de estar, verdadeiros espaços públicos.

Sem nunca ter sido capital da Colônia ou do Império, São Paulo se desenvolveu apartada dos principais influxos políticos e culturais vindos da Europa — a Corte Portuguesa e a Academia Francesa de Belas Artes —, tornando-se base para a exploração e conquista do interior continental. Situada num planalto que se prolonga a partir da Serra do Mar, a cidade é atravessada pelo rio Tietê, que, ao contrário da maioria dos rios, evita o litoral e corre para o interior, contribuindo para formar o rio Paraná. Assim, tendo crescido muito rapidamente a partir do início do século XX, através do cultivo do café e do desenvolvimento industrial, o estado construiu a mais importante rede ferroviária do país voltada para a hinterlândia[3], favorecendo uma particular consciência sobre as extensões continentais, a grande escala e a arquitetura como construção do território, envolvendo a transformação técnica da natureza.

Convidado, certa vez, a estabelecer uma comparação entre os projetos do edifício da FAUUSP e da Faculdade de Arquitetura da Universidade do Porto (faup, 1987), de sua própria autoria, Álvaro Siza observou tratar-se de situações muito distintas. Segundo ele, a generosidade dos espaços do edifício paulistano corresponde à "escala do território brasileiro", ao passo que na Europa se trabalha com limitações muito grandes.[4] Pois, de acordo ainda com Siza, o que permite a identificação do edifício da FAUUSP com o território brasileiro, ou da cidade de São Paulo, não é exatamente o seu tamanho, mas uma qualidade espacial que resulta dessa dimensão: o "caráter" que o edifício pode assumir, interpretando-se adequadamente o programa, quando pensado como uma sucessão contínua de ambientes em torno de uma "praça" comum de distribuição e convívio. No caso da escola portuguesa, a edificação teve de fragmentar-se em vários corpos separados.

Tais características, próprias à arquitetura de uma geração heroica, que construiu seus edifícios durante os anos de dura repressão em uma ditadura militar, continuam a se atualizar na produção das novas gerações em São Paulo. Características como a de um raciocínio que nega a partição exagerada do programa e concentra núcleos herméticos (áreas molhadas, dormitórios) a fim de não interromper a continuidade espacial dos edifícios, evitando o confinamento exagerado dos ambientes. E que busca explicitar não apenas os elementos construtivos (materiais, instalações), mas, principalmente, a mensuração indivisível do espaço: sua extensão material íntegra de fachada a fachada, por exemplo, desobstruída pela limpeza estrutural. Partido que faz dos edifícios instrumentos de medida, da leitura perceptiva do espaço e, em maior escala, da paisagem — daí a recorrência de expressões como "régua" ou "marcação urbana" em muitos dos memoriais dos projetos da nova geração paulista.

Hoje, ao postularem-se como "arranjos programáticos" ou como meras "disposições espaciais", ao invés de procurarem configurar uma "forma urbana", os projetos de grande escala dos jovens escritórios de São Paulo manifestam uma visão sistêmica do urbanismo, que procura, através de ações estratégicas, amparar a indeterminação, na expressão, mais uma vez, de Paulo Mendes da Rocha, desenhando a "imprevisibilidade da vida".[5] Nessa lógica mais "operativa" do que "linguística", digamos assim, é possível reconhecer um conjunto de intervenções recentes dessa nova geração.[6] Um exemplo claro é o projeto feito pelo escritório MMBB para o concurso "Bairro Novo" (2004), em São Paulo. Ali, a ação projetual do grupo se concentra no desenho legível da infraestrutura pública (arruamentos, logradouros, canais, pontes, passarelas, estações de tratamento de água), recusando determinar modelos rígidos para a porção de cidade destinada à ocupação privada, isto é, ao mercado imobiliário. Posição marcada por um certo realismo estratégico, que se afasta conscientemente tanto do revivalismo nostálgico de modelos historicistas, por um lado, quanto da ordenação universal e abstrata do urbanismo moderno, por outro.

Outro exemplo notável são os Centros Educacionais Unificados (CEUs), conjunto de escolas públicas projetadas pelo Departamento de Edificações da Prefeitura de São Paulo (Edif), com a coordenação de Alexandre Delijaicov, André Takiya e Wanderley Ariza em 2001. Levando em conta o princípio de racionalidade construtiva, bem como a necessidade de agilidade na realização de um número expressivo de unidades (45, em dois anos), o projeto faz uma clara opção pela pré-fabricação, utilizando peças pré-moldadas de concreto e escadas metálicas. Situados em meio a áreas precárias das periferias de São Paulo, caracterizadas por um casario baixo e irregular, os CEUs são focos agregadores de urbanidade local, aglutinando atividades recreativas e culturais que extrapolam o uso escolar durante os finais de semana, abrindo-se para os moradores da vizinhança. São também, portanto, espécies de centros comunitários de bairro. Aqui, o legado ético da Escola Paulista permitiu a construção de um verdadeiro sistema de equipamentos urbanos, extremamente eficazes na construção de sociabilidades mais generosas e coletivas na cidade.

Voltando à matriz da Escola Paulista, o edifício da FAUUSP carrega consigo um ideal civilizatório, relativo à importância e à responsabilidade do viver compartilhado, no qual a liberdade não é um atributo fácil nem imediato, mas algo que se conquista aos poucos. "Quem der um grito, dentro do prédio, sentirá a responsabilidade de haver interferido em todo o ambiente", escreve Artigas no memorial do projeto. Pois ali "o indivíduo se instrui, se urbaniza, ganha espírito de equipe",[7] completa. É importante frisar aqui a ideia de urbanidade, pois a imensa liberdade que o edifício inspira necessita de uma mediação fundamental, que é o respeito ao lugar do outro como compartilhamento de liberdades. Está aí uma das características centrais da chamada Escola Paulista de arquitetura: o combate ao predomínio da instância privada, no Brasil, sobre a esfera pública. É o que, na teoria social, chamamos de patrimonialismo: a tendência, muito própria a países colonizados e de tradição escravocrata, a tratar os assuntos públicos com base nas relações pessoais de favor. Não por acaso Artigas projetou tantas casas. Casas que se contrapõem frontalmente ao idílio doméstico, ao fetiche da intimidade, às ideias de privacidade, segredo e compartimentação, ao conforto burguês. A arquitetura entendida como infraestrutura foi o melhor meio de atingir esses objetivos. E criou uma "escola" arquitetônica que permanece a mais longeva e ativa no Brasil hoje. Uma "escola" para a qual o desenho do edifício não é apenas um exercício formal e volumétrico, mas também, e sobretudo, uma verdadeira atividade política.

1 Ver Álvaro Puntoni; Ciro Pirondi; Giancarlo Latorraca; Rosa Artigas (orgs.). *Vilanova Artigas*. São Paulo: Instituto Lina Bo e P. M. Bardi e Fundação Vilanova Artigas, 1997, p. 125.

2 Paulo Mendes da Rocha, "Genealogia da imaginação", in Rosa Artigas (org.), *Paulo Mendes da Rocha: projetos 1957-1999*. São Paulo: Cosac Naify, 2000, pp. 71-72.

3 Território afastado do litoral, das margens dos grandes rios ou dos centros industriais e comerciais; interior, retroterra. Do alemão *hinter* (trás) e *Land* (terra)

4 Álvaro Siza, "Entrevista com Álvaro Siza", in *Caramelo n.* 9, São Paulo: GFAU, 1997.

5 "O que desenha a imprevisibilidade da vida é uma construção, nítida e rigorosamente técnica, mas que não determina fim, modo e meio, programa. Ampara a indeterminação, a imponderabilidade da liberdade individual". Paulo Mendes da Rocha, "A cidade para todos", em Rosa Artigas (org.), 2000, op. cit., pp. 171-172.

6 Ver, por exemplo, Ana Vaz Milheiro; Ana Luiza Nobre; Guilherme Wisnik (orgs.). Coletivo: *arquitetura paulista contemporânea*. São Paulo: Cosac Naify, 2006.

7 Vilanova Artigas, in Álvaro Puntoni; Ciro Pirondi; Giancarlo Latorraca; Rosa Artigas (orgs.), 1997, op. cit., p. 101.

Arquitetura e cultura metropolitana: CCSP e SESC Pompéia.

Renato Anelli

Projetados e construídos quase ao mesmo tempo, o CCSP e o SESC Pompéia representam exemplos bem-sucedidos de arquitetura de uso público, compatível com a dimensão metropolitana recém-conquistada pela cidade. O Centro Cultural de São Paulo (CCSP), de Eurico Prado Lopes e Luiz Telles, foi projetado e construído entre 1977 e 1982[1]. Já o projeto de Lina Bo Bardi e equipe para o Serviço Social do Comércio – SESC Pompéia teve sua primeira etapa entre 1977 e 1982 e a segunda etapa entre 1982 e 1986[2].

Pode causar surpresa que, nestes dois projetos, os espaços abertos para o uso livre tenham sido construídos sob a vigência de um regime ditatorial. É necessário entender o papel dessas obras naquele momento histórico, que tinha fortes especificidades, para evitar simplificações da relação entre arquitetura e política. A segunda metade da década de 1970 foi marcada pela interrupção do crescimento econômico da primeira metade. A ascensão de movimentos sociais e sindicais resultou em novas estratégias do estado para atender a tais demandas, evitando mudanças radicais do regime. Nesse quadro, tanto a prefeitura de São Paulo, nomeada sem eleições, quanto o SESC, uma instituição privada, foram responsáveis pela introdução de novas políticas sociais.

O veloz crescimento demográfico da cidade de São Paulo, de 1,3 milhão em 1940 para 8,5 milhões em 1980, ocorreu através da acomodação da migração interna, do campo para a cidade em industrialização, em assentamentos periféricos, pobres e precários. Reconhecia-se a relação intrínseca entre crescimento e pobreza[3]. As periferias exigiam a descentralização dos equipamentos de atendimento público, tais como saúde, educação, esportes e cultura. Foram escolhidas áreas nas interfaces entre centro e periferia, criando vetores de descentralização. O CCSP foi posicionado no eixo sul, ao longo de uma antiga estrada para o litoral. Para construir seu segundo equipamento em São Paulo, o SESC escolheu o bairro Pompéia, região de moradias operárias e fábricas desativadas no eixo oeste para o interior do estado[4].

Usos

Concebido inicialmente como uma ampliação da Biblioteca Municipal Mário de Andrade situada no centro, o CCSP teve seu programa de atividades transformado em 1979: além da biblioteca, quatro salas de teatro, dois auditórios, um teatro de arena, áreas de exposição e guarda de acervos, além de amplas áreas de acesso livre. A revisão do programa fez parte do "Projeto Periferia", no qual núcleos de bairro assumiam o papel de centros culturais interligados em rede com os equipamentos centrais[5].

O SESC na Pompéia ampliava o programa tradicional dos serviços sociais da instituição, criada em 1945. Esportes, recreação e cultura são reunidos sob a concepção social do lazer. A oferta de espaços fora da habitação e do emprego para a recuperação do trabalhador era inspirada no intelectual católico francês Joffre Dumazedier[6]. Em uma série de seminários realizados no SESC, Dumazedier consolidou a ideia de orientar a oferta de espaços que estimulassem a fruição relaxada pelos usuários[7]. O projeto acompanhou esse novo conceito, mudando o nome de "Centro Cultural e Desportivo Pompéia" para "Centro de Lazer - Fábrica da Pompéia". Uma chaminé fabril soltando flores foi seu primeiro logotipo.

Partido arquitetônico

Os arquitetos dos dois projetos foram bem-sucedidos na interpretação dos novos programas em arquitetura, mas suas estratégias foram radicalmente distintas. Dentro de uma concepção moderna e abstrata, o CCSP é protegido do entorno urbano por taludes artificiais. Uma rua interna, espaço contínuo e linear, conecta as atividades distribuídas em planos situados em diferentes níveis. Já no projeto do SESC Pompéia, manteve-se a rua interna da antiga fábrica percorrendo os vários galpões existentes, transformados em praça coberta, restaurante, teatro, oficina de artes aplicadas, sala de exposições, e formando um percurso até as torres do complexo esportivo. Sua ação foi de requalificá-los para que substituíssem seu significado original de trabalho pelo de lazer. Para isso, a arquiteta lançou mão de sua experiência com cenografia, criando figuras capazes de estabelecer empatia com os usuários. A *promenade architecturale* se tornou uma narrativa figurativa a ser vivida.

O CCSP tem um caráter de infraestrutura urbana: uma trincheira linear que se ajusta ao espaço resultante de desapropriações para a construção da estação de metrô

Vergueiro, no alto da encosta, e da via expressa, no fundo do vale. O espaço interno que se desenvolve entre dois taludes paralelos protege o projeto das duas avenidas expressas, através de jardins planos e inclinados. Esse é o primeiro ato do projeto. O programa se distribui verticalmente, em planos horizontais, sendo os mais acessíveis localizados nos planos superiores junto à rua e os que necessitam resguardo, nos planos inferiores. O terraço-jardim, de acesso público, leva o visitante para fora do espaço protegido, oferecendo a única perspectiva ampla para a cidade.

Os planos da rua interna, quando interrompidos, oferecem visões das atividades nos planos inferiores e superiores. O exemplo do teatro de arena é radical: os shows ocorrem entre vedações transparentes, sendo vistos por todos os visitantes que atravessam o complexo, sem interferência sonora.

Estrutura

Apesar da riqueza espacial dos vãos e transparências, o sistema construtivo do CCSP apresenta deficiências. Inicialmente concebido em concreto armado, foi adaptado para um sistema misto, com uso adicional de perfis de aço laminado. A geometria estrutural ultrapassou a capacidade de detalhamento dos projetistas, enquanto que a pressa para a finalização da construção, em razão do calendário eleitoral de 1982, agravou a situação. Mesmo assim, o conjunto final é instigante em seus arroubos experimentais.

O SESC Pompéia foi construído de outro modo, com a arquiteta e sua equipe presentes permanentemente no canteiro de obras, definindo especificações e detalhes no próprio decorrer da construção. Não se tratando de edifício tombado como patrimônio histórico, foi possível grande liberdade de intervenção na fábrica, como a remoção dos revestimentos, deixando tijolo e concreto aparentes. O principal espaço de convivência foi criado no galpão maior, transformado em praça coberta através da substituição de planos de telhas cerâmicas por telhas de vidro. O mobiliário de madeira laminada[8] foi concebido como parte da arquitetura, organizando os amplos espaços de vivência. Algumas formas são tratadas figurativamente, como personagens de uma narrativa – o espelho d'água é o "Rio São Francisco", a torre de caixa-d'água é a "Chaminé", o guarda-corpo é a "flor de Mandacaru". Além de acolher os frequentadores, o passeio através desse espaço cênico busca o diálogo simbólico com seu repertório cultural.

Programas culturais

O CCSP combina a programação cultural com um acervo construído por Mário de Andrade durante sua gestão no Departamento Municipal de Cultura da Prefeitura de São Paulo (1935 -1938). Suas pesquisas etnográficas da cultura popular, realizadas em viagens pelo Brasil na década de 1930, constituem registros sofisticados de manifestações culturais até então pouco conhecidas devido a sua dispersão pelo território nacional. Mantido originalmente na Biblioteca Mário de Andrade, este acervo auxiliou na introdução do casal Lina e Pietro Bardi, já nos anos 1940, à cultura popular do país que adotaram[9]. Após a construção do CCSP, esse acervo foi transferido para lá, alimentando importantes exposições, publicações e pesquisas.

As exposições organizadas por Lina Bo Bardi após a inauguração do SESC Pompéia atualizaram seu entendimento da cultura popular brasileira. A primeira, "Design no Brasil: história e realidade", retomava ideias anteriores e acrescentava produtos de design recente, como computadores, carros e aviões[10]. As exposições seguintes aprofundaram a interação com as origens rurais dos novos paulistanos imigrados. Para os jovens já crescidos na metrópole havia outras estratégias, como o festival "O começo do fim do mundo", que revelou a força do punk rock nas periferias paulistanas. Nos dois anos seguintes, o teatro sediou o programa Fábrica do Som, onde os jovens grupos de rock paulista eram transmitidos pela TV Cultura para todo o país. O Pompéia se transformava em "fábrica de sonhos"[11], centro dinâmico de atração, produção e difusão de cultura popular no seu sentido amplo, não restrito às raízes coloniais da cultura brasileira.

Centro e periferia

O sentido de irradiação de cultura do centro para a periferia, presente na origem do CCSP, teve seu oposto no SESC Pompéia, pensado como centro de interação e renovação da cultura popular metropolitana. Nas décadas que se passaram desde a inauguração, quando a sociedade brasileira experimentou seu mais longo período democrático, esses dois polos foram referenciais para o quadro político brasileiro assim como para a arquitetura, que procurou transformar essa metrópole através da cultura.

Os motivos que lhes conferem enorme capacidade para atrair e acomodar pessoas ultrapassam a facilidade de acesso e as características dos programas. Mesmo usando estratégias opostas, é claro que suas arquiteturas têm grande responsabilidade para sua popularidade ainda hoje.

1 Eurico Prado Lopes e Luiz Telles, colaboradores Armando Alberto Prado, Christina de Castro Mello, Ernesto Theodor Walter, José Mario Nogueira de Carvalho, Raul Masatoshi Kan e Rita de Cássia Vaz Artigas.

2 Lina Bo Bardi, colaboradores Marcelo Ferraz, André Vainer e Marcelo Suzuki.

3 Lúcio Kowarick, São Paulo, 1975: *Crescimento e pobreza*. São Paulo: Edições Loyola, 1976.

4 O SESC Consolação foi a primeira unidade paulista e teve seu primeiro bloco inaugurado em 1967.

5 Cristina Rodrigues Pereira,*Tres obras arquitectónicas y una ciudad en transformación: Estación de Subte São Bento, Centro Cultural São Paulo y SESC Fábrica Pompéia en la ciudad de San Pablo.* Master thesis, Buenos Aires: Universidad Torquato di Tella, 2015; Fernando Serapião, *Centro Cultural São Paulo: espaço e vida* - 1. ed. - São Paulo: Editora Monolito, 2012; Carol Anseloni, "Centro Cultural São Paulo: En tiempos de represión y desarrollo urbano", in: Registros (Mar del Plata), v. 14, p. 48-60, 2018.

6 Dumazedier frequentara o Brasil no começo da década de 1960, convidado pelo Movimento de Cultura Popular de Pernambuco, com o qual Lina Bo Bardi interagiu na preparação da exposição Nordeste em Salvador.

7 Renata Carneiro Bechara, *A atuação de Lina Bo Bardi na criação do SESC Pompéia (1977-1986).* Master thesis, São Carlos: Instituto de Arquitetura e Urbanismo USP, 2016; Joffre Dumazeidier, *Vers une civilization du Loisir.* Paris: Ed. du Seuil, 1962.

8 Utilizou um sistema com madeira de espécies brasileiras de reflorestamento, desenvolvido por Vinício Walter Callia na sua empresa Laminarco.

9 Nas publicações do casal existem referências recorrentes às pesquisas iniciadas por Mário de Andrade. Um primeiro exemplo foi o artigo "Ex-votos do Nordeste" (Habitat 1, 1950. p. 72), referindo-se ao livro de Luis Saia *Escultura popular brasileira* (São Paulo: Editora Gazeta, 1944).

10 Exposições "Nordeste" (1963) e "A Mão do povo brasileiro" (1969).

11 O termo "fábrica de sonhos" é atribuído a Dumazedier por Erivelto Busto Garcia em seu texto "Fábrica de sonhos e o começo do fim do mundo", in: Marcelo Ferraz; André Vainer (Org). *Cidade da Liberdade: Lina Bo Bardi e o SESC Pompéia.* São Paulo, Edições SESC, 2013. p. 11.

O chão como projeto

Ana Luiza Nobre[1]

"O Brasil é um grilo de seis milhões de quilômetros talhado em Tordesilhas."

Oswald de Andrade, 1928

O arquiteto português Alexandre Alves Costa definiu a arquitetura brasileira como "uma linha horizontal levantada do chão"[2]. Ainda que parcial, essa leitura destaca um veio central da produção arquitetônica contemporânea num país onde os pilotis corbusierianos proliferaram como em nenhuma outra parte do planeta a partir da década de 1930, até encontrar expressão máxima nas superquadras de Brasília. Bem antes do plano piloto de Lucio Costa para a nova capital (1957), porém, tanto as palafitas quanto as redes de dormir indígenas já expressavam o esforço de suspender a edificação do chão. Um chão instável (porque sujeito a deslizamentos, assoreamentos, alagamentos, inundações periódicas), senão inexistente (porque permanente alagado). E com frequência associado a uma natureza tão áspera quanto temível, da qual seria sempre prudente guardar alguma distância.

Para entender a relação da arquitetura brasileira com o chão, portanto, é preciso ter em mente o meio em que se situa; um meio tropical marcado por temperaturas elevadas, umidade, odores fortes, chuvas abundantes, animais selvagens e insetos, com uma vegetação que se agarra aos pés, penetra e triunfa sobre tudo.

Numa das obras fundadoras das ciências sociais brasileiras (*Raízes do Brasil,* 1936[3]), Sergio Buarque de Holanda já apontava para a distância entre a atividade agrícola tradicional e os processos de exploração da terra introduzidos no que hoje é o Brasil pela lavoura açucareira. E isso por terem sido usadas menos técnicas de cultivo do solo já dominadas no Velho Mundo, como o arado, que práticas de caráter rudimentar adaptadas dos indígenas, como as queimadas. O autor atribui essa característica a diversos fatores. Dentre eles as dificuldades ligadas ao manejo do arado diante da impenetrável vegetação tropical e a abundância de terra – "terra para gastar e arruinar, não para proteger", diz. Ou seja, segundo uma lógica de exploração da terra mais identificada com a mineração que com a agricultura. Mais com a extração que com o cultivo.

Tal leitura ajuda a entender a "cultura da terra arrasada" que ainda hoje campeia no Brasil[4]. Bem como as raízes de uma dissociação entre arquitetura e geologia que tem contribuído para a proliferação de desastres fatais. Mas na relação estabelecida com o chão por uma certa arquitetura brasileira - que encontra em São Paulo sua mais forte expressão - ecoa também o longo histórico de conflitos fundiários e disputas pela terra que tem origem numa linha traçada sobre um mapa impreciso, do outro lado do Atlântico, antes ainda que as naus portuguesas tocassem a costa brasileira. Uma linha abstrata que instituiu o direito de posse e a repartição de terras originalmente habitadas por nativos num continente ainda sem nome, sem forma e sem fim.

Vale notar que a demarcação de terras indígenas é definida desde 1988 como um direito pela Constituição Federal Brasileira. Mas nem por isso esse direito está assegurado. Há atualmente no país 462 terras indígenas - o equivalente a 12% do território nacional - das quais só 8% estão regularizadas[5]. Em muitos casos - como na aldeia do Pico do Jaraguá, localizada dentro da cidade de São Paulo -, povos indígenas são confinados a áreas que estão longe de corresponder a suas práticas culturais e ferem um de seus princípios básicos: o de que a terra não pertence ao homem, o homem é que pertence à terra. Não por acaso, tanto o agravamento dos problemas ligados à demarcação de terras indígenas[6] quanto as pressões derivadas da expansão do agronegócio têm sido apontados como fatores determinantes para o suicídio crescente entre indígenas brasileiros, que hoje é quase o triplo da média nacional[7].

Por mais que esquemático, esse quadro ajuda a entender o marco ao mesmo tempo técnico-arquitetônico e político-simbólico que é o Museu de Arte de São Paulo - MASP (1961-8). Sem dúvida a construção em suspenso permanece indissociável, no Brasil, de uma experiência moderna que encontra na arquitetura de Oscar Niemeyer seu vértice e limite. A operação de elevação garantiria, afinal, um grau de autonomia e depuração condizente com uma concepção de forma em busca de uma liberdade radicalmente moderna, mesmo que paradoxalmente ancorada numa idealidade clássica.

Mas aquilo que desde o MASP se torna um traço distintivo da arquitetura contemporânea paulistana - sob o risco mesmo de reduzir-se a uma fórmula - é uma postura política-ideológica que tende a associar o chão (*rés-do-chão*) a espaço público (*res-publica*). Ou mais precisamente, a liberação do chão à crítica ao processo altamente perverso de urbanização do Brasil e à luta pela transformação da estrutura fundiária das cidades brasileiras. Parte significativa dos melhores projetos para São Paulo nas últimas quatro décadas inscrevem-se, efetivamente, nessa linhagem. A referência primordial, quase sempre, é o projeto de Lina Bo Bardi, em que o platô ao nível da Avenida Paulista mantém o horizonte do antigo mirante e instala um plano horizontal onde podem ser negociados os múltiplos sentidos da coisa pública. Ao mesmo tempo, o programa museológico é seccionado em dois: elevam-se as salas principais de exposição e enterram-se os espaços secundários, ocultando-os dos olhos da avenida. Elevar e enterrar - duas forças de sentido contrário - operam assim em conjunto e em vez de anular-se se complementam, orientadas por uma leitura atenta da geografia e da história urbana de São Paulo. O que resulta é um chão livre e independente da massa do edifício, embora por ele amparado. Um chão de escala metropolitana, que funda um espaço público e cívico decisivo no centro nervoso da maior cidade do Brasil.

Não por acaso, se a elevação do volume edificado tem como antecedentes algumas obras-primas da arquitetura brasileira - como o edifício inaugural do Ministério da Educação e Cultura (Lucio Costa, Oscar Niemeyer, Affonso Eduardo Reidy, Carlos Leão, Jorge Machado Moreira e Ernani Vasconcellos, com Le Corbusier como consultor, 1936) e o Museu de Arte Moderna (Affonso Eduardo Reidy, 1953), ambos no Rio de Janeiro, e o conjunto do Parque do Ibirapuera, em São Paulo (Oscar Niemeyer, 1951-4) -, o MASP marca um ponto de viragem no que diz respeito à relação com o chão. Abre-se com ele uma vertente que se define pelo assim chamado "vão livre". Livre de apoios estruturais intermediários, livre de limites e da própria noção de propriedade, livre do poder repressivo encarnado na arquitetura. Livre, enfim, no sentido da sua extraordinária disponibilidade urbana. Isto é, já não tanto na sequência direta do pilotis corbusieriano - baseado na dupla intenção de desimpedir o horizonte de ambientes cada vez mais densos e criar um solo permeável em oposição à tradição urbana da quadra fechada e da rua-corredor. Mas fundamentalmente como expressão arquitetônica de uma concepção de espaço público indissociável da luta política pela reforma urbana, pela democracia e pelo direito à cidadania no Brasil. Um espaço público entendido, afinal, como um solo comum, aberto e disponível a todas as pessoas, todos os usos e toda a potência da vida urbana.

Evidentemente a suspensão do chão, por si só, não configura espaço público. Alguns dos melhores espaços públicos de São Paulo estão em parte ou integralmente sob a terra, como as estações da primeira linha de metrô da cidade, projetadas nos anos 1960-70 sob a coordenação de Marcelo Fragelli (São Bento, Sé, Liberdade e outras), e a integração metroferroviária da Luz (2002-4), uma das últimas obras construídas de João Walter Toscano. E claro, também o Centro Cultural São Paulo, de Eurico Prado Lopes e Luiz Benedito de Castro Telles (1976-82), edifício-talude que em pleno período ditatorial transformou uma ilha de terra residual num dos espaços de maior vitalidade da cidade. E não podemos deixar de mencionar o edifício da FAUUSP (1961-9), de João Vilanova Artigas e Carlos Cascaldi, onde o semienterramento, somado à grande praça coberta, confronta-se com uma série de desafios sociais, ambientais e urbanos. São obras que nos lembram de que todo espaço público é espaço político. E como tal, envolve um debate sobre territórios, fronteiras e limites que é também da ordem da arquitetura. Ou melhor, do projeto da arquitetura e do chão sobre o qual nos equilibramos cotidianamente.

1 Este texto vincula-se à pesquisa em andamento da autora ("Tanto chão: Inquérito à arquitetura contemporânea em Portugal"), que conta com apoio do CNPq/Conselho Nacional de Desenvolvimento Científico e Tecnológico.

2 Alexandre Alves Costa. "Lembrando Lucio Costa". In: *Unidade.* Porto: FAUP, set número 6, 1998, pp.73-76.

3 Sergio Buarque de Holanda. *Raízes do Brasil.* Rio de Janeiro: José Olympio, 1986.

4 Expressão popular que resume práticas destrutivas em várias esferas, sobretudo ligadas a "limpeza do terreno" e desmatamento de várias ordens para fins de construção, plantio ou criação de pasto. Só em 2017, por exemplo, foram detectados mais de 200.000 focos de queimadas pelo país - cerca de metade na floresta amazônica, em áreas de expansão da fronteira agrícola da soja. Ver http://www.inpe.br/queimadas/portal (Acesso em 8.mar.2019)

5 "Bolsonaro transfere para a Agricultura a demarcação de terras indígenas e quilombolas." (O Globo, 02/01/2019) Ver https://g1.globo.com/politica/noticia/2019/01/02/bolsonaro-transfere-para-a-agricultura-as-atribuicoes-sobre-demarcacao-de-terras-indigenas-e-quilombolas.ghtml (Acesso em 8.mai.2019)

6 No governo Michel Temer (2016-18) nenhuma demarcação de terra indígena foi finalizada. Seu sucessor, Jair Bolsonaro, declarou já em campanha sua intenção de rever tais demarcações de modo a permitir sua exploração comercial e venda. Após eleito, o atual presidente entregou essa atribuição a uma liderança ruralista.

7 "Taxa de suicídio entre indígenas é três vezes maior que a média nacional" (O Globo, 21/09/2017) in: https://oglobo.globo.com/sociedade/saude/taxa-de-suicidio-entre-indigenas-tres-vezes-maior-que-media-nacional-21850401 (Acesso em 08.mar.2019)

O parque e a laje: A Marquise do Ibirapuera, por Oscar Niemeyer

Vanessa Grossman

Não há, talvez, no mundo, dentre as grandes obras da arquitetura moderna, um espaço público que seja mais intensa e espontaneamente apropriado pelas massas do que a Marquise do Parque do Ibirapuera em São Paulo, projetada por Oscar Niemeyer com cinco colaboradores: Hélio Uchôa, Zenon Lotufo, Eduardo Kneese de Mello, Gauss Estelita e Carlos Lemos[1]. A popularidade, na melhor acepção do termo, desta espécie de intervalo definido pela projeção horizontal de uma cobertura de concreto leve e sinuosa parece superar todos os entraves, em termos de acessibilidade, que poderiam vir a comprometer a sua frequentação.

Essa grande laje de 600 metros de extensão foi originalmente concebida como elo de ligação de um conjunto arquitetônico maior que foi inaugurado em 1954, na ocasião das celebrações do IV Centenário da cidade que a acolheu, consistindo em três grandes pavilhões temáticos destinados a exposições. O seu acesso principal se daria através de uma praça de entrada monumental delimitada ainda por um museu de arte e um auditório. Apesar de ter sido ideada como passeio coberto, ela tem dimensões suficientemente generosas que a permitem acolher, por si, atividades coletivas, com vãos variando de 6 m nas extremidades até 75 m na parte central.

A "Marquise", como é conhecida, faz parte de um dos maiores parques urbanos da América do Sul, localizado em um dos bairros mais nobres e centrais da maior metrópole desta porção do continente, e de intrincado acesso à população menos privilegiada, que muito longe dali reside. De fato, não é exclusivamente a sexagenária Marquise, mas sim o Ibirapuera como um todo — um dos poucos equipamentos verdes coletivos de São Paulo — o atrativo para as massas oriundas da chamada "periferia" que atravessam a cidade de ponta a ponta em busca de lazer, cultura, esportes e bem-estar. Porém, é seguramente a Marquise a verdadeira ágora do Ibirapuera, e possivelmente de toda a cidade, por ali se reunirem os mais diversos representantes de uma das mais ricas culturas urbanas nacionais, de distintas classes, gêneros, raças, credos e faixas etárias, dos quais se destaca uma forte presença jovem[2].

Porém, não é somente do ponto de vista quantitativo, em termos do número de usuários, que a Marquise se destaca, mas sobretudo qualitativo. A Marquise tem a particularidade de apresentar uma certa atmosfera carioca da praia, ao mesmo tempo intimista e coletiva, incrementada pela singular urbanidade paulistana ao se transformar, principalmente nos fins de semana, ao mesmo tempo em palco e auditório para as mais variadas manifestações que emanam de paulistanos à vontade: não de sunga e biquíni, mas se apoiando nos mais diversos artífices comerciais, culturais e esportivos urbanos. Ela abriga vendedores ambulantes; patinadores, skatistas e ciclistas, iniciantes e profissionais; rodas e brincadeiras de criança; espetáculos não programados de hip hop, funk, capoeira, "zouk" e outras danças, e performances artísticas; congregações de jovens do "metal", da cena *queer* e de outros movimentos urbanos; tanto animais de estimação quanto um sem-número de pombas. Ali, a cultura popular urbana encontra aquela considerada erudita ou oficial, a partir do momento em que seus usuários dos mais ordinários esbarram no público especializado das muitas exposições programadas nos pavilhões que a Marquise conecta. A cada fim de semana ou feriado, a Marquise se transforma em um grande "estar".

Esta frequentação exacerbada vem a compensar, no conjunto da obra de Niemeyer, o alegado insucesso, neste mesmo quesito, de alguns espaços coletivos que o arquiteto carioca concebeu e que se prestam a alvo frequente de criticismo. Das esplanadas de Brasília ao Memorial da América Latina, muitos destes espaços foram julgados pelo tribunal da crítica por estarem habitualmente esvaziados de frequentadores e assim terem seus usos, ou mesmo funções cívicas, comprometidos. Em decorrência de seu destino histórico, a "estrutura" dos espaços públicos de Brasília é até hoje interpretada como tendo sido projetada pelo arquiteto de modo a "facilitar" a ação dos militares e assim frustrar a assembleia das massas[3].

A lógica por trás da apropriação desenfreada e justaposta da Marquise — como se a cada um o espaço sob sua sombra legitimamente pertencesse — poderia ser aludida à combinação entre duas entidades que parecem ali estar em uma relação simbiótica: o parque e a laje. A primeira, um programa; a segunda, um elemento arquitetônico a ser programado. Uma é rara e a outra, autóctone em São Paulo. Enquanto os chamados "Bairros Jardins", que foram urbanizados na cidade pela inglesa Companhia City, fundada em 1912, são privilégio de pouquíssimos, as marginais de seus rios, que outrora se prestavam ao lazer e ao esporte com fauna e flora originais, foram projetadas já há quase um século como autoestradas. Diferentemente do contexto carioca, em São Paulo a carência de espaços ao ar livre dedicados ao lazer e ao esporte coletivos, como praias, florestas, parques e outros verdes naturais ou construídos, é muitas vezes suprida pela laje. Se o shopping center é o principal destino *indoor* de paulistanos de todas as classes e idades, a laje de cimento armado é talvez o dispositivo mais marcante do lazer, pontuando o horizonte da interminável periferia da cidade. A laje plana, encarnando um dos cinco pontos da arquitetura moderna de Le Corbusier — o terraço-jardim —, é a forma de acabamento mais barata para as tipologias habitacionais periféricas, ou a iminência de um pavimento adicional[4]. Programada a bel-prazer, sobre ela são pendurados varais, montadas piscinas infláveis e churrasqueiras improvisadas, organizadas festas e, sobretudo em São Paulo, esquadrões de crianças, jovens ou mesmo adultos são formados para empinar pipa, potencializando seus poucos metros quadrados em verdadeiras batalhas de laje contra laje.

Contudo, não seria verossímil alienar o papel da arquitetura no que diz respeito à notoriedade da Marquise, onde o lazer é conquistado sob a laje. Enquanto o piso é a projeção exata deste plano flutuante meândrico, pintado de branco, demarcando uma horizontalidade plena, as 106 colunas que o sustentam dão ritmo ao grande "estar", ditando focos de densidade e partitura às atividades que reverberam a altercação entre trabalho e tempo livre na cidade. Esta estrutura é ainda reforçada pelos oito pilares em V situados nas suas quatro extremidades, definindo um pé-direito variável, de 3 m a 4,25 m, "em curva e em declive" como a apresentavam, à época, os seus construtores[5]. O conjunto é marcado pela tensão entre o rigor geométrico da implantação e forma dos pavilhões — de planta trapezoidal, retangular ou circular — e a sinuosidade livre da Marquise que os liga. Para o seu desenho, Niemeyer deu continuidade à exploração das possibilidades plásticas do concreto já forjada por ele na Pampulha, em Belo Horizonte, na década anterior, característica que o crítico Mário de Andrade definiu como "Escola Carioca" em 1944[6]. Espalhando-se pelo parque como concreto líquido, esta extensa laje sinuosa deveria desempenhar, no Conjunto de Niemeyer para o Ibirapuera, o "papel ordenador" que na Pampulha era realizado pelo lago, o que fez da Marquise uma espécie de "espelho d'água de concreto"[7]. Porém, no Ibirapuera a Marquise tomou a frente da cena do projeto de Niemeyer. Apesar da expressividade formal atribuída a cada um dos pavilhões como na Pampulha, mais do que mera infraestrutura, a Marquise se transformou em superestrutura.[8]

Com praça e auditório suprimidos do projeto original, na construção, pelo poder público, durante anos a "entrada" da Marquise não foi completada, o que levou Niemeyer a considerar que a "arrojada marquise parece algo inacabado (e, realmente, o é), ou mal iniciado: sai de um ponto qualquer, desgarrado"[9]. Este efeito de inacabamento foi ainda enfatizado por "stands" erigidos sob a Marquise, que vieram a comprometer a "amplitude panorâmica" e a "leveza" almejadas[10]. Nesta mesma lógica, o que começou, em 1959, como um pavilhão temporário de exposição projetado por Lina Bo Bardi acabaria por consolidar, desde 1968, a sede permanente do Museu de Arte Moderna de São Paulo (MAM). Apesar da *mea culpa* da arquiteta, que ainda reformou o MAM nos anos 1980 "ao invés de liberar a Marquise para reconstituir o projeto original de Niemeyer"[11], o vão daquela laje jamais seria completamente livre. Foi talvez a persistência deste efeito de "inacabamento", produzindo uma tensão constante entre o "papel ordenador" original e uma função desordenadora, que condenou o modernismo pristino da Marquise a um espaço de informalidade, onde tudo parece ser possível para os seus frequentadores, até mesmo a passagem do anonimato à fama.

Houve, da parte de Niemeyer, um último gesto polêmico para reordenar o Conjunto. Ao ser comissionado para a retomada do projeto do auditório, propôs demolir uma parte da Marquise para criar a suprimida praça na área envoltória da nova construção, completada em 2002. A despeito da intenção deste que era o autor do projeto original, a demolição foi sustada graças à intervenção dos órgãos de proteção dos bens culturais da cidade[12]. Em 2015, ano anterior ao tombamento do Conjunto como patrimônio nacional, o projeto da praça havia sido retomado por Paulo Mendes da Rocha. O arquiteto pretendia implementá-la no local atualmente ocupado por estacionamento para que se tornasse o principal ponto de ingresso ao parque, privilegiando a locomoção a pé ou por transporte público. O intuito era o de garantir a acessibilidade ao usuário.

Porém, nem a pendência da praça parece implicar a acessibilidade da Marquise, que é hoje tangível até mesmo via Internet. Ela se transformou no principal destino dos "rolezinhos", encontros de jovens da periferia ativados por redes sociais que foram banidos dos shopping centers. Emoldurados pelo branco da laje tortuosa, com o fundo verde do parque, os organizadores dos eventos — os chamados "influenciadores" — concretizam momentos de fama ao reunir milhares de seguidores, que para ali correm excedendo quaisquer percalços materiais, alguns culminando em confusão e violência, mas outros em uma mera busca por fotos e abraços.

1 Agradeço à Fundação Oscar Niemeyer pelo acesso a documentos, e a Ciro Miguel pelo auxílio à pesquisa e pelo seu papel de leitor.

2 Ana Estela de Souza Pinto, "Rolezinhos do beijo lotam marquise do Ibirapuera com até 20 mil jovens," *Folha de São Paulo*, 5 de fevereiro de 2017, disponível em https://www1.folha.uol.com.br/cotidiano/2017/02/1855091-rolezinhos-do-beijo-lotam-marquise-do-ibirapuera-com-ate-20-mil-garotos.shtml

3 Cf. "Brasília by Rem Koolhaas", agosto de 2011. Disponível em *Revista Centro*, http://revistacentro.org/index.php/koolhaasen/

4 Cf. "Cultura da laje nas periferias". Profissão repórter. Edição do dia 27 de setembro de 2011.

5 Citado em Ruth Verde Zein. " A Marquise do Ibirapuera".*Revista AU*, nº226, janeiro de 2012. Disponível em http://au17.pini.com.br/arquitetura-urbanismo/226/artigo275965-2.aspx. Ver também

6 Mario de Andrade, *Brazil Builds* (1944). In: Alberto Xavier (org.). *Depoimento de uma geração*. São Paulo: Cosac & Naify, 2003, p.179.

7 Paulo César Garcez Marins. "O Parque Ibirapuera e a construção da identidade paulista". *Anais do Museu Paulista - História e Cultura Material*, São Paulo, v. 6-7, 1998-1999, p.26.

8 Este protagonismo, garantido pelo uso que ela veio a conquistar, foi ainda intensificado pela não interferência de ajardinamento no seu entorno imediato. Ao que tudo indica, este foi um desígnio de Niemeyer que culminou com o descarte do projeto original de paisagismo do Ibirapuera atribuído, em 1951, ao paisagista Roberto Burle Marx. Cf. Fernanda Araújo Curi. "Burle Marx e o Parque Ibirapuera: quatro décadas de descompasso (1953 - 1993)". *Anais do Museu Paulista*. São Paulo, Nova Série, vol. 25, nº3, setembro-dezembro 2017, p. 103-138. Ver ainda Fernanda Araújo Curi. Ibirapuera, metáfora urbana. O público/ privado em São Paulo, 1954-2017. 2018. Tese (Doutorado em História e Fundamentos da Arquitetura e do Urbanismo) - Faculdade de Arquitetura e Urbanismo.

9 Oscar Niemeyer, "Mutilado o conjunto do Parque". Módulo, nº1, março de 1955, p.18.

10 Ibid., p. 20. Ver também Oscar Niemeyer. *Minha arquitetura*. Rio de Janeiro. Revan, 2000. p.31.

11 Cf. Mara Gama. " Um prédio polêmico". *Folha de São Paulo*, 14 de julho de 1998, disponível em https://www1.folha.uol.com.br/fsp/especial/fj14079811.htm

12 Cf. . Benedito Lima de Toledo. "A polêmica sobre a Marquise do Ibirapuera." *Folha de São Paulo*, 18 de dezembro de 2005, disponível em https://www1.folha.uol.com.br/fsp/cotidian/ff1812200512.htm

Arquitetura, lugar público e exceção

José Tavares Correia de Lira

"Le Brésil n'a pas de peuple" [1], escreveu o fisiologista francês Louis Couty em 1881, às vésperas da abolição da escravidão: entre seus 500 mil senhores no topo e os dois milhões e meio de escravos e índios, "inúteis ou quase", na base, havia uns seis milhões de brasileiros que "vegetavam" em fazendas e cidades e não mais que três capazes de ascender à condição de cidadãos livres e produtivos. O bordão ecoou anos a fio, inclusive entre os brasileiros. Em 1906, quase vinte anos depois da Abolição, em plena República, o folclorista Silvio Romero o evocou para saudar a nomeação do escritor Euclides da Cunha à Academia Brasileira de Letras: reiterando a leitura de Couty, ele enfatizou a natureza igualmente inoperante das elites nacionais[2]. Se o diagnóstico funesto hoje soa inconcebível, a imagem de um país sem povo, sem classe média nem camadas dirigentes, aos moldes europeus, viria a permear boa parte do pensamento social brasileiro até bem avançado o século vinte.

É de se notar que essa noção de povo se assenta em preconceitos raciais e restrições legais de uma ferocidade etnocêntrica típica de intelectuais formados no evolucionismo, fossem eles estrangeiros ou nacionais. Ela em geral denota cidadãos cosmopolitas, eleitores instruídos, burgueses moralizados ou operários organizados. Se a validade de tais imagens nas sociedades europeias é relativa, no Brasil, onde as heranças do genocídio indígena, da escravidão africana e do patriarcalismo perpetuam-se no presente, muito do que chamamos de lugar público impõe às camadas populares situações variadas de desigualdade, violência e exclusão.

Mesmo em uma cidade como São Paulo – que em meados do século vinte emergiu como emblema da modernização do país, da passagem do escravo ao cidadão e do rural ao urbano-industrial – tais atavismos nacionais e seu cortejo de atrocidades não seriam facilmente ultrapassados. O sociólogo Florestan Fernandes, pai da sociologia paulista do desenvolvimento, escreveu em 1959 um belo ensaio sobre a metrópole em formação[3]. Nela, o aprofundamento da concorrência havia aperfeiçoado a distribuição das atividades e espaços sociais, inclusive entre as famílias mais modestas, mas não lograra forjar um substrato material verdadeiramente urbano. Se a ordem patrimonialista vinha se desagregando com a valorização da impessoalidade, a atitude privatista ante os assuntos de interesse coletivo revelava o peso das permanências coloniais. Se, portanto, o progresso material produzira condições favoráveis ao funcionamento da democracia e da sociedade de classes, ele também criara a ilusão de que a vida local se dava em condições similares às de grandes cidades de países desenvolvidos. Ao contrário, o caráter tumultuoso e descontínuo da urbanização vinha localmente reduzindo a influência dinâmica das tensões e conflitos sobre o rendimento das instituições e os padrões de vida, em boa parte ainda tacanhos. Entre outras coisas, ele se referia ao mau funcionamento das infraestruturas de transportes, energia, saneamento, abastecimento d'água e de víveres, assistência social e saúde, segurança e outros serviços públicos.

A despeito do diagnóstico perspicaz acerca dos paradoxos paulistanos, as dificuldades da leitura de Florestan em superar os pares moderno/atrasado, civilizado/popular, podem ser bem ilustrados por dois processos urbanísticos contemporâneos: a realização do Parque Ibirapuera e a conversão da Avenida Paulista em nova centralidade metropolitana. O parque, executado sob o comando do magnata Ciccillo Matarazzo entre 1951 e 1953, fora concebido para sediar as pomposas comemorações dos 400 anos da cidade, abrigando no magnífico conjunto projetado por Oscar Niemeyer a sede definitiva da Bienal de Arte de São Paulo e as feiras industriais ali doravante centralizadas. Se não é irrelevante o seleto programa institucional do empreendimento, a sua implantação nos arredores de exclusivos bairros-jardins nem o – ainda hoje – deficiente transporte público para o parque, é imprescindível considerar a crescente popularização do Ibirapuera nas últimas décadas, especialmente de sua Marquise, cuja forma, tipologicamente inclassificável, foi sempre avessa a definições de uso precisas.

A Avenida Paulista, por sua vez, aberta em 1891 para abrigar algumas das famílias mais abastadas da cidade, logo seria convertida em importante sítio de ostentação. Com 2700 metros de extensão em linha reta, a avenida veria, partir dos anos 1950, seus suntuosos palacetes serem rapidamente substituídos por edifícios em altura, assumindo desde então o papel de principal centro financeiro da cidade, em torno do qual gravitariam os rumos locais da especulação imobiliária avançada. Distante do tsunami de informalidade e degradação ambiental que tomava conta das periferias, essa nova centralidade ilustrava exemplarmente a lógica da desordem no subdesenvolvimento, a meio caminho entre a busca de normatividade e a racionalização da exceção.[4] O aparecimento nas últimas décadas, nos arredores da Paulista, de um conjunto expressivo de equipamentos culturais, a inauguração em 1991 da linha 2 de metrô sob a via e, a partir de 2015 sobretudo, a interdição do trânsito de automóveis aos domingos e feriados geraram, em paralelo a seu esvaziamento como polo de negócios globais, uma transformação visível na região, com o aparecimento de novos usos e nova população, em grande parte jovem.

Seja no Ibirapuera, seja na Paulista, espaços originalmente burgueses, vêm se observando, portanto, processos de apropriação similares àqueles que em capitais brasileiras litorâneas há mais tempo se verificam em suas praias. Fortemente elitizadas no mercado residencial e marcadas pela mistura étnica e social no usufruto de suas qualidades ambientais, a praia urbana encontra no Ibirapuera, na Paulista e, em certo grau, também no Minhocão, um equivalente paulistano. Ao mesmo tempo que denunciam processos brutais de segregação, condensam pressões micropolíticas de reterritorialização vis-à-vis as dinâmicas formais de redemocratização do país no em finais dos anos 1980.

De fato, estruturas como a marquise do Ibirapuera, as escadarias do edifício Gazeta, o vão livre do MASP, as galerias do Conjunto Nacional, as lajes do Centro Cultural São Paulo, mas também as vielas, pátios, passarelas e rampas dos SESCs Pompeia e 24 de Maio falam de uma arquitetura que, entre suas virtudes, pauta-se pela abertura ao indeterminado, ao instável e ao perturbador da vida metropolitana. Em todas elas é notável o zelo com que se elabora, por exemplo, a margem entre exterior e interior, as conexões com a cidade, os elementos de circulação e outros espaços propícios a reuniões e acontecimentos coletivos, institucionalmente programados ou não.

Veja-se, por exemplo, a enorme profusão de fluxos e situações que o desenho a um tempo sedutor e indecifrável da Marquise de Niemeyer parece estimular no Ibirapuera. Ou a força magnética do mirante do MASP de Lina Bo Bardi, essa grande praça pública da Avenida Paulista que desafia o paredão de concreto que a encerra, a densidade e verticalidade dos arranha-céus lindeiros e a cobiçada propriedade privada do solo para acolher os mais variados gêneros performativos da cultura popular, juvenil, periférica ou militante. Ou a incorporação da topografia urbana no jogo de terraços, escadas, pátios e passarelas imaginado por Eurico Prado Lopes e Luiz Telles no CCSP, catalisando contingentes diários de estudantes e grupos das mais diversas tribos em torno de demandas culturais cotidianas, momentos de evasão e ritos identitários. Ou ainda o que ocorre no SESC-Pompeia e no 24 de Maio, de Bo Bardi e Paulo Mendes da Rocha/MMBB respectivamente: suas diferenças patentes não escondem, em ambos, uma assertiva fortemente urbana, equacionando com veemência tanto as relações entre projeto, programa e experiência espacial quanto as soluções sem programa rígido, que articulam o edifício com seus usos e usuários em potencial, ao mesmo tempo infletindo no entorno e ecoando seletivamente seus valores.

São todos eles projetos que não apenas se mostraram capazes de reposicionar o modernismo arquitetônico no Brasil, mas que desenvolveram exemplarmente hipóteses das mais instigantes à produção contemporânea. Não somente em zonas do globo marcadas por apostas muito modernas de viabilização social, como nos próprios polos mundiais de canonização. Operando cada qual de sua forma, promovem um deslocamento na problemática disciplinar rumo ao enfrentamento do objeto como peça de uma organização territorial maior, capaz de adensar funcional e eroticamente certas economias morais de existência popular [5] na metrópole, incertas ainda que vorazes, breves ainda que muitas, fora da ordem e capazes de tudo pôr à prova[6].

Como outros marcos de experimentação arquitetônica em São Paulo, operam, pois, nas fímbrias da excepcionalidade. Sugerem possibilidades de articulação do espaço comum sem esquivar-se aos processos de disputa, dissolução, construção e ruína próprios a toda grande cidade. Surgindo como realizações de exceção em um processo urbano dos mais anômicos, nele funcionam como um pormenor numa pintura: às vezes imperceptível, mas igualmente capaz de dar sentido a todo um quadro. São como um refúgio aos prazeres e perigos da vida social, como engrenagens de anti-produção ou de produções sociais residuais, dissolventes, nem sempre controláveis, porque desejantes, movediças, macunaímicas. À semelhança das que irromperam no último Carnaval com a performance e o samba-enredo de timbre warburghiano da Mangueira: uma "História pra ninar gente grande", feita de "versos que o livro apagou", sem heróis emoldurados mas povoada de "Marias, Mahins, Marielles, malês" e de outras tantas figuras fora do retrato[7]. Talvez esteja aí, em suas petições de presença, na capacidade de dar passagem aos fantasmas da civilização, a chave de decifração dessa arquitetura em sua incontestável eficácia pública.

1 Traduzido do francês: "O Brasil não tem povo."Louis Couty, *L'Esclavage au Brésil.* Paris: Librairie de Guillaumin et Cie, 1881, p. 87

2 Sílvio Romero, *Discurso pronunciado aos 18 de dezembro de 1906, por ocasião da recepção do Dr. Euclides da Cunha.* Porto: Chardron de Lello & Irmão, 1910

3 Florestan Fernandes, "O homem e a cidade-metrópole" in *Mudanças Sociais no Brasil.* São Paulo: Difusão Européia do Livro, 1960, pp. 266-283.

4 Lucio Kowarick e Vinicius Caldeira Brant, *São Paulo 1975: crescimento e pobreza.* São Paulo: Loyola, 1976; Francisco de Oliveira, "A economia brasileira: crítica à razão dualista", in *Estudos Cebrap*, n. 2, 1972; idem, "O Estado e a exceção - ou o Estado de exceção?", in *Revista Brasileira de Estudos Urbanos e Regionais*, vol. 5, n.1, mai 2003, pp. 9-14.

5 Edward Thompson, "A economia moral da multidão inglesa no século XVIII", in *Costumes em comum.* São Paulo: Companhia das Letras, 2008, pp. 150-202.

6 Caetano Veloso, "Fora da Ordem", in *Circuladô*, 2005.

7 O samba da Mangueira evoca a potência de homens e mulheres comuns, e suas lideranças e movimentos indígenas, negras, femininas, populares entre outros, no passado e no presente. Cf Danilo Firmino, Deivid Domênico, Mamá, Márcio Bola, Ronie Oliveira, Tomaz Miranda, *História pra ninar gente grande.* Rio de Janeiro: Estação Primeira da Mangueira, 2019.

Em prol de um (raro) contato estético com a rua na São Paulo atual

Fraya Frehse

Que contribuição as edificações multifuncionais em exibição dotadas de assinaturas arquitetônicas incisivas - marquises, museus, centros culturais, um mercado, um centro educacional, um prédio - oferecem à vida cotidiana dos habitantes da São Paulo do presente? Minha resposta se pauta numa perspectiva sociológica sensível à historicidade das regras de natureza simbólica que orientam as relações que os pedestres, através de seus corpos, (re)produzem dia a dia entre si e com bens materiais e/ou simbólicos nas ruas e praças empiricamente existentes - em suma, na rua. A meu ver, os projetos selecionados compartilham, para além de suas variadas estruturas, formas, funções e escalas, um mesmo incentivo a que ao menos seus usuários, quando não também não-usuários, travem contatos estéticos de natureza arquitetônica com a rua na cidade, como espaço simultaneamente físico-material e social. Já que tais contatos, pautados em representações arquitetônicas sobre o que é "belo" em relação à rua, são incomuns na São Paulo atual, estimulá-los é a contribuição singular dessas edificações.

Assumindo-se que o espaço é produzido pelas relações que os seres humanos, através de seus corpos, travam em lugares tanto com bens materiais e/ou simbólicos quanto entre si[1], a rua conta com uma materialidade física e social gerada historicamente também por interações sociais passíveis de serem denominadas, com Erving Goffman[2], "contato". Interfere na produção do espaço da rua um conjunto de sinais e trocas verbais e não verbais que, integrando a "linguagem corporal" de quem interage[3], opera toda vez que dois ou mais indivíduos se encontram em copresença física ou intermediada simbolicamente[4]. Sob esse prisma metodológico, é conceitualmente revelador contemplar as infraestruturas arquitetônicas em exibição à luz da história sociocultural dos padrões de contato corporal dos pedestres com a rua em São Paulo. Se, como veremos a seguir, (i) agora que concretizados, os projetos viraram lugares esteticamente carregados de uma arquitetura favorável ao contato físico e simbólico com a rua, uma retrospectiva histórica sintética evidenciará (ii) a excepcionalidade dessa ênfase projetual em São Paulo e (iii) sua contribuição ímpar no mínimo para o dia a dia dos usuários das obras em foco.

(i) A arquitetura das edificações em exibição e a rua
Sua aparência física sinaliza por três vias distintas para arquitetos que alçaram a rua a objeto privilegiado de tratamento estético de viés arquitetônico. Penso, de um lado, na prioridade projetual absoluta à escala do pedestre liberto de veículos automotores. Não é à toa que a maioria dos projetos prescinde de estacionamentos. De outro lado, destaco dispositivos arquitetônicos que ampliam o contato físico ou, ao menos, visual entre as edificações e as ruas e praças do entorno: em relação ao primeiro, vãos livres e escadarias, e quanto ao segundo terraços, rampas e janelões.

Enfim, algumas obras evidenciam um contato metafórico com a rua. Não somente a toponímia em seu interior remete explicitamente a "praças" e, em um caso, a "calçada". O mobiliário é funcionalmente análogo àquele de vias e logradouros públicos em São Paulo – embora com diferenças significativas. Relembro, por exemplo, placas cuidadosamente estilizadas de sinalização para os usuários, ao invés daquelas que, em péssimo estado físico de conservação e embaralhando tipografias diversas, se destinam aos pedestres na cidade. Tampouco faltam suportes físicos para o apoio corporal dos usuários que portam designs autorais inconfundíveis, bem diversos dos relativamente poucos bancos de praça que persistem em São Paulo.

Se todos esses recursos deixam evidente o propósito projetual de manter os usuários em constante contato físico ou, ao menos, simbólico com a rua física e social pela mediação da estética arquitetônica, resta em aberto o que essa ênfase revela sobre a colaboração das edificações para a vida cotidiana dos habitantes de São Paulo. Afinal, projetos de espaços multifuncionais com foco físico e metafórico na rua não são, de modo algum, exclusivos dessa cidade. Para tanto, nada como um pouco de história.

(ii) Da historicidade dos padrões de contato corporal com a rua em São Paulo
Menos de um terço dos atuais 465 anos de São Paulo tem transcorrido em ruas e praças legalmente "públicas", isto é, acessíveis por lei à maior quantidade de tipos humanos[5]. Até a abolição oficial da escravidão africana (1888), a rua dessa cidade ainda rural de quase 64 mil habitantes foi socialmente evitada por aqueles cuja posição social elevada dispensava de passar ou permanecer fisicamente ali com regularidade[6]. A figura do transeunte apenas lentamente ganhava consistência social em vias e logradouros apinhados dia a dia sobretudo de pedestres envolvidos em trabalho braçal e na sociabilidade a este ligada: escravos legalmente sujeitos a toques diários de recolher, afora os chamados libertos e livres, gente econômica e sobretudo socialmente pobre.

Desde então evidentemente muito mudou, e a circulação de transeuntes e principalmente de veículos é hoje um poderoso padrão de uso corporal da rua na cidade. Poderoso, mas não hegemônico. Afinal, uma regra de comportamento corporal do passado escravista – a permanência física regular de pedestres na rua para fins econômicos e de sociabilidade – permanece atual. Vias e praças submetidas quase sem intervalos a políticas em prol do automóvel são agitadas por uma diversidade imensa de pedestres que *não* circulam em meio ao trânsito de humanos e máquinas: vendedores ambulantes, artistas e artesãos, pregadores e pedintes, os autodenominados moradores de rua. Se suas motivações residem em fatores econômicos e sociais que não cabe aqui discutir, o fato é que 131 anos depois de se tornar legalmente acessível a todos, a rua é espaço referencial da vida cotidiana de *não-transeuntes*[7].

À luz dessa síntese retrospectiva, evidencia-se a excepcionalidade das edificações em exibição. Seus autores alçaram a preocupação projetual privilegiada um espaço não apenas historicamente marginal, em termos sociais. Também é de natureza histórica uma das contradições sociais profundamente atuais da rua em São Paulo. Apesar de toda a pressão político-administrativa e socioeconômica ali em prol da mobilidade, tão decisiva no mundo globalizado do presente, a imobilidade historicamente tão antiga dos pobres urbanos frequentemente prevalece na rua em São Paulo.

É verdade que essas circunstâncias não explanam integralmente por que prevalecem na cidade hoje ruas e praças públicas amplamente despojadas de um apuro estético minimamente análogo ao das infraestruturas arquitetônicas em foco. Mas elas permitem reconhecer que a peculiaridade dessa ênfase projetual se deve também a uma história sociocultural que, através dos corpos dos pedestres, se (re)produz na rua dia a dia – e a (re)produz.

(iii) A raridade da contribuição do conjunto expositivo
Sob essa perspectiva, não surpreende que as edificações em foco potencializem um tipo de contato que é raro em São Paulo

hoje: nas edificações ou fisicamente a partir delas, no mínimo seus usuários são incentivados a interagir esteticamente com a rua. O que equivale a dizer: são estimulados a contatar física ou ao menos simbolicamente, pela mediação da estética arquitetônica, a diferença sociocultural e desigualdade social que esse espaço, como nenhum outro na cidade, acolhe há séculos. A situação provavelmente incomoda, mas também pode encantar usuários que se deparam com não-transeuntes potencialmente ou copresentes nesses lugares de beleza arquitetônica, ou bem próximos dali. De fato, tal apuro estético prevalece em locais de acesso privado.

Assim há como esclarecer, por fim, por que o meu argumento se refere *ao menos aos* usuários das obras em exibição. São estes que prevalecem fisicamente ali. Apesar dos vãos livres e da gratuidade de boa parte das atividades funcionais nesses lugares, não-transeuntes em geral não os usam: pelo que pude observar, nos horários de funcionamento das infraestruturas em foco, eles predominam nas ruas e praças das redondezas ou nos limites arquitetônicos indicativos de entradas - aliás, frequentemente vigiadas por seguranças. Quanto ao porquê disso, são sugestivos dados que coletei sobre o contato corporal de não-transeuntes com infraestruturas arquitetônicas outras do centro de São Paulo em 2013-2014. Eles apontam que as edificações encantam pela beleza arquitetônica e incomodam pelo constrangimento vivenciado em face dos olhares, trajes, gestos, posturas e expressão emocional dos usuários - em suma, de sua linguagem corporal.

Nem por isso, as obras deixam de incentivar também não-transeuntes ao raro contato estético aqui destacado. Afinal, traduzindo toda essa história sociocultural de contatos corporais com a rua em cimento, pedra e vidro, as obras expressam materialmente, tanto para usuários quanto para não-usuários, como as contradições sociais implícitas no contato corporal dos paulistanos com a rua se apresentam num momento temporal preciso: quando esta é submetida à sensibilidade estética do arquiteto.

1 Fraya Frehse. "Relational Space through Historically Relational Time - in the Bodies of São Paulo's Pedestrians." *Current Sociology*, vol. 65, n. 4, 2017, pp. 511–532.

2 Erving Goffman. "The Interaction Order: American Sociological Association, 1982 Presidential Address." *American Sociological Review*, vol. 48, n. 1, 1982, p. 6.

3 Erving Goffman. *Behavior in Public Places*. New York: The Free Press/Collier-Macmillan, 1963, p. 33.

4 Erving Goffman. "The Interaction Order: American Sociological Association, 1982 Presidential Address." *American Sociological Review*, vol. 48, n. 1, 1982, p. 6.

5 Lyn Lofland (1985). *A World of Strangers*. Prospect Heights: Waveland Press, p. 19; Fraya Frehse. *Ô da Rua!* São Paulo: Edusp, 2011, passim.

6 Fraya Frehse. *O Tempo das Ruas na São Paulo de Fins do Império*. São Paulo: Edusp, 2005; Fraya Frehse. *Ô da Rua!* São Paulo: Edusp, 2011.

7 Fraya Frehse. "On Regressive-Progressive Rhythmanalysis.", in: Jenny Bauer and Robert Fischer (eds.). *Perspectives on Henri Lefebvre*. Berlin/Boston: De Gruyter, p. 107.